HISTORY AND PROPHECY:

OSWALD SPENGLER AND THE

DECLINE OF THE WEST

KLAUS P. FISCHER, Ph.D.

MOORE PUBLISHING COMPANY
Durham, North Carolina 27705

Library of Congress Catalog Card Number: 76-57812
ISBN: 0-87716-080-5

To Fern

Oswald Spengler, 1935

CONTENTS

PREFACE

This book was primarily written for students and for the general educated reader, though it is hoped that professional historians—to whom Oswald Spengler is still a bête noire—will also benefit from the major cultural issues presented in it. My purpose in writing this book has been twofold: to recreate the thought of Oswald Spengler as fairly as human objectivity permits, and to demonstrate the relevance of his ideas to our troubled age. In pursuing this goal, I have been only too conscious of the pitfalls involved. It is not easy to describe the center of a philosopher's vision without letting one's own ideas and feelings intrude upon the material. Although I scrupulously tried to present Spengler's ideas as I think he saw them, I feigned no pretended objectivity. In the humanities, as Spengler himself was well aware, "scientific objectivity" is not always a virtue because it discourages the frank expression of personal moral convictions. Accordingly, I say precisely what I personally think, and I make it clear that I am saying it. In other words, I do not attempt to hide behind the overarching cover of Spengler's work, as some reactionary writers have done, in order to express my own ideological biases. In this age of moral crisis an author owes it to his readers to let them know exactly where he stands. This was also one of the major convictions of Oswald Spengler. I hope that I have lived up to it.

Finally, I would like to pay tribute to Spengler for helping me rediscover the truth of my own German heritage, including both its glorious accomplishments and its wretched disasters.

Santa Barbara, Spring, 1976.

INTRODUCTION: HISTORY AS A GRAND-DESIGN

I

In the last few years, the name of Oswald Spengler, so long relegated to the curiosity shop of historical oddities, has suddenly been recalled from obscurity by prominent politicians, leading journalists, and troubled academics. No one, to be sure, knows exactly what Spengler did, but everyone knows that he predicted the impending demise of European and American civilization. Since we are currently in the throes of a profound cultural crisis, Spengler has become "relevant" again; and by implication, so has the practice of enlisting history for the purpose of prophecy. But before we invoke Spengler, or the idea of historical prophecy, let us be sure that we understand the source of our appeals. The purpose of this study is to shed some light on Oswald Spengler's role as an historical prophet and, indirectly, to stimulate renewed interest in his synoptic treatment of world history—an enterprise that has almost disappeared from the academic scene.

Oswald Spengler belongs to that species of thinkers who are not content with merely describing the past, but who seek to use their acquired historical knowledge for the purpose of predicting the future. The legitimacy of this venture has been questioned by most practicing historians in recent years. It is a well-known fact that the two reigning theories of history at the present time—"history as art" and "history as science"—both disparage the notion of historical prophecy.[1]

The proponents of scientific *rigueur,* enamored by the precision of the natural sciences, constantly urge the historian to adopt scientific procedures, but they usually couple this desideratum with the condescending rejoinder that history will, of course, never be able to approximate the scientific ideal. The best we can hope for, the social scientist would say, is that historians refine their terminology and tighten their explanations. The discovery of objective laws of history, which can be quantitatively ascertained and thus rendered predictable, is a futile venture because the subject matter of history will always be resistant to exact scientific observation and measurement.[2]

In confessing their failure to raise history to the level of an exact science, the proponents of "history as science" have time and again reinforced the basic premise of their opponents, namely, that history is an unique inquiry with its own methods of explanation. The champions of "history as art" assert that scientific observation, measurement, and prediction can only be attained in the natural sciences, where the objects of study are uniform physical events which are invariable throughout time and space. Unlike science, however, history has for its subject matter unique human events which cannot be scientifically observed, measured, summed up in mathematical formulas, and predicted. Since the objects of study are fundamentally different in science and history, it follows that the methods by which we explain them must also differ. Thus, both science and history have their own subject matter, their own language, and their own methods of explanation.[3]

Philosophers who believe in the unity of scientific explanation, regardless of the subject matter in question, have strongly opposed all arguments asserting the uniqueness of historical explanation. For over a century now, they have urged their opponents to tell them precisely how an historical explanation differs from a scientific one. In other words, how does the collection, evaluation, and verification of historical data differ from the scientific approach towards evidence and proof? R. G. Collingwood, a leading idealistic philosopher of history and a strong opponent of the scientific approach to history, has argued that past events possess two attributes: a material or outward form and an inner or "thought-side."[4] It is precisely this dual aspect of events, he asserted, which constitutes the difference between natural science and history. The task of the historian, as Collingwood saw it, would be that of

> ... penetrating to the inside of events and detecting the thought which they express... In this way the task of the historian is more complex than that of the scientist. In another way it is simpler: the historian need not and cannot (without ceasing to be an historian) emulate the scientist in searching for the causes of laws of events. For science, the event is discovered by perceiving it, and the further search for its cause is conducted by assigning it to its class and determining the relation between that class and others. For history, the object to be discovered is not the mere event, but the thought expressed in it. To discover that thought is already to understand it.[5]

The understanding of past thoughts, according to Collingwood, is achieved when the historian re-thinks or re-enacts them in his own mind. As Collingwood expressed it, "the history of thought, and therefore all history, is the re-enactment of past thought in the historian's own mind."[6] He then proceeded to sketch his own principle of explanation, the much disputed principle of "empathetic understanding."

Whether the practicing historian accepts the doctrine of empathy would, of course, depend on his philosophic orientation. In any case, Collingwood's theory has not convinced those who embrace the ideal of scientific explanation. These thinkers would argue that few events exhibit a "thought-side," since historical movements are generally in the nature of collective action. This being so, Collingwood's theory would only be applicable, if at all, to individuals rather than to collective wholes such as institutions, nations, classes, and parties. Moreover, Collingwood's much vaunted method of explanation, the theory of empathetic understanding, does not constitute a legitimate principle of explanation. As Carl Hempel, the most articulate spokesman for the scientific ideal, has said: "This method of empathy is, no doubt, frequently applied by laymen and by experts in history. But it does not in itself constitute an explanation; it rather is essentially a heuristic device; its functions is to suggest certain psychological hypotheses which might serve as explanatory principles in the case under consideration."[7] However, what really counts in a scientific or historical explanation, Hempel argued, is the universal validity of a general hypothesis, a validity based on "empirically well-confirmed assumptions concerning initial conditions and general laws."[8]

In this seemingly open-ended controversy between the Collingwoodians and the Hempelians, neither side has scored a major victory, since both are arguing from different premises. The lines and the arguments are as rigidly drawn today as they were a hundred years ago when the controversy between the proponents of the human sciences (*Geisteswissenschaften*) and the natural sciences (*Naturwissenschaften*) first began in earnest.[9] In recent times, the arguments of these two schools have become so esoteric that even the professional historians are baffled, scarcely knowing which side to take.

Assuming that the historian were to listen exclusively to the scientific idéologue, what kind of history-writing would result? One thing is certain, it would be an account of abstract forces, movements, facts, and causes; it would not concern itself, except peripherally, with man's inner life — his dreams, ideals, hopes, fears, or aspirations. In other words, the human element would receive short shrift because the scientist, in his quest for accuracy, often tries to eliminate "the human element" from his explanation. The social scientist, Leslie White, for example, repeatedly insists that cultural processes can be explained without taking human organisms into consideration, and that a good scientific explanation does not take people into account at all.[10] Purposive personalities, acting on unpredictable impulses, are often a distinct embarrassment to the scientist whose basic goal is to ascertain events in quantitative terms. But to do so, the scientist must assume that human beings, like natural events, behave rationally and logically — an assumption which the facts of history often belie. If most historians became dedicated social scientists, a large dimension of man's past would disappear.

But would history-writing improve under the auspices of those who, like Collingwood, eschew the external side of events in favor of human thought? Perhaps this would be a more desirable approach, but not necessarily a more accurate one. Collingwood's theory, assuming that it were applied consistently, would transform history into the history of thought; it would pay only scant attention to collective human behavior and recurring uniformities. The Collingwoodian approach possesses another, and far more serious, disadvantage: it lacks a normative principle of explanation. Having empathy with some past agent, or re-thinking the thought of a past figure, is a subjective psychological process; it is not an objective method of verification.[11]

Exclusive reliance on either school of historical thought would undoubtedly improverish the writing of history. It is therefore salutary that most historians are confirmed eclectics when it comes to historical methodology. However, the present ideological strife between competing theories of history has left its mark on historical practice. Being preached at by the dogmatic theorist, the practicing historian has reacted by becoming excessively cautious, narrow, and over-specialized. To the educated layman, who wants to turn to history for a sense of meaning and orientation, current history-writing often appears devoid of relevance. Hugh Trevor-Roper has admirably summed up the present situation when he observed that

> ... a kind of hopelessness has overcome many conventional historians. For how, they ask, can one ever compete with the enormous weight of this ever-lengthening, ever-deepening past? Their answer has been to draw in their horns. Always seeking finality, fearful of giving any answer which some new document will reverse, ... they have become narrow specialists, knowing more and more about less and less, and saying less and less about it. And this timidity of the specialist in turn intimidates the layman. For when the experts are unable to master even such minute periods of history, how can the layman, who lacks their training, hope to understand any historical problem? Besides, the answers of the expert seem to the layman not only uncertain, but trivial. For if history is to interest the layman at all, it must be because it has some general significance.[12]

II

Fortunately for both the layman and the historian, there is a more synoptic approach to the past. We shall call this third historical inquiry the grand-design method. The grand-design thinkers generally recognize the importance of both science and art as a means of recreating the past. Being confirmed generalists, they see merit in the premises of both the social sciences and the humanities. In fact, many grand-design historians have tried to synthesize the findings of other schools on a higher level. Thus, they uphold the humanistic claim that history is a unique discipline, while at the same time insisting that the past is governed by general laws analogous, though not similar, to the laws of the natural sciences.[13] Many grand-design thinkers would agree with Collingwood that the study of history is largely, if not wholly, the study of past thoughts or values, but they would reject his assertion that past ideas cannot be subsumed under the rule of certain general laws. Whatever their philosophic orientation may be, the grand-design historians all try to comprehend both the spiritual and the material in man's past in terms of some uniform law, rhythm, pattern, or regularity. Among the grand-design historians are ranged some of the greatest speculative minds of modern times: Giambattista Vico, Johann Gottfried Herder, G. W. F. Hegel, Karl Marx, August Comte, Herbert Spencer, Oswald Spengler, and Arnold Toynbee.

These thinkers try to comprehend the broad sweep of history from the perspective of an all-encompassing paradigm. Although their models and their conclusions may widely differ, they all share this ingrained bias for final answers. It is well to recall in this respect that the grand-design school was an outgrowth of theology. Every grand-design historian strives to find an answer to the ultimate riddle of history: is there a meaning or purpose in man's past? It is this metaphysical impulse which has driven them beyond the boundaries of ordinary historical inquiry. Every historian, of course, wants to create order out of past events and to present a coherent account that can pass the test of his profession. But the average historian, especially if he belongs to an academic guild, is not possessed by the same metaphysical spirit as is the grand-design historian, who seeks not only to explain the past, but to discover its innermost purpose.

The grand-design thinker holds that there is both a meaning *in* history and a meaning *of* history. The practicing historian would agree with the first belief, but he would deny the second as unknowable or meaningless or both. The question whether history as a whole has a meaning, he would say, cannot be answered by our present methods of explanation and is therefore not a legitimate problem of historical inquiry. It is on this issue that the grand-design historian parts company from his cautious colleagues, for he cannot abandon his inner conviction that history as a whole is meaningful and that it can be explained by an all-encompassing system.

The quest to comprehend history-in-the-round has enmeshed the grand-design historians in several theory questions regarding the source, the object, and the direction of change in history. In seeking solutions to these problems the grand-design historians are guided by the same instinct: they all display a marked predilection for the all-inclusive, the definitive explanation. This should not be surprising in view of their psychological obsession with finding an historical master key.

In their speculations about the source of change, the grand-design historians share the conviction that the nature of change resides in one primary phenomenon rather than in a plurality of occurrences. Marx, for example, argued that the primary force of change was economics, and that all other human activities would automatically change in accordance with changes in economic conditions. "Assume a particular state of development in the productive faculties of man," he wrote to his Russian admirer Annenkov in 1846, "and you will get a corresponding form of commerce and consumption. Assume particular degrees of development of production, commerce and consumption and you will have a corresponding form of social constitution, a corresponding organization of the family, of orders or of classes, in a word, a corresponding civil society. Assume a particular civil society and you will get a particular political system which is only the official expression of civil society."[14] In postulating a primary agent of change, Marx thought that he could predict a broad range of social, political, religious, and artistic consequences. Since all social institutions are based on underlying economic forces, it follows that a change in the economic substructure (*Unterbau*) automatically results in a change of its ideological superstructure (*Überbau*). As Marx confidently put it, "in acquiring new productive forces, men change their mode of production; and in changing their mode of production, in changing the way of earning their living, they change all social relations."[15]

G. F. W. Hegel, Marx's mentor, approaches the problem of change from the same perspective, though he differs from Marx in describing change in spiritual rather than in material terms. In Hegel, as in Marx, we find the typical grand-design attempt to comprehend history in one full sweep and on the basis of a few premises. The source of all change, as of all reality, according to Hegel, is found in ideas. All ideas are innate and suffused with the spark of divinity. One idea is prominent: the idea of freedom. This idea originates in God, is implicit in nature, and manifests itself in history as Spirit.

The source of change, then, is Spirit manifesting itself in history as the progressive dialectical unfolding of freedom from the Oriental East (where only one was free), to the Greco-Roman world (where some were free), to the Germanic world (where all are free). Hegel's philosophy of history is a theodicy, a description of God's design in history.

Hegel's idealistic explanation of change shares much in common with the great theological system of St. Augustine. Both Hegel and Augustine argue that change is initiated by a supernatural agent, not by man himself. History thus becomes a showplace in which God makes use of man to serve his own end. It goes without saying that all such monistic explanations of historical change involve one form of determinism or another. Marx, it is true, locates the source of historical change in man himself; but in predicating change on economics, he unwittingly makes man's destiny contingent on impersonal forces beyond his control. As he put it in no uncertain terms in *Das Kapital*, "individuals are dealt with only insofar as they are the personifications of economic categories, embodiments of particular class relations and class interests."[16]

To understand the sources of change presupposes a knowledge of that which changes. Here, again, the grand-design historians have adopted the broadest perspective. Since they are committed to explain the entire sweep of history, it naturally follows that they would investigate the largest rather than the smallest entities of change. Indeed, the grand-design historians assert that the meaning of history must be gleaned from the behavior of collective wholes. Studies of microscopic events, they would say, may satisfy our antiquarian curiosity, but they do not contribute anything to our knowledge of broad historical movements — unless, of course, they are studied as instances of regularities in the behavior of some large historical entity: a class, a society, a nation, or a culture. This explains why each grand-design historian has focused his attention on the recurring patterns within a given historical entity. To know the rhythm, the pattern, or the regularity of an historical entity, he would say, is to know its direction and its future — in short, its meaning.

Grand-design historians, of course, have differed about the nature of these historical entities or holisms. Hegel preferred to study the spirit of great nationalities; Marx, the structure of economic systems such as ancient slavery, feudalism, and capitalism; Comte, the development of the human mind through the successive phases of theology, metaphysics, and science; and Henry Adams, the movements of society along a scientifically-determined path.

The majority of grand-design historians, however, has singled out culture as the most suitable entity for study. Herder, Vico, Spengler, or Toynbee would all agree that there is only one satisfactory approach to the bewildering mass of detail in history: the perception and delineation of forms or holisms (*Gestalten*). If we do not organize the details, the grand-design historian would say, historical events will be nothing more than isolated ice caps, floating aimlessly through history. The best way to organize historical phenomena, large or small, is to delineate the groups or classes to which they belong. Implicitly, every historian operates from these simple premises of organization; but not every historian would accept the grand-design principle that historical knowledge increases when our approach becomes synoptic, and that it decreases when it becomes specialized or fragmented. In other words, the grand-design historian has completely inverted the accepted scientific (empirical) procedure of reductive analysis which studies phenomena by breaking them into their component parts and by submitting each of these parts to microscopic scrutiny. This approach, the grand-design historian would argue, is theoretically and practically mistaken. In history, as in science, the holistic vision always precedes the microscopic investigation of its parts. Practically speaking, studies of minute historical detail have distorted rather than enriched our overall conception of history.

Most practicing historians, of course, recognize the importance of organizing historical details, but they are notoriously uncomfortable with broad regularities, rhythms, patterns, or configurations. H. A. L. Fisher, for example, has confessed in a much quoted passage that "men ... have discerned in history a plot, a rhythm, a predetermined pattern... I can only see one emergency following upon another ... , only one great fact with respect to which, since it is unique, there can be no generalization."[17] Presumably, Fisher meant broad recurring patterns; for — as Philip Bagby has rightly observed — "if he had meant no pattern at all, he would have refuted himself with every word he wrote."[18] Every grand-design historian would regard Fisher's attitude as an intolerable nominalism.

The grand-design historian, then, believes that the riddle of history can only be solved by finding the source of change and by applying the knowledge thus acquired to the largest collective enterprise by which men express their lives. Knowing the major agency of change and the principal object to which it must be applied, there only remains the task of plotting the direction of that changing object. The third stage of grand-design history is the most controversial because directionality involves prophetic and ethical judgments. In other words, identifying an agency which directs the flow of events invariably raises the question whether the movement of history in a given direction is purposive? Moreover, it raises the further question whether such a purpose, assuming that it has been defined, is good or bad, strictly determined or subject to human control?

III

Grand-design historians have subscribed to two major patterns of change: linear and cyclical. The linear historians, Christian or secular, assume that a single entity such as mankind journeys on a straight line from a starting point (*terminus a quo*) to a final end (*terminus ad quem*). By and large, those who subscribe to the linear pattern have been optimists of one sort or another, viewing history as a straight path towards the city of God or as an irreversible meliorative development towards the city of Man.

Linearism is a Christian contribution to historical thinking; its major tenents, derived from biblical revelation, hold that history is universal, providential, apocalyptic, and periodized.[19] The Christian envisions the history of mankind as a uniform development in time from the Fall, to the Mosaic community, to the coming of Christ, to the inexorable fulfillment of the Christian law. This Christian story of history exhibits all the elements we have associated with the grand-design school: it possesses a definitive explanation of historical change (providence), a universal subject of change (mankind), and an unalterable direction of change (from the Fall to Redemption).

Consciously or unconsciously, every grand-design historian has been influenced by the Christian view. Modern proponents of progress, for example, have retained all the metaphysical premises of Christian historiography — linearism, universalism, and prophecy. The only thing that has changed in their systems is the replacement of religion by science as a motivating force of historical progress. But the religious dimension is still there in transmuted form because the metaphysical premises of Christianity (linearism, universalism,

and prophecy) are always invoked as a guarantee to progress.
Thus, modern prophets of progress such as Turgot, Condorcet,
Hegel, Marx, Comte, or Spencer have unwittingly grafted a
secular and scientific experience on a basically Christian
metaphysics. They have merely poured new wine into old
bottles under such labels as "scientific progress," "The
classless society," or "biological evolutionism." As Edward
Sullivan shrewdly observed,

> the naturalistic rationalism of the Enlightenment
> had no place for the supernaturalism of traditional
> Christian eschatology, and yet it could not divest
> itself altogether of the Christian teleological
> conception of life and history. A belief in the
> perfectibility and the indefinite progress of the
> human race on earth tended to take the place of
> the Christian faith in the life of the world to come
> as the final goal of human effort. [20]

Another way of conceiving the pattern of historical events
is cyclical.[21] The ancients believed in historical and cosmic
cycles, and so did Machiavelli, Vico, Herder, Nietzsche, and
Toynbee in modern times. Oswald Spengler also takes his
place among the cyclical grand-design historians. The cyclist
holds that historical events regularly repeat themselves in a
pattern of birth, growth, maturity, and old age. He believes
that history is a kaleidoscope of ever-changing events, a
world without permanence and therefore without enduring
values and institutions. Although everything changes, chance
itself is not chaotic, for it obeys the law of cycles. If change
is cyclical, so is that which changes such as an individual, a
class, a society, or a culture.

The cyclists are more profound than the linear grand-design
historians because they base their theories on a simple truth

of life: all things grow, mature, and wither away. This recognition of impermanence has made the cyclists acutely conscious of the tragic element in life. As a result, most cyclists are pessimists of one sort or another who hold that life always destroys our fondest hopes or aspirations. History and life, according to the cyclists, are subject to a never-ending rhythm of opposites: life and death; progress and regress; persistence and change; good and evil.

Implicit in this cyclical view of history is therefore the idea of inevitable degeneration. Consequently, most, if not all, cyclists have been philosophers who were haunted with thoughts of immanent decline regarding their own class, society, or culture. The cyclical view, however, does not preclude a certain modicum of optimism because decline merely portends the end of one life cycle and the beginning of a new one. According to this view, decline is always coupled with the growth of something new and vital. The only thing on which most cyclists are insistent is that an entity, once it has become senescent, cannot regenerate itself. In this respect much would depend on the length and the stage of the cycle in question. It makes a lot of difference whether a regular revolution of the cycle occurs every few generations or only after long intervals of time. Few cyclists, it should be pointed out, have given serious attention to this thorny problem. Moreover, few cyclists have seriously pondered the problem of cyclical uniformity — that is, the uniform change of all human activities in terms of one cycle of childhood, youth, manhood, and old age. In other words, may there not be several cycles which obey the rhythm of different clocks? Perhaps the life cycle of a certain style of art may not correspond to the life cycle of a political institution. Conceivably, the former may outlast the latter or vice versa.

Here we have touched on a metaphysical assumption which

every cyclist simply takes on faith — the belief, namely, that all human activities in a certain time and place are subject to the same cyclical law. In justifying this belief, the cyclist would probably reply by saying that every inquiry ultimately rests on one or several fictions. Science, for example, rests on a number of metaphysical assumptions which must be accepted on faith. As David Hume has demonstrated long ago, science cannot claim a logical necessity for its major assumptions: that nature is uniform, that every effect has a cause, that the essence of reality is material, and that nature operates rationally and logically. Every inquiry is based on such fruitful fictions. Scientific fictions seem to persuade us more because a greater number of observable and measurable facts can be adduced to support them.

In any case, each cyclist bases his system on a belief in cyclical growth, arguing that cultures, like organisms, pass through regular cycles of birth, youth, maturity, and old age. It is from this metaphysical belief that he derives his major historical theories. Assuming that each historical entity is subject to the cycle of growth, the cyclist draws the conclusion that an entity such as a culture must be vital and creative when it is young, senile and unproductive when it is old. There is also widespread agreement among the cyclists that the vitality of a culture is based on religious faith. Even agnostics like Spengler argue that every creative impulse in a culture is sustained by a mighty religious faith. Conversely, senility sets in when faith is no longer inwardly binding or compelling to the members of a society or a culture. Such a stage in the life history of a culture usually occurs when science and rationalism replace religion as the supreme value in men's lives. Each cyclist argues that science, especially when it is coupled with technology, fosters excessive preoccupation with material rather than spiritual values, and thus removes man's only protection against the sin of idolatry

— the worship of such false idols as wealth, power, and material pleasures. According to the cylists, the sharp edge of scientific criticism is incapable of creating or sustaining a sense of purpose that can inspire pyramids and temples; castles and cathedrals; statues in Parian marble and frescoes in the Sistine Chapel; the Ten Commandments and the Gospel of Christ.

The critical spirit of science sows the seeds of doubt and reorients man's concerns from the spiritual to the material plane. This growth of skepticism and doubt is all the more ominous since it usually coincides with the rise of industrialism in most cultures. The consequences of rationalism — free thought, skepticism, and doubt — combine at this stage with the consequences of industrialization — gigantic cities, the emancipation of the masses, complex bureaucracies, and widespread political and ideological warfare. The last stage of a culture, according to the cyclist, is a world without values and without meaning, a formless, anomic, cynical, and — above all — a violent world. As Pitrim Sorokin put it, "rude force and cynical fraud will become the only values in all inter-individual and inter-group relationships."[22] The final death-knell will be sounded when skepticism and doubt affect the body politic — that is, when patriotism and national consciousness are no longer accepted as worthy ideals by the average citizen. The historian Andrew Hacker, to cite a recent example, has diagnosed this condition as a present malaise in the American character. As he bluntly states it, "a willingness to sacrifice is no longer in the American character; and the conviction that this country's beliefs and institutions merit global diffusion is in decline. What was once a nation has become simply an agglomeration of self-concerned individuals; men and women who were once citizens are now merely residents of bounded terrain where birth happens to have placed them."[23] From this and other

symptoms of decline, Hacker draws for America the lesson
Spengler had long drawn for the whole western world:

> We have arrived at a plateau in our history: the
> years of middle age and incipient decline. We are
> now at that turning-point ancient philosophers
> called *stasis*, a juncture at which it becomes
> pointless to call for rehabilitation or renewal. Such
> efforts would take a discipline we do not have, a
> spirit of sacrifice which has ceased to exist.[24]

IV

Andrew Hacker's gloomy forecast differs only in matters of
detail from other cyclical scenarios of cultural decline. The
consensus among the cyclists is that a culture disintegrates
when a majority of men loses faith in its institutions and its
shared ideals. Most cyclists would agree with Toynbee in this
respect that such incipient decline manifests itself as "a failure
of creative power in the minority, an answering withdrawal of
mimesis on the part of the majority, and a consequent loss of
social unity in the society as a whole."[25] The final or winter
phase of a culture is a period of disease, which either takes
the form of mass death or collective psychosis. At the same
time, disease — as paradoxically as it may sound — always
portends new vital life. As the cyclist Egon Friedell has
expressed it, "wherever something new is born, there is
weakness, sickness, and 'decadence.'"[26] In other words, the
existence of decadence, corruption, and social chaos portends
life as well as death, renewed hope as well as despair. In the
eyes of the cyclist, such is the nature of life and history.

Is there no hope of regeneration? Is the process of

disintegration inevitable; and if so, why? The cyclists are generally of two minds on this issue of inevitable degeneration. One group, whom F. L. Polak has aptly called "unconditional pessimists,"[27] holds that all cultures are higher forms of life which obey the unalterable cycle of childhood, youth, manhood, and old age. According to this group, which includes Karl Friedrich Vollgraff, Peter Ernst Lasaulx, Oswald Spengler, and Ludwig Klages, cultures are doomed when they reach their downswing. The second group, best represented by Arnold Toynbee, is made up of "conditional pessimists." These are the "escape hatch theorists," the "prophets of doom and gloom unless..."[28] Typically, they warn that we are hanging on a precipice, and that stringent measures are necessary to reverse the downtrend. They also hold that the only salvation lies in a religious revival of one sort or another. If such a spiritual awakening does not take place, they would argue, all is lost.

If a grand-design historian were confronted by a skeptic who wanted to know what justification he had for making such dire (or hopeful) predictions, he would probably reply that his knowledge of recurring events in the past entailed knowledge of these events in the future. Regularly recurring events in the past, he would say, produce the recurrence of similar events in the future. On the face of it, this appears to be sound scientific procedure. The scientist, too, derives his knowledge of future events from known past events and from universal empirical laws on which these events are based. It has been shown time and again, however, that the kind of laws which the grand-design historians have formulated are not universally valid from an empirical point of view. At best, these laws possess the status of generalizations, but they do not exhibit the structure of universal empirical laws that we associate with the natural sciences.

As scientific shamans, then, the grand-design historians

have not been very convincing because they have not succeeded in formulating historical laws analogous to the laws of physics. Does this invalidate the grand-design position? By no means. The opponents of the grand-design school have in no wise demonstrated the impossibility of framing historical laws. The only thing they have shown is that the historical laws which have been formulated so far do not possess the attribute we associate with a typical scientific law (i.e., the law of inertia, gravity, Boyle's law, Ohm's law, etc.).

In retrospect, we can see that the grand-design thinkers made a serious error in emulating the natural sciences, while at the same time insisting that they were pursuing an intrinsically different (i.e., historical) enterprise. As we shall see, Spengler often committed this error when he posed as both positivist and idealist. Spengler and the grand-design thinkers are at their best and most persuasive when they take their stand on a metaphysical belief. The existence of grand historical patterns regularly repeating themselves is an *a priori* conviction about the structure of life and history. Since it can never be fully confirmed nor fully disproved, much depends on the kind of evidence that the grand-design historian can marshal in order to persuade us of its existence and validity.

Admittedly, the perception of broad recurring patterns in the past depends in large part on the subjective vision of the perceiver; and so does the empirical evidence which is adduced to support it. But this is true of every single historical generalization. The subject matter of history is so oceanic, the facts, like tiny drops of water, so infinite, that every generalization can be based on the "facts." In other words, the infinite richness of history seems to validate the most divergent and, sad to say, the most contradictory points of view. This gives history its daemonic aura. The often-repeated cliché that every generation has to re-write history conceals a very disconcerting message: history seems to prove everything and nothing.

To escape from the chaos that is history, men have searched far and wide for a cognitive anchor amidst the confusing welter of detail. The grand-design historians, I believe, have provided us with the most meaningful orientation. They may not have "proved" the scientific validity of their theories, but they have given us breadth of vision, profound insights, and a sense of orientation. Above all, they have taught us that the past is relevant, and that insight into the past is approximately proportionate to vision of the future.[29]

V

Oswald Spengler was one of the last historians who wrote history in the grand style. Universal history-writing is no longer a fashion. The specialists have taken over and they have defined the larger discipline by the smaller. But we do not have to be satisfied with this fragmented approach which Will Durant has so aptly called "shredded history." The time has come, I believe, for a revival of the grand style, the style of Spengler and Toynbee. Hero-worship, of course, is out of the question. We should recognize the great faults committed by the grand-design historians and benefit accordingly. Spengler, like Toynbee, had great faults; but his virtues far outweigh his mistakes. It is my firm *belief* that Spengler has never been equalled in his universality, his breadth of vision, and his dazzling wealth of suggestive insights. He was one of the supreme historical intellects of all times.

If this is so, why has he never received the recognition that his genius deserves? Why has he been treated with so much derision and lack of understanding? The answer to these questions is the purpose of this book.

A. THE MAN BEHIND THE THEORY:
YEARS OF GROWTH, 1880-1920

I

Blankenburg am Harz, where Spengler was born on May 29, 1880, is nestled in the Harz mountains — a region which the poet Goethe immortalized in his famous tragedy of *Faust*. Goethe found the locale with its mighty oaks and dark caverns an ideal setting for his *Walpurgisnacht* — the witches' sabbath. If geography is an index to a man's thought, then the carboniferous landscape of the Harz is more likely to nourish visionary souls than stout-hearted believers in the light of pure reason. Indeed, central Germany has produced a disproportionate number of mystics during the course of German history. Meister Eckhart, the great medieval mystic, came from central Germany, as did Jakob Böhme and Paracelsus. Oswald Spengler belongs to the same proud lineage of visionary thinkers.

Spengler's ancestors migrated to the Harz Mountains from southern Germany in the seventeenth century because they could no longer make a living in their native land. The Spenglers were attracted to the Harz mountains when they heard that there was a flourishing mining industry. Unfortunately, their expectations were not fulfilled because the mining industry gradually declined, forcing the Spenglers to choose different occupations. The children of Oswald's grandfather had already abandoned mining for other professions. Bernhard Spengler, Oswald's father, became a minor postal official. From what we know about him, which

22

is not very much, he seems to have been a model of the German bureaucrat: obedient, hard working, fastidious, and patriotic. His educational background was eminently respectable, for he attended *Gymnasium* (high school) and studied at the Polytechnical College in Braunschweig. Like his ancestors who had worked in the mines, Bernhard Spengler was a practical and hard-working man with a marked dislike of intellectualism for its own sake. He tried to instill the same values and attitudes in his son Oswald, but not always with success.

The maternal side of Oswald's family was quite different: in contrast to the Spenglers, who prized the practical virtues of the lower middle class, the Grantzows were more at home in the company of unconventional artists. Oswald's great grandfather, Friedrich Wilhelm Grantzow, was a Berliner. Little is known about him, except that his father had married a Jewish girl — a tidbit which we owe to the Nazis who were eager to discredit some of Spengler's ideas.[1] Oswald's grandfather, Gustav Adolf Grantzow, was a dancing instructor who broke with accepted Protestant tradition by marrying a Catholic girl from Munich. The couple had four daughters — Mathilde, Anna, Adele, and Pauline. Mathilde and Anna became moderately successful actresses; Adele, the most gifted, followed in her parents' footsteps by becoming an accomplished ballerina. From 1865 to 1876, at the height of her artistic career, she performed in front of the crown heads of Europe. Despite her wealth and fame, Adele was a melancholic and highly unstable girl. Her untimely death was so tragic that Oswald's mother felt obliged to keep the details a secret from her children. Adele injured her knee and suffered a blood infection. Forced to choose between amputation, which would have meant the end of her career as a dancer, and death, Adele preferred death by blood poisoning to life as a cripple. Before her death, Adele had bought her parents a large villa in Blankenburg. In 1876, the year of her death, the house was occupied by her father and by her sister Pauline.

Pauline, the mother of Oswald, was the least talented member of the Grantzow family. In appearance, she was plump and a bit unseemly. Her disposition, which Oswald inherited, complemented her appearance and frail physique: she was moody, irritable, and morose. Pauline met Oswald's father on one of her daily trips to the post office, where she would accompany her father to buy a newspaper. The suspicion has been raised that the good-looking Bernhard Spengler married Pauline when he learned that she had inherited a sizeable fortune. Perhaps pity also played a part in Bernhard's decision to marry the sad-looking girl. In any case, two years after they were married, their son Oswald was born (1880). Within five years Pauline Spengler gave birth to three more children — Adele (1881), Gertrude (1882), and Hildegard (1885).

In 1886, when Oswald began grammar school, Bernhard Spengler received a promotion and was transferred to the remote village of Soest, a town so unattractive that their new landlord referred to it as a pigsty which only lacked the roof to be complete.[2] Quarters in Soest were very cramped. The children had to sleep in one room, where Oswald would keep everyone awake by his incessant crying.[3] Although Oswald was in many ways a normal youngster, eager to play and cause mischief, he was also a very high-strung boy. Sometimes he displayed such nervousness that a doctor had to be fetched. Oswald's nervousness may have been caused in part by the tense atmosphere in the parental home. His father was always weighed down by the oppressive burden of his paper work — to the point where he would often bring unfinished files and reports home in order to allay his nagging fear of losing his job. Not surprisingly, such excessive preoccupation with his work made Bernhard Spengler tense and irritable, causing him to neglect his family.

Oswald undoubtedly felt the absence of his father's love and affection. Father and son gradually drifted apart, especially after Oswald became engrossed in literature and the arts. When the father began to sense a budding literary talent in his son, he waxed uneasy. Although well-educated himself, he regarded the arts with the complacent indifference typical of the pragmatic bureaucrat. He was afraid that his son might choose a literary career, which, in his opinion, was tantamount to a life of unconventional Bohemianism and dire poverty. On the whole, father and son went their own ways; neither one showed much interest for the desires or hopes of the other. Oswald rarely mentioned his father in later life, though he sometimes approvingly recalled his father's conscientiousness and his dedication to hard work.

Oswald was even more indifferent to his mother than he was to his father. Pauline Spengler displayed few, if any, maternal feelings for her children — least of all for her three daughters. In fact, she disliked them all, especially Gertrude, the prettiest. Although she gave Oswald preferential treatment, she never gave him love or affection. The Spengler home was therefore lacking in warmth and affection, since both parents were indifferent to their children and to each other. A visible sign of this parental indifference was the lack of concern shown about the children's clothes. The Spengler children were often exposed to the cruel mockery of other children because of the old-fashioned and ugly clothes they wore. As the children matured, the atmosphere in the parental home worsened. Spengler's mother became increasingly embittered, venting her frustrations on her children. Her dislike of Gertrude became almost pathological. One day she attacked the poor girl because she had not defrosted a chicken. When Gertrude, who was still half asleep, defended herself and inadvertently scratched her mother, the old lady was so infuriated that she took the case to court![4] As Hildegard later summed it up: "such was our home and my youth."[5] Elsewhere, she sadly remarked about the parental home that "if human beings have ever grown up without mutual love, it was us."[6] What Oswald thought of his mother in later years may be gleaned from a shocking reference he made about her in a letter to Adele. His sister had been forced to interrupt her artistic career because her mother refused to pay for it after she learned of her daughter's Bohemian life style in Berlin. When Adele asked Oswald for advice, he recommended that she bide her time until her mother's death. Apparently, he regarded his mother's death as the only solution to Adele's financial problem.[7]

In childhood, as in later years, Oswald suffered from terrifying fears, especially at night. Some of his childhood nightmares were still as vivid to him in old age as they were when he first dreamed them. His recurring nightmares involved crawling bugs on his blanket, barrels being emptied, staggering problems of arithmetic, the torture of slaves, and flying through the air. In some of his dreams his bed and blanket grew in infinite size; in others, his room would change form as the walls slid and turned. One of the most horrible dreams was about a hideous worm peeping out of an arm; and when Spengler tried to pull its head out, a second head had grown in its place, then another and another.[8]

Oppressed by these dark fears and suffering from parental neglect, the boy naturally tried to escape from this harsh reality. He did this by creating for himself a world of pleasant fantasy. "I was always a dreamer," he once confessed, for "all experiences dissolved into fantasies."[9] His penchant for fantasy sometimes tended to blur the difference between fact and fiction. In his autobiographical fragment, entitled *Eis Heauton*, Spengler candidly acknowledged his enchantment

with fantasy. "The great vice of my life," he exclaimed in a moment of self-castigation, "is lying. I always spoke untruths."[10]

What Spengler probably wanted to say was that he loved to embellish reality with the touch of his own temperamental feelings. As a young boy he loved to transform the world around him into a fairytale. In fact, fairytales delighted him so much that he decided to spin his own tales. One was called "Afro-Asia," another "Greater Germany." What strikes us about these youthful stories is Spengler's ingenious gift for blending poetry and history. As such, these childhood tales are not too dissimilar from his later writings, which have frequently been seen as imaginative poems. Spengler himself always insisted that man's past could only be recreated poetically, never scientifically. The works of the mature Spengler were in many ways only more sophisticated versions of the young man's historical poems.

II

In 1891, Spengler's family moved to the growing industrial city of Halle in Saxony. For eight years Oswald attended the Francke *Gymnasium*, a religious school that had been founded in the eighteenth century for the purpose of inculcating Protestant (pietistic) values. His mother insisted that Oswald be placed in the second grade since he had already attended more than a year of the *Gymnasium* in Soest. It was a poor decision. Inasmuch as the Francke schools were far more rigorous than the regular schools, Oswald soon fell behind in his school work and had to repeat the second grade. During his high school years Oswald did not display outstanding talents, though when he liked a particular subject, he did very well in it. His favorite subjects included mathematics, history, and geography; his least favorite subject was German. The reason for his dislike of German probably stemmed from the poor choice of reading material, which was boring and annoyingly moralistic. Spengler's sister Hildegard, who attended a branch institution of her brother's school, once used the expression "brave mare" in a school essay, a phrase which prompted the marginal remark "indecent expression" by her teacher.[11]

Spengler later grumbled about the religious character of the Francke *Gymnasium*. However, he conceded that the school had given him a firm grounding in both science and the classics. The religious atmosphere of the Francke school never left a deep impression on him. Although he was confirmed in the Protestant faith in 1895, he already looked upon religion, his own and that of others, as a dead ritual rather than a vital internal experience. His confirmation at the age of fifteen did not move him emotionally or intellectually; it was a ceremony to be performed because it was the thing to do. Years later, Spengler often envied the kind of faith that springs from within and then goes on to move mountains. He never had that experience himself. In fact, he argued that decaying cultures are incapable of deep religious convictions. He blamed the Francke Gymnasium for its attempt to combine religious piety and secular learning. All such experiments, he held, are doomed to failure, for no modern institution can honestly rear both a pietist and a twentieth century technocrat. Spengler insisted that true religion is not of this world; and as soon as it descends into the materialism of this world, it inevitably becomes mock religion.

Although Spengler was not a brilliant student, he performed above average in most of his subjects. He learned Latin, Greek, and French in school because they were considered indispensable for a well-rounded liberal education. Later he taught himself Italian, English, and a little Russian.

He excelled in mathematics and history, but did very poorly in sports because of his weak heart. It goes without saying that Spengler learned the classics of western civilization by heart, as evidenced by the dazzling display of his erudition in the *Decline of the West*. Since many modern authors, especially Nietzsche, Wagner, and Ibsen, were decried in school , he read them on the sly. All in all, Spengler received an excellent education in high school, an education noted for its depth and universality. A German education was then a prized experience, for it provided a student with a truly synoptic overview of man's knowledge. There was only one thing wrong with it: German education did not stress the practical aspects of learning nearly as much as it did the theoretical. The admonition of the eighteenth-century humanist G. C. Lichtenberg, who chided German educators for producing a stoop-shouldered race of bookworms, was still true in Spengler's day. German students were famous for firing off a salvo of learning at the slightest provocation, but they knew little about the practical side of their learning.

Now Spengler was acutely conscious of this shortcoming in himself, and he made strenuous attempts to combat it. In later life, he often attributed his lack of grace to his education. Spengler's awkwardness, however, was more rooted in his character than in his education, though the heavy theoretical emphasis of his education undoubtedly accentuated his lack of social polish. What prevented Spengler from intimate contacts, especially with girls, was his basic shyness and his fear of committing a *faux pas*. He compensated for this weakness by adopting habits of pomposity and formality. Later, he would add the protective mantle of the all-knowing prophet to compensate for his lack of self-assurance. Some historians have described such attitudes as being typical of the German intellectual, who tries to compensate for his lack of balance, grace, or self-assurance by dogmatic posturing and annoying over-expressionism.[12]

Shyness must have been an agony to Spengler when he grew up. In *Eis Heauton*, he candidly admitted: "shyness made my youth a torture."[13] The unbearable thing about his bashfulness was that it prevented him from getting close to the opposite sex. In fact, he often lamented about his "awful fear of everything female."[14] Was his absence of female companionship in later life — Spengler never married — the result of these fears? His biographer hints that impotence might have been a problem, for one of Spengler's projected novels was entitled "Impotence."[15] In this fragment, a young man suffers from occasional impotence, especially with women he really loves. Was that young man Oswald Spengler? The idea of impotence would recur frequently in Spengler's works in the form of cultural sterility. Already as a young man he perceived his own age as a barren wasteland, brightened by only occasional glimmers of creativity.

In 1899, Spengler passed his *Abitur*, the final examination leading to a German high school certificate. A photograph of that year reflects a spectacled, serious-looking young man with thick black hair and a mustache. The intensive stare of the eyes and the seriousness in mien are strongly reminiscent of the young Nietzsche. Looking at Nietzsche or Spengler's picture as a young man, one cannot avoid the feeling that these two had never tasted the innocence or frivolity of youth. Both were prematurely mature and prematurely old. If we look at Spengler's photograph at the age of thirty-five, only fifteen years after he graduated from high school, we see a wholly different person. By that time he had not only changed physically but intellectually. He had grown completely bald and looked as though he had gone through a harrowing intellectual experience. Juxtaposing Spengler's photographs at various stages of his life reveals much about his character and experience; it shows, above all, the intensity of his intellectual life. At the age of thirty-seven, about the time when he finished the first volume of the *Decline*, he looked like a man well into his fifties!

Upon completion of his *Abitur*, Spengler began his studies at the University of Halle. For several semesters (1899-1901) he bored himself with mathematics and the natural sciences. In the meantime, his father's health deteriorated steadily; in the summer of 1901 he died from the complications of a painful operation. Although Spengler later asserted that he was never very close to his father, he was disconsolate by his death at the time. When someone close to us passes away, we try to search for the meaning of that person's life. Spengler felt that his father had left a meaningful legacy through his exemplary devotion to the state. When he later recommended the Prussian spirit of state service, he was thinking about his father's unswerving duty to king and country.

After his father's death, Oswald needed to escape from his immediate surroundings. Accordingly, in the fall of 1901 he transferred to the University of Munich. Although he had not as yet settled on a profession, he had vague plans about pursuing a teaching career in the natural sciences. At this time he was still too captivated by student life to think seriously about a life-long career. Munich, still basking in the afterglow of the dream king Ludwig II, appealed to Spengler's artistic temperament. He was full of praise for the city's architecture and for its cultural life. Munich has always had a closer affinity to southern than to northern Europe; and its cultural life has reflected the lighter, more exuberant spirit of the Catholic south. As such, the city has always stood in sharp contrast to the ascetic and serious Protestant north. Perhaps Spengler was even then thinking of making the city his permanent home.

We know little about his studies in Munich, except that he was uncertain whether to pursue the humanities or the natural sciences. He read eclectically but widely and voraciously. Even then he showed a keen interest in contemporary issues: the problems of German foreign policy, the rise of socialism, *avant-garde* movements in the fine arts, and the impact of Darwin, Spencer, and Haeckel.

In the fall of 1902, Spengler went to the University of Berlin for the fall semester; then it was back to Halle for the concluding semesters. He had now decided to become a school teacher; but before taking his state teacher's examination, he first planned to finish his Ph.D. For his dissertation topic he had chosen the philosophy of Heraclitus, a daring subject for a young scholar because Heraclitus had only left a few and highly cryptic fragments of his thought. The interpretation of these paradoxical fragments presupposed considerable linguistic and philosophic ability. In the fall of 1903, Spengler submitted his thesis (*Heraklit- eine Studie Über den energetischen Grundgedanken seiner Philosophie*) and went to Halle for the oral defense. He failed. Spengler was not overly shaken by his failure because he felt that the decision was justified. In preparing his thesis, he had not consulted a single professor, so that his doctoral committee never had the opportunity to warn him about possible pitfalls before it was too late. Although his professors agreed with his overall approach, they felt that he had not provided sufficient documentation. Six months later, Spengler took his oral examination again and passed. In 1904, he passed his state teacher's examination in the natural sciences.

Spengler was only twenty-four years of age when he received his Ph.D. With some anxiety and trepidation he now set out on his first teaching assignment — a year's probationary teaching in a small north German town.

III

Spengler spent only a little over five years in the teaching profession (1905-10). From the outset he regarded teaching as a means to support his real interest in life — writing and research. He did not enter teaching because it satisfied some noble inner need in him. As soon as the opportunity for financial independence presented itself, he abandoned his teaching post immediately. His first teaching assignment was in the little town of Lüneburg, located about forty miles south of Hamburg in the Lüneburg Heath. He stepped off the train, inspected the town and the school, and was so horrified by the prospect of being trapped in a small-town milieu that he returned to Blankenburg with a nervous breakdown. Having recuperated, he served briefly as a substitute teacher before trying another assignment. When he was offered to teach in Saarbrücken, he gladly accepted because the city was situated in the heartland of German industry, quite apart from possessing the attraction of being located close to the French border. Spengler was to make several trips to France and other countries during his brief teaching career.

After successfully completing his year of student teaching (*Seminarjahr*), Spengler accepted another position in Düsseldorf (1906-7). Finally, in the winter of 1907, he received a permanent position in Hamburg, where he was to teach mathematics, natural sciences, history, and German. Spengler liked the patrician city of Hamburg, though he often suffered from agonizing migraine headaches in that damp city. Apparently, Spengler was a very good teacher, admired by his colleagues and loved by his students. But his heart was simply not in his work. He never had a high regard for school teachers because they lacked the scholarly habits which he admired. When he was teaching, he always made it a point to avoid the foibles commonly attributed to schoolteachers: pedantry, narrow provincialism, and incivility. He dressed in the latest fashion, tried to be *au courant* in the scholarly accomplishments of his profession, and made special efforts to broaden his cultural horizon by attending the theater or visiting museums. In Düsseldorf he was often seen in the local casino, something unheard of for a respectable *Oberlehrer*.

In the meantime, things were not going well at home. His sister Adele, who resembled her famous aunt in everything but talent, was stubbornly bent on pursuing a musical career in Berlin. Since she had only a modest talent, her hopes of becoming a famous pianist were frequently disappointed. One of her few concerts in Berlin was a dismal failure, prompting the malicious comment by one reviewer that "Miss Spengler mucked about with Beethoven and cold fingers."[16] The reviewer's advice was that she should expend her energies elsewhere. When Adele's mother learned of her Bohemian life style in Berlin, she stopped sending money, thus forcing Adele to return to Blankenburg. Adele's obsession about becoming a great virtuoso would ultimately lead to bitter disappointment and suicide. Spengler's two other sisters, Hildegard and Gertrude, tried to cope as best they could with the embittered mother. Hildegard married a music teacher by the name of Fritz Kornhardt. Her mother was somewhat chagrined that she did not make a better match, but she was appeased when she learned that Hildegard was pregnant. Unfortunately, she never saw the birth of her first grandchild, for in February 1910, she suddenly died.

A death in the family often brings out the worst in the survivors, especially when the deceased has left an unjust will. There was considerable acrimony over the spoils when Pauline Spengler died. Adele seems to have been the most greedy, displaying little reverence for the departed mother. She quickly dissolved the household by selling most of the furniture. Each family member then went his own way. Adele soon squandered her inheritance of 30,000 Marks and was penniless by 1917. The others were more thrifty, especially Oswald. In fact, his mother's death was a turning-point in his life, for the money he inherited from her death enabled him to retire from teaching. In March 1911, he took a leave of absence and returned to Munich with the intention of pursuing a literary career. It was a daring gamble on his intellectual and financial capabilities. Perhaps the idea of writing a great historical work, which could only be finished in complete solitude, was a motivating factor in Spengler's decision.

When Spengler arrived in Munich in the spring of 1911, he had only the vaguest notion about his future. He wanted to pursue a literary career, but he did not know precisely what he wanted to write about. His numerous sketches for short stories, plays, and novels reflect his uncertainties at this time. Except for a few short stories, Spengler has left us only fragments of his great literary ambitions. In view of his failure to produce a major work, it is not surprising that his unfinished fragments sound one common theme: an artist cannot fulfill his creative potentialities in a decaying culture. In the *Decline of the West*, Spengler gave a prominent place to this theme of thwarted potentiality.

One of Spengler's short stories, later published in his collected essays, was entitled "The Victor." With the Russo-Japanese war of 1905 as its background, the story depicts the heroism of a little Japanese warrior who sacrifices his life for the glory of his country and his culture. Spengler's narrative bristles with sanguinary adjectives and glorifies death as a holy experience.[17] Although the story is weak both in conception and execution, it tells us a great deal about the author's state of mind. Did Spengler glorify the will to power in order to compensate for his own weaknesses? There is much to be said for this theory. We know that Spengler was extremely short-sighted and in poor physical condition. Like Nietzsche, his idol, he suffered from constant headaches and other maladies. The army turned him down several times because of his poor physical condition. Imagining himself a mighty warrior endowed with superhuman strength was one way for compensating for his own limitations. Spengler's obsession with struggle, discipline, and toughness, however, cannot be solely attributed to his psychological frame of mind. Historians who have studied the late nineteenth century are almost unanimous in describing that age as being appallingly violent in spirit — if not always in deed. In fact, the late nineteenth century both institutionalized and intellectualized force and struggle. There was a profound conviction among statesmen and thinkers, supported by the evidence of contemporary science, that nations were engaged in a ceaseless struggle for survival, and that only the strongest nations stood the chance of emerging victoriously from it. Both Darwinism and Marxism, the two reigning ideologies of the West, not only identified struggle as an inevitable fact of nature, but insisted that violence was physically as well as morally desirable. The corollary was inescapable: if struggle is natural, then peace or cooperation is unnatural. Thinkers of all nationalities were almost delirious in proclaiming the virtues of struggle. Heinrich von Treitschke, the influential German historian, wrote: "war is both justifiable and moral, and . . . the ideal of perpetual peace is not only impossible but immoral as well."[18] The French writer Maurice Barres echoed the same sentiments and rhapsodically spoke of war as a holy experience: "The soil of the trenches is holy ground; it is saturated with blood; it is saturated with spirituality . . . the French make war as a religious duty."[19] And across the ocean, the American Admiral Alfred T. Mahan declared that "no greater misfortune could well happen than that civilized nations should abandon their preparations for war and take to arbitration."[20] Wherever one looked, Europeans, and Americans too, were making a cult of strife and war. As Jacques Barzun has said it so well, "no one who has not waded through some sizeable part of the literature of the period 1870-1914 has any conception of the extent to which it is one long call for blood."[21]

Spengler shared the assumptions of his age about force and struggle. He agreed with Treitschke or Admiral Mahan that war was a regenerating force in the life of a nation that had become spiritually decadent. In many of his writings, Spengler proclaimed struggle as a healthy condition of mankind; conversely, he called peace or pacifism a terminal disease of mankind. Sometimes he literally revelled in gory and brutal images, as when he spoke of "the intoxication of the senses when the knife cuts into an enemy's body, and when the smell of blood and the groaning are perceived by the triumphant senses."[22]

Spengler's glorification of struggle, force, and toughness, however, represents only one aspect of his personality, concealing a profound softness at its center. Although he was firmly convinced that nature was vicious and cruel, he could never resign himself to accept such a reality. There is always a tone of sad and sorrowful resignation when he talked about the merciless jungle of life. It seems that the tender-minded part of his personality was always in a tug-of-war with his tough-minded one. He could only accept the cruelty of this world by intellectualizing it, thereby rendering it bearable. In other words, like so many tender-minded intellectuals, he tried to come to terms with harsh reality by adopting tough ideas or convictions. This explains the martial sound of his writings and his carefully cultivated public image of the all-knowing, tough, and realistic prophet. Privately, however, Spengler was soft to the core of his being, as his sister Hildegard confirmed when she said that Oswald was a soft and unstable man who always needed to lean on someone.[23] Oswald wept easily and often, especially in the theater. A Baroque concerto or a poem by Hölderlin would move him to tears.

IV

Foreign observers of the German character have repeatedly pointed out that the Germans, more than any other people in Europe, exhibit a disconcerting tendency to combine great humane learning with an appalling habit of brutality and arrogance.[24] The Nazi experience seems to have confirmed the worst suspicions about this aspect of the German character. Of course, there is nothing innate about the German or any other national character. A people's character is molded by its shared historical experiences, not by certain innate predispositions. Nations, like individuals, define themselves in the process of their growth; they are what they are by virtue of their history. Since Spengler was a German through and through, it might be helpful to indicate briefly the nature of the historical situation in which he grew up. Spengler's Germanic origin throws significant light on his habits of mind, his likes and dislikes, and his perception of the world around him.

The fact that he was born only nine years after national unification explains much about his intellectual orientation. The Germans achieved nationhood very late in their history. For centuries, Germany was a political and geographic expression, a fragmented and disjointed jumble of independent principalities in central Europe. Within that "carnival jacket" of states, as Germany was mockingly referred to by her foreign detractors, one state gradually achieved supremacy — Prussia. Aided by the weaknesses of her enemies and the strength of her inveterate militaristic tradition, Prussia gradually extended her territories, her power, and her influence. Between 1864 and 1871, the Prussian state, led by its "Iron Chancellor" Otto von Bismarck, unified Germany and then imposed the militaristic character of its institutions on the rest of Germany. The Hohenzollern king of Prussia became the German Emperor; the Prussian capital of Berlin became the German capital; and Prussian institutions and habits of mind began to pervade all aspects of the national consciousness. The new Prussianized Germany possessed many good qualities. Even Prussia's most hostile critic, Friedrich Nietzsche, always stressed the positive aspects of the Prussian spirit: a respect for authority, a strong dedication to duty and hard work, and an ingrained sense for good order. At the same time, the militaristic spirit of Prussia was not always compatible with the spiritual values of higher culture. Friedrich Meinecke, the well-known historian of German thought and himself a Prussian, sadly acknowledged in his old age that there had always dwelt two souls in the Prussian breast — one capable of culture, the other hostile to it.[25] One was humane and individualistic, the outgrowth of the Protestant conscience, the other was brutal and collectivistic, the product of a long and rigid tradition of militarism. During the newly created German Empire the Prussian spirit of subservience to authority, symbolized by the semi-divine status of the Emperor, penetrated all aspects of life.

The aura of authority that was conveyed by the new German Empire was basically illusory. Beneath the grandeur of Hohenzollern power there lurked countless social forces antagonistic to the semifeudal monarchy. In times of rapid industrial growth, the monarchy adhered to the traditional values of its feudal or pre-industrial past. In many ways,

Spengler grew up in a hybrid society which saw the persistence of feudal political institutions within the context of modern capitalism and machine technology. The convergence of these antagonistic forces released acute social, political, and intellectual tensions which threatened the very fabric of German society. Other nations experienced the same floodtide of industrialization, but they possessed more stable institutions to cope with the consequences — gigantic cartels, labor unrest, periodic cycles of boom and bust, and complex bureaucracies. Germany neither possessed nor developed resilient institutions to cope with the rapid social and economic changes. The ascension of the politically immature and in many ways clownish Emperor Wilhelm II only aggravated the contradictions in German society. Wilhelm II symbolized the weaknesses of the new Empire. His bellicose and boisterous pronouncements never really concealed the inferiority and lack of assurance which animated them. Wilhelm was Germany writ large, for he represented a nation that had not found its identity, and that tried to cover up its weaknesses by wild posturing and dogmatic self-assertion.

The intellectual community mirrored the contradictions and anomalies inherent in the institutions of the new Reich. Bismarck had forged the new Germany by "blood and iron;" and in so doing, he had flung a challenge to the German intellectuals. How did the nation of "poets and thinkers" respond to the reality of power politics? The former enemies of Bismarck performed an astonishing *volte face* after the triumph of Prussian arms, abandoning their cosmopolitan and liberal ideals as so many pipedreams.[26] The awesome spectacle of Prussian might convinced many intellectuals that the essence of reality resided in power, not in abstract ideals. Having shifted their emphasis from the ideal to the real realm of existence, the German intellectuals were obliged to give a rationale for their acceptance of power politics. How did they envision power? Unlike the Englishman, who regards power as a pragmatic tool for the attainment of certain limited goals, the German intellectuals confronted the issue of power from the vantage point of their idealistic past. In other words, the Germans idealized power. Despite their rejection of abstract ideals, they could only grasp the meaning of power in abstract and highly theoretical terms. Thus, power was not just a pragmatic tool; it was the ultimate source and sanction of reality. Similarly, the state was not just a conventional set of institutions; it was the Divine Will as it exists on earth.

The German intellectuals, then, became political realists of the worst kind, glorifying power for its own sake. Acceptance of this premise entails the corollary that the strong always devour the weak. From this simple premise others inevitabily followed, namely, that the highest form of power was embodied in the military monarchy of Prussia, and that every citizen must submit himself in pious devotion to the state.

The glorification of power politics (*Realpolitik*) did not represent a viable synthesis of the real and the ideal. The synthesis was tenuous because the thorny problem of intellect and power had been resolved to the detriment of autonomous spiritual values. In other words, the German intellectuals, intoxicated by the triumph of Prussia's military institutions, profaned their idealism by making it subservient to the new values emerging from modern nationalism and industrialism. The spiritual tenor of German thought, rooted largely in pre-industrial Romanticism, was all too often crudely grafted onto the materialistic values of the machine age. Thus, sublime spirituality was often blended with gross materialism. Spengler's own thought can only be understood in this context, for it exemplifies the convergence of Bismarckian *Realpolitik* and German Romanticism.

V

Returning to Spengler's life in Munich, we are struck by his self-enforced isolation. Although he was not antisocial, he permitted very few people to intrude on his solitude. One close friend was Oscar Lang, a littérateur of far-ranging interests and abilities. Spengler helped him in putting together a book of readings in German poetry. Spengler was also on close terms with several artists, most notably with the sculptor Franz Cleve, who later made a fine bust of Spengler. Lang or Cleve were acquaintances to Spengler, not intimate friends with whom he could share his innermost ideas. Spengler's correspondence at this time confirms the dearth of real confidants. Between 1913 and 1918, he corresponded regularly only with Hans Klöres, a former colleague in Hamburg.

During these years of isolation, Spengler read hundreds of books in such diverse fields as art, literature, history, science, archeology, and philosophy. He would go to the library with a knapsack, scoop up a dozen books and read throughout the night in his little tenement apartment. It goes without saying that this monkish existence accentuated his loneliness. In his autobiographical fragment *Eis Heauton*, he often lamented that his contemplative existence had always deprived him of a normal life, and that it had focused his whole experience on his own encapsulated ego. If he had to write an autobiography, he said, it would be a confession of his soul rather than a description of the world around him. In moments of despair he regretted that he had missed so many opportunities to lead a normal family life. "I envy anyone who has lived," he remarked, "because I have only cogitated; and when I had the opportunity to live, I withdrew and let it pass me by, only to be overcome by bitter regrets when it was too late."[27] Spengler's haunting fear of being an alienated ego adrift in an indifferent world represents a recurrent theme in his thought, manifesting itself in his famous dichotomies: ego-world; microcosm-macrocosm; self-other.

We do not know precisely when Spengler conceived the ideas which gradually led to the *Decline of the West.* The idea for his subject may have originated when he saw Otto Seeck's work *The History of the Decline of Antiquity* in the display window of a bookstore.[28] Although Seeck's book may have given him the idea for his title, the belief that the West had shot its creative bolt and was now only capable of producing epigoni had been maturing in his mind long before he ever saw Seeck's book. Spengler had never been deceived by the proponents of progress who depicted the future in glowing optimistic terms. Where others saw progress, Spengler only perceived incipient decline. In part, his gloomy predictions undoubtedly stemmed from his own temperamental biases. At the same time, his pessimistic vision was based on very convincing historical evidence, past and present.

Gradually, Spengler articulated his feeling about widespread cultural decline by setting it into a wider historical perspective. He asked himself whether former cultures had experienced the same symptoms of decline as Europe did at the present time. If so, what were these symptoms and how could they be diagnosed? More specifically, how did cultures grow, mature, and wither away? These questions must have obsessed him for a long time. It only needed a spark to put him on the right path: the formulation of a coherent historical paradigm. Several events probably brought Spengler's inchoate ideas into sharp relief. One was the Second Moroccan crisis of 1911 in which Germany was thoroughly humiliated by Emperor Wilhelm's reckless diplomacy.[29] The aim of Germany was to preserve the territorial integrity of Morocco from French aggression. The Kaiser's policy was a dismal failure; Morocco fell under French hegemony and the Triple Entente, which Germany hoped to weaken, was greatly strengthened. Spengler sensed that the growing alliance system, the arms race, and the imperialistic entanglements would inevitably lead to catastrophe. As he looked at these developments, he came to the conclusion that Europe was about to be plunged into a major world war, and that the result would be cultural suicide for all concerned.

Oddly enough, Spengler never disavowed his belief in the Kaiser's aggressive foreign policy, even though he knew that it would eventually lead to war. As a German nationalist, he firmly believed that Germany must play a role in the world commensurate with its stature as a first-rate power. Spengler envisioned Germany as an ascendant power surrounded at all sides by ruthless enemies. He believed that Germany could only survive in this jungle if it mobilized all of its internal resources for the outer fight. International success, however, presupposes domestic tranquility. Spengler warned that Germany could not survive the impending world wars unless it put its domestic house in order. He realized that social harmony would be difficult to achieve because the Industrial Revolution, which was then sweeping over German society, was spreading deep class antagonisms in its wake. Spengler's solution to this social problem was a paternalistic monarchy which pursued broad socialist policies. He reasoned that the monarchy emboidied the general will, and that its classless character would enable it to transcend the narrow vision associated with particular interest groups. When he admonished the monarchy to pursue socialistic policies, Spengler was not advocating Marxian socialism. As we shall see later, Spengler regarded Marxism as a cancer on the body politic because it stimulated class warfare, expropriation of the expropriators, the dictatorship of the proletariat, and the destruction of the state. All these Marxist goals were odious to Spengler. By socialism Spengler meant "Prussian Socialisms." Designed to preserve rather than to destroy the state, Prussian Socialism means obedience to the state, love of duty, and unflagging dedication to one's work. Although every German citizen owes the state his unswerving support, the state, in turn, owes the citizen certain tangible rewards for his loyalty. These ideas of the state enjoyed wide support among intellectuals during the pre-war years. When the war broke out, these theories became enshrined in the German war effort in order to accentuate the difference between German *Kultur* and Anglo-American decadence.[30]

Like so many of his contemporaries, who cheered when war was announced, Spengler welcomed World War I as a healthy counterpoise to years of peaceful stagnation. Spengler was not a very good prognosticator of events during the war. Although he was right in predicting future annihilation wars, he was wrong about the future of his own country. Even in 1918, he stubbornly clung to hopes of a German victory. Spengler did not shirk his responsibility to the fatherland during the war. He wanted to sign up for the army, but was rejected again because of his poor health. The initial enthusiasm for the war, which Spengler had shared with his fellow Germans, gradually gave way to doubt and disillusionment. World War I did not bring joy to Spengler or anyone else. As the situation on the home front grew desperate, Spengler increasingly felt the pinch at home. When his interest on his foreign investments was stopped, he found it more and more difficult to eke out a living. To supplement his meager income, he was forced to write book reviews and to hold occasional lectures. Even this proved to be inadequate. The food situation was appalling, especially during the last two years of war. Other necessities were also getting scarce: the flow of gas and electricity, for example, was interrupted for many hours a day, forcing Spengler to write much of the *Decline* by candlelight. Sometimes it would get so bitterly cold that Spengler put a chair on top of the living-room table to be closer to the ceiling, where it was warmer. Bad news now came streaming in from all sides. In 1917, his high-strung sister Adele committed suicide; one year later, Fritz Kornhardt, Hildegard's husband, fell on the western front. The pessimistic Spengler, however, still believed in a German victory. In fact, he labored around the clock in order to finish the *Decline of the West*, hoping that its publication would coincide with a German victory!

The first volume of the *Decline* was substantially finished in 1917 and appeared in print a year later with Braumüller of Vienna. The second volume appeared with C. H. Beck of Munich, as did all subsequent editions of the *Decline*. It is unlikely that Spengler's book would have become a great popular success had Germany won the war. The book owed its success to Germany's defeat and to the general malaise of western culture after World War I.

Spengler himself was utterly crushed and dejected by Germany's defeat, asking again and again how such a cruel fate could have befallen the fatherland.[31] The years immediately following the war were indeed desperate for Germany. From 1918-23 Germany was enveloped by anarchy and confusion: Revolutions broke out in several German states, including Munich; the Emperor abdicated and fled to Holland; the still reigning monarchs all abdicated their thrones; the communists attempted to seize power; and Germany was forced to sign the humiliating peace treaty of Versailles. Only gradually was a semblence of order restored by the interim Social Democratic regime. A constituent assembly was elected and drew up a democratic constitution at Weimar. Almost over night, Germany had become a parliamentary democracy. Few people wanted it. The only persuasive reason for accepting democracy at this time seems to have been the mistaken assumption that it would please the allied powers and convince them to grant lenient peace terms. Nothing of the kind happened. The peace terms were not lenient, but Carthaginian. Perhaps the greatest tragedy was that the democratic forces in Germany had to bear the brunt of the allies' vindictiveness. It was the democrats who tacitly accepted the blame for the German defeat by signing the Versailles Treaty. The right-wing forces neatly stepped aside and put the onus of defeat on the democrats. As a result, the Weimar Republic was born with the permanent stigma of defeat and humiliation. In 1919, few observers expected the Republic to survive the year.

It was in this atmosphere of defeat that Spengler's *Decline of the West* made its appearance. Not surprisingly, the book became an instant bestseller and its author became so famous that some historians have referred to 1919 as "the Spengler Year."[32] Although only a few experts perused Spengler's heavy book from cover to cover, the message was simple enough for everyone to understand: Germany may have lost the war, but its tragic fate was common to the whole western world. In showing that Europe and America shared equally in the inevitable decline of the West, Spengler did much to soften the impact of the German defeat. The *Decline of the West* offered the down-cast German a kind of palliative for his dejection; it made him gloat with a malicious pleasure at the prospect of seeing everyone eventually dragged down into the mire. This, as much as its dazzling scholarship, made the *Decline* such a popular success in the early 1920's. By 1926, only eight years after the book was first published, over a hundred thousand copies had been sold — an amazing fact in view of the book's scholarly character.

VI

Although the public was captivated and impressed by Spengler's book, the scholars were almost unanimous in condemning it.[33] Brought up in an age that prided itself on its scientific approach to scholarship, the professional historians were bound to be critical of Spengler's synoptic view of history and of his firm belief in intuition. Historians inveighed against his claim that intuition could disclose more about the past than dispassionate scientific inquiry. They also disliked his morphological method, which they regarded as a poor substitute for the scientific approach. The hostility of the historical profession toward Spengler's work was the hatred of a guild whose professional canons had been flouted by an outsider. Where the historical profession prized scientific modes of inquiry, Spengler recommended intuitive insight, empathetic understanding, and imaginative flair. Where the professional scholars called for specialized monographs, Spengler insisted on broad cultural investigations. To borrow a phrase coined by Will Durant, Spengler was a historian-in-the-round who despised shredded history for its own sake. Spengler conceded that specialized monographs are important, but only when they succeed in throwing some light on broad historical movements. An historian is not worthy of the name unless he has acquired a firm grasp of the unities underlying historical variety.

In the *Decline of the West*, Spengler tried to show that cultures were the largest historical unities. He also attempted to show that historical events would always appear as a meaningless welter of detail unless the historian had a firm grasp of the nature and scope of culture. The only meaningful kind of history-in-the-round is the history of human cultures. Spengler had no illusions about the difficulties involved in such an enterprise. To reconstruct the life of a whole culture requires extraordinary skills in many fields such as politics, economics, art, religion, music, or science. Apart from acquiring the necessary scholarly tools which enable him to decipher man's cultural expressions, the historian of culture must also pay close attention to the tempo or style which animates the life of a culture. In other words, he must seek to elucidate the rhythm of development in the life history of a culture. Finally, the cultural historian, as Spengler envisioned him, owes his reader more than a descriptive explanation of past events. Even if he has shown how cultures grow, mature, and wither away, he must still go one step further by telling his readers what it all means. The historian shirks his duty, Spengler believed, if he does not inform his reader what the future has in store for him. The success of his book was proof positive to Spengler that he was right in mingling history and prophecy.

In explaining the meaning and the direction of history, Spengler satisfied a deep craving in the public mind for a sense of orientation. The professional historians had long abandoned the quest of finding meaning in the historical process as a whole. Having been trained to investigate bits and pieces of history without commitment to broad generalizations, academic historians were usually reticent in their conclusions. They were convinced that questions about the purpose or meaning of history did not belong to the world of scientific scholarship. When Spengler's work appeared, they saw in it the kind of history-writing which they had been taught to avoid because it was metaphysical or "pre-scientific." Living under the dispensation of the scientific outlook, they denounced Spengler as a throwback to "pre-critical" thinking.

Spengler's critics not only objected to his universalist approach, but to the conclusions he had drawn from his findings. His major crime, it seemed, was to have predicted the demise of the West. In canvassing the scathing critiques of Spengler's book, one cannot avoid the suspicion that the scholars cared less about the truth or falsity of his position than they did about its unedifying conclusion. Even when the scholars tried to analyze the *Decline of the West,* they all did so from the point of view of their narrow fields of specialization. As Manfred Schröter has rightly observed, this was precisely the wrong approach to Spengler's work.[34] A specialist in Egyptian or medieval history who has never thought about history-in-the-round is not competent to judge a universalist like Spengler or Toynbee. Even a hundred specialists, all exposing minor errors in Spengler's work, are still not entitled to render judgment on the overall soundness of his approach. This can only be done by someone who is willing to consider the merits of Spengler's premises, not by someone who dislikes his conclusions or who finds fault with trifling details.

The gnawing criticism of Spengler's enemies reached its culmination in a special issue of the scholarly journal *Logos,* in which seven specialists, all from the point of view of their own specialties, tried to discredit Spengler's ideas as unsound, unscientific, and unwholesome. The brief introduction, entitled "Escort" was so comical that it could have been written by a well-meaning maiden aunt. What followed, however, was less comical. A friendly reviewer of Spengler's work admirably grasped the essence of the controversy when he wrote:

Seven thoroughly decent professors have bandied together in order to kill Spengler. One of them expressly states that they perpetrate the deed willfully and with deliberation. Juridically, this is called attempted murder; literarilly, it is condemnation by mocking ridicule. Scene of the crime is the most eminent journal of German intellectual history, the organ of Rickert and Max Weber, of Simmel and Wölfflin — one that treats philosophy as an affair of culture rather than academic pedantry. This effectively heightens the punishment. The perpetrators advance with philological finesse. In one hundred and fifty scholarly and sometimes clever pages, they prove with great subtlety that Spengler does not possess sufficient knowledge in the seven fields of specialization and is therefore not competent to judge the nature of the Greek calendar or the small plastic art of Egypt in the fifth dynasty. Then why grapple with the dilettante Spengler? Answer: the seven enemies of Spengler want to protect the German nation from a work of delusion in which "inferior quality is served up in place of superior;" and they admonish "the son of the fatherland" to look to respectable historical scholarship. But they add that respectable historical inquiry is unfortunately incapable of satisfying the present need for a synoptic view of the contemporary scene.[35]

This tacit confession of incompetence saved Spengler's life. The public, after all, could care less about the distinction between the fifth and sixth dynasty in Egypt. The general reader wanted to know from the historian how the past affected his future. In refusing to address themselves to such issues, the professional historians lost face in the estimation of the general public. Spengler, on the other hand, owed his popular success precisely because he answered questions which the scholars refused to consider. The hostility of the academic community toward Spengler derived largely from the popularity of his works. The scholars could not abide Spengler for his bold vision, his daring hypotheses, his intuitive approach, and — above all — his popular success. After reading the special issue of the *Logos*, Spengler condemned the critiques as a disgrace to German scholarship.[36] He complained that his critics, in their eagerness to ridicule and condemn, had completely missed the gist of his position. The whole disgraceful affair, he said, was but another example of arrogant scholarship seeking to silence a novel idea. As with past discoveries, however, Spengler was hopeful that the power of change would force the scholars to incorporate his discoveries into their accounts of the past.

Spengler's pugnacious temperament did much to exacerbate the whole controversy. In a short and combative article, entitled "Pessimism?" (1921), he blasted his critics for having misunderstood the purpose of his book. The *Decline of the West*, he insisted, was not a philosophical work, but a representation of life. He wanted to show, he said, how man in the past expressed his life in action and deed as much as in word or thought. As to the accusation that the pessimistic conclusion of the book would paralyze modern man, Spengler replied that the recognition of impending disasters should inspire the opposite of stoic resignation.[37] His book, he reiterated, was actually a rationale for action. "Every sentence which is not written to serve life," he asserted, "seems superfluous to me."[38] Spengler was always afraid that he might be cast in the role of a pedantic scholar who has his head in the clouds. In his reply to his critics he depicted himself as an active person who lives in the world of phenomena and who writes down what he has experienced rather than what he has dreamed up.

Spengler was often his own worst enemy. Others defended him better than he did himself. One of his earliest, and most successful, defenders was Manfred Schröter, a professor of philosophy at the Technical University of Munich. In 1922, Schröter published a very sapient summary of the Spengler controversy under the title: *Der Streit um Spengler, Kritik seiner Kritiker (The Controversy around Spengler: Critique of His Critics)*. Schröter carefully dilineated the various points of disagreements between Spengler and his critics, and demonstrated that both sides had largely talked past each other. This act of clarification alone lowered the emotional temperature of the controversy. Although conceding that Spengler's work suffered from certain dogmatisms and pitfalls, Schröter reminded the critics that they had not met Spengler on his own ground. He concluded by saying that even if most of the adverse comments about Spengler's work were true, Spengler's overall vision would still be undiminished in its basic truth. Schröter believed that the *Decline of the West* had withstood the best that German criticism had to offer.

Schröter's book did much to break the ice between Spengler and the academic community. Gradually, some eminent scholars endorsed many, if not all, of Spengler's theories. One of the first to do so was Eduard Meyer, Professor of Ancient History at the University of Berlin. In an address to the German Historical Congress of 1924, Meyer praised Spengler's comparative method and the major conclusion Spengler had drawn from it, namely, that the West was in decline.[39] At the same time, he rejected Spengler's monodological interpretation of self-contained cultures. Meyer's reasonable attitude did much to remove the cloud of suspicion that had hung over Spengler's writings. After 1924, the Spengler controversy had largely subsided in Germany.[40]

Reaction to the *Decline* outside Germany varied from country to country. In Spain, where the tenor of intellectual life had always been more pessimistic than elsewhere in Europe, the *Decline* was well received. José Ortega y Gasset, Spain's foremost philosopher, was a supporter and frequent correspondent of Spengler's. His own major work, *The Revolt of the Masses*, was Spenglerian in tone as well as substance. In Italy, most scholars fell in behind Benedetto Croce, who admired some of Spengler's ideas, but generally dismissed the *Decline* as a pale imitation of the eighteenth century Italian thinker Giambattista Vico.[41] The French intellectual community, reared on Cartesian rationalism, reacted to Spengler's mysticism and intuitive insights with incomprehension. The French were especially perturbed by the belligerent tone which pervaded the pages of the *Decline*; they suspected that some of Spengler's slogan might be turned by the Germans into levers of political action.[42] On the other hand, one of the soundest appraisals of Spengler's doctrines, equalling that of Schröter in fairness and perception, was the French work *Oswald Spengler: Un Philosophe Allemand Contemporaine* by André Fauconnet. Spengler himself praised Fauconnet's book and opened a lively correspondence with the French professor.

In England, the *Decline of the West* received a cautious but respectable hearing. This was largely owing to the fairness of the historian G. P. Gooch, who had always kept a sense of proportion about the cultural differences between Germany and England. A more negative verdict was delivered by the Oxford philosopher R. G. Collingwood who faulted Spengler's critical view of history and his morphological method. Granting Spengler a "brilliant power of discrimination,"[43] he rejected his rigid monism and his pseudo-positivism.

Strangely enough, it was in America, the home of reseate optimism, that the *Decline of the West* was most enthusiastically received. The decadence of the Roaring Twenties undoubtedly had something to do with it. Spengler

seems to have stirred the Puritan conscience in America,
bringing out all the latent guilt of decadence and riotous
living. In America, as in Germany, Spengler became the voice
of the conservatives and the haunting ghost of the liberals.
The first volume of the *Decline* was published in 1926 by
Alfred Knopf; two years later volume two followed. The
translation of Charles Francis Atkinson was magnificent, for it
fully conveyed the beauty and emotional range of Spengler's
prose. By 1940, over twenty thousand copies of the *Decline*
had been sold in the United States. The scholarly world in
America, as in Germany, was largely hostile to Spengler.
Unlike their German colleagues, however, the Americans were
far more polite and restrained in their critiques.

Perhaps the most favorable reception of Spengler's work
occurred in South America. In Argentina, Professor Ernesto
Quesada had lectured on Spengler as early as 1921, when he
delivered a series of lectures on Spengler's philosophy of
history. Later, he published his lectures in book form under
the title: *Sociologia relativista Spengleriana*. Queasada was a
man of wide experience, who served in government as well as
academia. His travels took him all over the world in the
1920's and '30's; and on some of his travels he would usually
visit Spengler in Munich. Owing to Quesada's efforts
Spengler's ideas disseminated throughout South America.
Ortega y Gasset, who also taught in Argentina in the 1920's,
undoubtedly helped in bringing Spengler's ideas to the notice
of the Latin American public.

An important cycle of Spengler's life had ended with the
publication and the reception of the *Decline of the West*. His
prolonged struggle for recognition was now over. Encouraged
by his growing fame, Spengler abandoned his scholarly
isolation and threw himself into the world of political
controversy. The final act of his life was about to begin.

Spengler, age 19   Spengler, age 30

Spengler, while writing the *Decline*.   Spengler, age 37

Oswald Spengler in 1926

Oswald Spengler, 1931

Oswald Spengler, 1917

Fritz and Hildegard Kornhardt, geb. Spengler, 1907

B. THE MAN BEHIND THE THEORY:
MATURITY AND OLD AGE, 1920-36

I

In the 1920's, the prophet of the *Decline* entered the political arena in order to lend weight to his theories. A quick outburst of polemical writings flowed from his pen between 1919 and 1924: *Prussianism and Socialism* (1919); "Pessimism?" (1921); "France and Europe" (1924); "Tasks of the Nobility" (1924); "Political Duties of German Youth" (1924); and "Reconstruction of the German Reich" (1924). Written during the chaotic years of the fledgling Weimar Republic, these writings sounded one common theme: Germany must rekindle its conservative tradition and adapt it to the new realities of the twentieth century. If the tone of Spengler's prose seems shrill and even hysterical to us now, we must remember the chaotic times in which he lived. In Munich, violence had been endemic since Kurt Eisner proclaimed a Socialist Republic in late 1918. Eisner's assassination several months later ushered in years of right and left-wing agitation, culminating in the infamous Hitler Putsch, to which Spengler was an eyewitness.[44] In the rest of Germany, these years were marked by the reception of the hated Versailles Treaty, widespread political instability, the invasion of the Ruhr by the French, and catastrophic inflation. Spengler himself was undernourished, haggard-looking, and mentally exhausted from his work on the *Decline of the West*. Moreover, he was financially ruined because the war had wiped out his savings and investments. In anguish, the all-knowing prophet cried out: "Why has Destiny treated us this way?"[45]

Spengler's life and thought in the 1920's roughly paralleled the shifting fortunes of the ill-fated Weimar Republic. The traumatic birth of the Republic, spanning the years 1919-23, saw Spengler frantically enmeshed in political controversy. The middle years of the Republic (1923-29) were generally peaceful and prosperous for both Spengler and Germany. Disillusioned by politics, he withdrew from public debate and cultivated his scholarly interests. Then came the floodtide. The world-wide depression and the recrudescence of political extremism rocked the very foundation of German society. Between 1929 and 1933, the last years of the Republic, the major political event was the rise of National Socialism. For Spengler, the resumption of political anarchy meant the end of his self-enforced isolation. Once more, he plunged into the fray, contributing his share of confusion to the political questions of the day! Although he mistrusted the Nazis, he reluctantly endorsed some of their ideas. Hitler's Revolution after seizing power gave Spengler pause to think. Regretting his former support of Hitler, he now voiced his open disdain. Under the Hitler regime, Spengler became an embittered prophet without a forum. In 1936, he died in isolation and loneliness. These are the important episodes which stand out in Spengler's later life.

While Spengler was laboring on the second volume of the *Decline*, political events intruded upon his solitude and caused him to distill some portions of the work into a separate pamphlet entitled *Prussianism and Socialism*. The book was a masterpiece of political propaganda, comparable to Marx's *Communist Manifesto* in its blending of history and prophecy. Spengler's aim was to warn his readers of the impending threat of Marxian socialism. In 1919, the possibility of a Bolshevik revolution was a clear and present danger; and in order to forestall such an impending triumph of communism, Spengler suggested a clever alternative: state socialism based on Prussian principles. Spengler tried to convince his fellow Germans that there was no need for Marxism since Germany already possessed a viable non-Marxist brand of socialism. We have seen that these ideas had germinated in his mind since the turn of the century. Even then he had resigned himself to the fact that socialism was the wave of the future. At the same time, he had always insisted that socialism would sweep across Europe and America in different forms, adapting itself to the contour of the various national landscapes. The type of socialism best suited to Germany's national heritage, Spengler believed, was Prussian socialism.

Spengler's clarion call to Prussian socialism did not make many converts among the working classes. His greatest success was with the conservatives, who praised his ideas in *Prussianism and Socialism* as a genuine antidote to decadent Marxism. Admiral von Tirpitz was one of the first to endorse Spengler's ideas. Writing to Spengler in 1920, he expressed the hope that the Marxist-polluted working class would take *Prussianism and Socialism* to heart.[46] Tirpitz was not the only famous public figure was saw in Spengler an intellectual dear to his own heart. Spengler soon found himself in the company of some very celebrated figures such as the Bavarian crown prince, Walther Rathenau, Erich Ludendorff, Hans von Seeckt, and others. His real initiation into conservative circles came in 1919 when he lectured to the conservative *June Club*. Here he met Arthur Moeller van den Bruck, who was soon to electrify the public with his book *The Third Reich* (1923). Both Spengler and Moeller made such a striking impression on their listeners that the meeting ended with an enthusiastic endorsal of their ideas.[47] In the *June Club* Spengler encountered men who shared his distaste for parliamentary democracy and his hatred of the Versailles Treaty. Here, too, he found men whose convictions were rooted in the Prussian tradition, men who were not apologetic about their monarchist sentiments.

Spengler's political activities during these confusing years were motivated primarily by his strong fear that the future of Germany was imperilled. He felt that it was his duty as an intellectual to affect events through his ideas. We have seen that this formed an important part of his convictions. Academic isolation, he insisted again and again, is social irresponsibility. Every thinker worth his salt must attempt to make his ideas socially or politically relevant. Spengler was clearly reacting against the traditional attitude of the German intellectual who had always prided himself on his splendid political isolation. Spengler warned that Germany could ill afford such an attitude of self-delusion. He called on the German intellectual to dedicate himself to society, even if it involved considerable risk, frustration and hardship.

Yet, Spengler's ambition of combining theory and practice was never realized. After several years in the limelight, he retreated into privacy. What had gone wrong? The answer is that Spengler had been insulated far too long from public life to become a man of action over night. Besides, temperamentally he was not suited for the world of political struggle. At first, his participation in public debates seemed to have enriched his life. He made new and lasting friends, especially among captains of industry, who fascinated him because they possessed practical knowledge and the ability to move men. The industrialist Paul Reusch, who was one of the founding fathers of industrialization in the Ruhr, struck up a lasting friendship with Spengler after the war and actively championed some of his ideas.[48] Ties of friendship and admiration also bound Spengler to the Hamburg exporter Roderich Schlubach, the newspaper mogul Alfred Hugenberg, the industrialist Karl Helfferich, and the industrial magnate

Hugo Stinnes. In the company of some of these men, Spengler's own ambitions were greatly stimulated. He toyed, for example, with the idea of emulating William Randolph Hearst by founding his own newspaper cartel.[49]

Although nothing came of Spengler's grandiose ambitions, he was at least trying to be sincere about his conviction that a good thinker is one who puts his ideas into practice. In pursuance with this belief, he went on lecture tours; he made contact with men of power; and he tried to appeal to youth. An important figure in his life at this time was Elizabeth Förster-Nietzsche, the sister of the great philosopher. It was she who introduced Spengler to a wide variety of famous political and academic notables. His friendship with Nietzsche's sister began in 1919 when he received an award from the Nietzsche Archive in Weimar. A close friendship of fifteen years followed. In the 1930's, however, Spengler felt obliged to withdraw from the Nietzsche Archive because it was being turned into a shrine for National Socialism.

By 1924 Spengler was becoming weary of public debate. He was visibly uncomfortable with the fame and notoriety his political writings were inspiring both at home and abroad. His good friends warned him not to dissipate his genius on trival political issues. Spengler took the advice of his friends, partly because he had always felt ill at ease in an atmosphere of constant political tension, and partly because he knew that he was basically a man of theory rather than of action. For all these reasons, including his deteriorating health, Spengler decided to retreat from public life and resume his scholarly interests.

II

When Spengler returned to the solitude of his study, he

tried to continue where he had left off in the *Decline of the West*. The intervening years had not been a complete loss because Spengler benefited by the flood of criticism which his great work had evoked all over the world. Most of the criticism was vituperative and unconstructive; but there was enough insightful criticism which caused him to rethink some of his major premises. The most persistent objection to the *Decline*, apart from the widespread disagreement with its ominous conclusions, was its rigid monodological treatment of culture. Spengler had posited eight self-sufficient cultures, each developing unique philosophic, literary, artistic, and religious styles of expression. This view committed him to an uncompromising relativism. In the *Decline of the West*, historical man as such does not exist: there are only Faustian, Apollonian, Magian, or Chinese men — all speaking different languages, thinking different ideas, and perceiving different things. Is there nothing intrinsically human which these men share in common, irrespective of their cultural surrounding? Spengler thought that there were distinctly human traits which transcended all superimposed culture traits. The elucidation of these universally human attributes, especially as they manifested themselves in man's prehistoric past, became Spengler's great obsession. In a projected work, probably begun in 1925/26 and entitled *Urfragen (Primal Questions)*, Spengler wanted to fill a gap in the *Decline of the West*. As he put it, he sought to "portray the universally human element, the phenomenon man on this earth crust, the eternal and primevally human instincts, love, hunger, fear, war, hate."[50] The subtitle of *Urfragen* was "Entwurf einer Frühgeschichte der Menschheit" (Sketch for a Prehistory of Mankind). From his extant aphorisms, sketches, and notes, which have only recently been published, we learn that Spengler contemplated writing a new cultural history, designed at once to serve as a supplement and a complement to the *Decline of the West.*[51]

In the *Decline*, Spengler had portrayed the life histories of self-enclosed cultures; in his projected *Prehistory of Mankind*, he wanted to describe how prehistoric cultures interacted. Before the arrival of high cultures in the ancient Near East, Spengler now admitted, there was continuous cultural diffusion. Unfortunately, Spengler never completed his new vision of culture. His biographer suspects that he was afraid that his new interpretations might jeopardize the major premises of the *Decline.*[52] Having posed as the irrefutable prophet of the West, it was difficult for him to admit errors or to make major revisions in his system. Although there is some truth to this argument, the answer to Spengler's silence on these matters must be sought elsewhere. The truth is that Spengler had set himself an impossible task. He wanted to write a grand panorama of the human soul from its emergence in the eons of prehistoric times to its actualization in the high cultures. This plan was too immense and too visionary, for it involved a knowledge of prehistory and archeology which neither Spengler nor anyone else possessed. Even today we know little about man's spiritual questings before the appearance of written records. In Spengler's day even less was known of prehistoric man, certainly not enough to enable the historian to recreate early man's spiritual life. Spengler had the added disadvantage of being a novice in the field of archeology, although he made strenuous efforts to overcome his deficiencies. If we add to all these obstacles Spengler's failing health, we can see why he never finished his great project.

Although Spengler did not complete his cultural history, he continued to work on it until his death. As he grew older, the subject of man's early beginnings would haunt his intellect. Prehistory was then in its infancy as a science, attracting a number of bold conquistadors. One of the most colorful explorers of prehistoric man was Leo Frobenius, whom Spengler met in the early 1920's. Spengler was probably drawn to Frobenius because he was not only a successful African explorer, but because he was also a brilliant outsider who dared to question every canon of "respectable" archeological research. Frobenius was forever flitting back and forth between Europe and Africa, collecting prehistoric objects, assembling impressive exhibitions, and formulating bold speculative theories. His great dream was to build an Institute of Cultural Morphology; and it was in connection with these plans that he sought Spengler's help. Spengler tried his best to promote Frobenius' ideas because they closely approximated his own. For example, Frobenius advocated a view of culture which was very similar to Spengler's in the *Decline of the West*. Like Spengler, Frobenius postulated a spiritual theme or *Paideuma* as the motive force behind every cultural expression.[53] The *Paideuma* (Spengler's *Prime Symbol*), according to Frobenius, determines both the direction and the style of a culture. Frobenius also shared Spengler's idea of cultural cycles, holding that cultures traverse the successive phases of childhood (*Barbarei*), youth (*Kulturei*), and manhood (*Mechanei*). He also shared Spengler's view that cultures flourish in their youthful phases and then wither away when they grow old and sclerotic. The two men also agreed that the last phases of a culture are marked by increasing technological complexity; they disagreed, however, on the issue of cultural diffusion. Frobenius believed in cultural interaction, whereas Spengler adhered to the idea of cultural self-sufficiency, at least in his published writings.

Although Spengler learned much from Frobenius, he eventually broke with him when he perceived what he was really like: a dilettant and a showman. To be sure, Spengler admired boldness and unorthodoxy in a thinker, but his painful contact with the world of scholarship had convinced him of the importance of being taken seriously as a trustworthy authority. This is why he preferred the expert advice of respectable scholars such as Eduard Meyer, George Steindorff, Alfred Doren, Gustav Haloun, and Hans Erich Stier. He took great interest in new archeological discoveries and frequently visited scholarly conferences. Yet, during these years he absorbed more than he contributed to the field of Prehistory. The only major publication on the subject of Prehistory, save for a few articles, was his short essay *Man and Technics* (1931). It is commonly agreed that *Man and Technics* is Spengler's weakest book, although in fairness to him, we should remember that he intended to use this essay as a kind of prolegomenon to his great cultural history. All it was intended to do was to adumbrate some of his preliminary findings — nothing more. The book reiterates a prominent theme of the *Decline*, namely, that man's history is irremediably tragic. Since Spengler located the source of man's tragic fate in prehistoric times, he felt obligated to retrace the tragic heritage of man's primitive past. In *Man and Technics*, Spengler tried to show that primitive man was a magnificent predatory animal who possessed two major advantages over other beasts of prey: a superior brain and ambidextrous hands. Yet, man's advantage is also his tragic fate, for he remains a savage beast in spite and because of his superior intelligence. Although man's genius for invention allows him to escape from his primitive origin, his savageness remains basically unaltered beneath the veneer of civilized society. As Spengler saw it, man's tragedy arises from a perennial clash between his natural aggressive instincts and the unnatural taboos or moral dictates which he erects to contain his savageness. Technology, Spengler said, is man's way of compensating for his weaknesses. Man fashions tools or machines in order to protect himself or to improve his material condition. At the same time, his aggressive nature prompts him again and again to direct technology to war-like ends. As cultures mature, technology becomes more complex and more sophisticated, and so does the nature of warfare.

Spengler coupled this gloomy account of man's tragic condition with an equally pessimistic reminder that Faustian man was reaching the end of his rope. The book ends with the same prophecy as does the *Decline of the West*: Faustian man has dissipated his energy, compromised his ideals, and squandered his technical know-how. More youthful and more vigorous races, Spengler predicted, would probably take the place of Faustian man. Is there nothing we can do? There is, Spengler said: Let us stand fast and confront our impending destiny with resigned determination. Let us emulate the Roman guard who stood watch at Pompey during the eruption of Mount Vesuvius. He let the blazing lava envelop him because he had not been relieved![54]

Man and Technics did not stir up much excitement, although its pessimistic conclusions prompted a number of angry rebuttals. Spengler's remark that optimism meant cowardice, and that the only philosophy worthy of Faustian man was "manly pessimism," hardly endeared him to the average reader. In 1931, at the depth of the world-wide depression, Germans were listening to different prophets than Spengler. Adolf Hitler and his S. A. battalions were knocking at the gates of the Chancellery, ready to proclaim the "Thousand Year Reich." Before turning to Spengler's reaction to Hitler and the Nazis, let us take a more personal look at the private, as distinct from the public, Spengler. What sort of man was behind these gloomy historical prophecies?

III

A man who preaches doom and gloom is unlikely to be

happy or fulfilled in his private life. From what we know of Spengler's last years, there emerges the picture of a man who suffered intensely from the burden of his pessimistic convictions. Spengler suffered because he was honest with himself and his readers. There is no evidence, either in his writings or in his public pronouncements, that he derived pleasure from his gloomy visions regarding the future of Faustian man. Nor did Spengler ever write a single line to stimulate the perverse thrill for the macabre in his readers. The impending decline of the West, as Spengler was well aware, would undoubtedly be greeted with a sense of relief or even joy in some quarters; but Spengler himself never joined the ranks of the despisers of the West. What Spengler attacked was not the West, but the weaknesses of the West. Yet, the problem was that Spengler, unlike more hopeful analysts of the West, did not believe that the weaknesses of the West could be remedied. It was this irreconcilable dilemma which caused Spengler so much agony as a writer. Spengler, then, suffered from the worst affliction which could befall an historical prophet: he knew that his writings on the West were a *post-mortem*, not a positive program pointing to the resuscitation of the West.

Convinced of the truth of his ideas, Spengler resigned himself to a life of quiet desperation. Outwardly, however, there were few signs that he felt that way. The success of the *Decline* enabled him to move to a more spacious apartment in the Widenmeyerstrasse, which overlooked the Isar River. He furnished his new home with some exquisite objets d'art, acquired at auctions or sent to him by his admirers. Visitors were struck by Spengler's vast collection of books, which lined the walls; his paintings and vases; and his Turkey-red carpet on which he would pace up and down while formulating his ideas.[55] Although his financial situation improved markedly with his growing fame, he continued to live a rather austere bachelor's existence. His pleasures were modest: regular visits to the Theater, where he would cry profusely; a fine bottle of wine; a good supply of black cigars; and occasional travels to Italy.

Spengler's mental well-being did not match his new-found material prosperity. He was basically a very lonely man, uncomforable in his time and uneasy in the company of his own ideas. Apart from his sister Hildegard, who kept house for him, he had few friends with whom he could discuss personal problems. The only man who seems to have been close to him was Hans Albers, a clerk who worked for Spengler's publisher in Munich. Albers had met Spengler shortly after the publication of the *Decline of the West* and thereafter became the prophet's eager sounding board. On one of their frequent walks, Spengler had outlined the major themes of his second volume of the *Decline*. On one particular walk, Albers was so impressed by Spengler's view of socialism, that he urged his friend to publish his novel ideas immediately.[56] As we know, the result was Spengler's essay *Prussianism and Socialism.* Albers remained fiercely loyal to Spengler — so much so, that when Spengler died in 1936, Albers committed suicide by throwing himself in front of a train. Next to Albers, the only other person close to him was his sister Hildegard. Brother and sister felt a close kinship; but temperamentally, they were quite different. Hildegard's diaries, which are extremely frank in tone, reveal some of the less attractive aspects of Spengler's personality: his saturnine moods, his penchant for *Schadenfreude* (the glee experienced when one's enemies or friends suffer a reversal in their fortunes), his apparent obliviousness to the miseries of the average man, and his disconcerting habit to twist the truth in his personal affairs. At one point, Hildegard made an interesting slip of the tongue when she mused about the different images of Oswald Spengler — that is, Spengler as she knew him and Spengler as he was known to the world.[57]

To the public, Spengler presented the image of the clairvoyant prophet whose predictions would come to pass with unfailing regularity. This explains the pontificating tone of his writings; it also accounts for the boldness of his convictions. A man who feels himself an irrefutable prophet is unlikely to take kindly to criticism. Indeed, Spengler reacted to criticism with an air of disdain, conveying the impression that his detractors were either dolts or simply lacked his intuitive gifts. This feeling that he possessed special intuitive insights often caused Spengler to overestimate the novelty of his theories. The *Decline* bristles with self-confident phrases such as "never seen before;" "in this book is attempted for the first time;" "I put forward the natural, the Copernican form of the historical process;" or "so far a genuinely Faustian treatment of history has been entirely lacking."

The public Spengler, then, appeared to be a rock of certainty, a man of undaunted conviction. Privately, however, Spengler was consumed by nagging doubts, desperately seeking public approval and moral reinforcement. The public Spengler seemed quarrelsome and dogmatic, but the private Spengler was surprisingly polite and unassuming. His friends are in full agreement that Spengler was a superb conversationalist, who always listened politely, never interrupted a friend's discourse, and rarely revealed a flash of dogmatism.[58] Unlike his public utterances, which were shrill *in extremis*, Spengler's private conversations were always marked by unusual decorum. As one of his friends remarked, Spengler disliked harsh or emotional outbursts in private discussion; and when his partners became agitated on a certain issue, Spengler became more calm and reserved.

The contradictions between the private and the public Spengler do not end here. Publicly, Spengler called for submission to Prussian discipline; privately, however, he behaved like a confirmed Bohemian, keeping irregular and highly eccentric hours. He urged the Germans to close ranks behind the authoritarian state. Personally, however, he detested regimentation in any form, carrying his antisocial attitudes to the point where he would isolate himself for days on end without talking to a single soul. He stressed the importance of intimate relationships, the necessity of marriage and family, and the need for an organic community of believers. Yet, personally, he avoided intimate contacts and never married. In order to shield himself from the world, he made it a habit to hang a sign on his door which read: "OUT OF TOWN."[59] When he actually left town, the sign would be taken down. Yet, this self-imposed isolation was a torment to Spengler. For his autobiography, he toyed with such titles as "Loneliness" or "Life of the Outcast."[60]

The public Spengler, then, was not synonymous with the private Spengler. The man behind the theory was haunted by a persistent fear of being lonely, rejected, or worthless. He often felt himself inadequate to aspire to the rigor of his own public utterances. For example, he demanded nerves of iron and steel for Faustian man; but as to his own moral stamina, he sadly confessed: "I never went a month without thoughts of suicide."[61] This recognition of falling short of his own standards — an awareness which is conspicuous in all great moralists — was a painful experience to Spengler. He agonized about his weaknesses with the same brutal honesty as Rousseau did in the *Confessions*, with the difference that Spengler rarely tried to project his shortcomings on society at large. Spengler believed that, in the final analysis, the individual has to assume responsibility for his own weaknesses. Spengler was acutely conscious of his limitations; and privately he wondered whether he was entitled to promulgate standards which he could not meet himself.

Spengler never resolved the conflict between his public

image and his private self-image. A resolution was probably impossible. Privately, Spengler could not live up to the image of the iron-willed prophet. His glorification of the will to power and his appeal to unemotional hardness were betrayed again and again by his countless emotional instabilities. In the final analysis, Spengler was a soft man who could not bear his own perception of the world as a cruel jungle. His biographer tells us that he wept easily and profusely. The sight of an old woman with tangled grey hair would turn his hardened soul to jelly.[62]

In sum, the stern-looking, supremely self-assured prophet who transfixes us with his forbidding countenance on the cover of the *Decline* was Spengler as he wanted to see himself. The world has largely accepted this image. Spengler himself tried to live up to it; and in so doing, transformed his life into torment and sustained suffering. Yet, his own suffering heightened his perception of the tragic element in man's history. Few other historians have portrayed the tragic sense of historical life as profoundly as Spengler did. What made this insight all the more valuable was that Spengler brilliantly portrayed the grandeur and the beauty which are embodied in man's tragic past. Admittedly, much of what Spengler described was colored by his own pessimistic temperament, but it was also his keen sense for tragedy which enabled him, as it did few other historians, to illuminate a very important dimension in man's past.

IV

Spengler's withdrawal from public controversy had coincided with the return of relative stability in the rest of Germany. The middle years of the Weimar Republic

(1924-29), however, were marked by a very deceptive calm and an even more illusory prosperity. Germany's political situation, symbolized by the octogenarian President Paul von Hindenburg — whom his detractors called a "zero paving the way for Nero" — was as precarious as the new-found economic prosperity. When the American stock market crashed in 1929, the economic shock waves reached Germany in a matter of weeks, since American loans had in large part propped up the sagging German economy. The result was a deep depression, comparable in scope to that in the United States. The political repercussions were immediate: all the parties pledged to the violent overthrow of the Republic gained a new lease on life. In the election of September 1930, the Nazis polled more than 6.4 million votes and elected 107 deputies to the Reichstag. The communists also won a great victory, increasing their representation in the Reichstag from 54 to 77 seats. It became increasingly clear that moderate parliamentary democracy could not survive in a society that had become so hopelessly polarized by extremist factions. The newly elected Reichstag of October 1930 revealed that democracy had degenerated into anarchy as the Nazi deputies marched to their seats in full uniforms, singing and disrupting the proceedings. The communists behaved in the same rowdy fashion. This chaos inside the Reichstag was writ large in the rest of Germany, where extremists of all hues took their grievances to the street, clashing with each other and the police in bloody encounters. In desperation, the Brüning government invoked Article 48 of the constitution, which enabled the government to rule by executive decree. When Brüning fell from power in May 1932, the Nazis were already banging at the portals of the government. After the election of July 31, 1932, the Nazis were the strongest party and Hitler was the most powerful politician in Germany. As Alan Bullock put it, "with a voting strength of 13,700,000 electors, a party membership of over a million and a private army of 400,000 S. A. and S. S., Hitler was the most powerful political leader in Germany, knocking on the doors of the Chancellery at the head of the most powerful political party Germany had ever seen."[63] After several months of shabby political deals, in which Hitler deftly played his enemies against each other, President Hindenburg appointed Hitler to the post of Chancellor (January 30, 1933). The Nazi Revolution had begun.

The economic crisis and the recrudescence of political extremism roused Spengler from his isolation. Spengler's conservative bias naturally drew him to the proliferating right-wing parties, although he was still ambiguous about the Nazis. What he could not abide in their outlook was their utopianism and their racial gibberish. At the same time, he sensed the enormous dynamism of the movement and gave his guarded approval to some Nazi proposals. "Hitler is a Dummkopf," he told his sister Hildegard, "but the movement must be supported."[64] Having predicted the coming of Caesarism, he was still surprised by the form it assumed under Hitler's leadership. When Hitler came to power, he was at first willing to suspend judgment.

On July 25, 1933, Spengler was granted a personal audience with Hitler in Bayreuth. Like many of his conservative friends, he labored under the illusion that he could moderate Hitler's behavior by offering his expert advice! Although we do not know precisely what transpired during their hour and a half conversation, we know that Hitler did most of the talking. Spengler came away from the meeting with a sense of relief, referring to Hitler as a highly decent man who wanted to do what was best for Germany. Still, he was not overly impressed by Hitler's personality: "sitting next to him," Spengler mused, "one did not gain the slightest inkling that he represented anything significant."[65]

Rumor had it that before the two men separated, Hitler asked Spengler for one final advice. Spengler is said to have responded cryptically: "Watch your Praetorian guard!" A year later Hitler purged his Praetorian guard — the S. A. If Spengler actually offered this advice, it would have been his only one that was ever followed by a public leader!

Gradually, however, Spengler's views of Hitler and the Nazis changed drastically, especially after the movement revealed its utopian program. In his last book, *Years of Decision* (1933), published during the early months of the new regime, Spengler already portrayed the Nazis as dangerous dreamers, intoxicated by their bombastic rhetoric and blinded by their roseate visions. Only ten years before, Spengler had been brought face to face with the same kind of mass delusion. This was the time when the Nazis staged their first *Putsch*. He assumed that ten years of political experience had taught the Nazis the hard facts of life; but when he saw that they were no more circumspect in their actions than they were a decade ago, he knew that he had completely misread the movement. Now that the Nazis had seized the reins of power, Spengler shuddered at the consequences.

What Spengler found most unattractive in National Socialism was its virulent racism. He lambasted the belief in Aryan purity because such theories were not supported by historical evidence. The term race, he argued, has no meaning when it is defined in a biological sense — that is, when a physical difference is transmuted into a qualitative difference. The truth is, Spengler insisted, that race denotes a spiritual rather than a physical phenomenon.[66] Race refers to a recognizable group of people which share a common spiritual experience; it is a cultural bond that unites the members of a society by virtue of certain commonly recognized ideals and institutions. Spengler was too good an historian to classify races according to physical or even linguistic traits, and to deduce from this procedure qualitative racial differences, as the Nazis insisted on doing. He certainly recognized the differences between national groups, but he also believed that national differences stemmed from cultural rather than biological facts. Germans, Frenchmen, or Italians differ, but they also share certain similarities because they are all bearers of the Faustian spirit.

As to the Jew, Spengler ascribed his uniqueness to the peculiar cultural tradition which has molded his character. The Jew is neither superior nor inferior to anyone else; he is simply different. It is in his cultural distinctiveness, however, that the tragic fate of the Jew is emboidied. Spengler observed that the character of the Jew was molded by his position as an outsider in European society. Since outsiders are generally forced to adopt attitudes that are inimical to the mainstream of society, they are perceived as a threat to the society that has excluded them. In time of crisis, these outcasts always serve as ready scapegoats to societies that cannot solve their own problems. Spengler was fully cognizant of the Jew's dilemma, and he believed that the only solution for the Jew lay in abandoning his Jewishness. In other words, he believed that the Jew must opt for assimilation or go under.

Spengler, then, was not a racist. Only racial inferiors, he once caustically remarked, preach racism.[67] By racial inferiors, he meant mental inferiors; and the mentally-retarded he specifically had in mind were the Nazis! If Spengler hated the Nazis for their racial nonsense, he despised them even more for their inflated aspirations. Hitler's boast of a "Thousand Year Reich" insulted his historical sense and only reinforced his growing fear that Nazi megolomania would lead Germany to destruction. Spengler was particularly worried about foreign reaction to the antics and grotesqueries of the Nazis. As he put it in his last book, the *Year of Decision*,

"The National Socialists believe that they can fend against and without the world at large, and that they can build their castles in the air without . . . reaction from abroad."[68]

Spengler's hostile reaction to National Socialism came as a surprise to many readers who had studied his political writings. For over two decades Spengler had advocated theories roughly analogous to National Socialism. In *Prussianism and Socialism,* for example, he had urged the adoption of state socialism based on the Prussian instinct of obedience, duty, and hard work. He had sketched an outline for an organic German community without social frictions, a society that would preserve the best elements of the feudal past within a new industrial setting. He believed that this was the only viable solution to the conflicts inherent in present-day industrial societies.

Since the Nazis advocated similar solutions, it is not surprising that Spengler has so often been viewed either as a precursor or a fellow traveller of National Socialism. Elizabeth Förster-Nietzsche, for example, simply could not understand Spengler's hostility toward Hitler; and when Spengler withdrew from the Nietzsche-Archive, she was dumbfounded. Writing to Spengler, she feigned complete bewilderment:

> To my great sorrow I hear that you have turned away from the Nietzsche-Archive and that you want nothing more to do with it. I regret it enormously and simply cannot comprehend the reason for it. I was informed that your attitude toward the Third Reich and its Führer is one of vigorous opposition, and that your withdrawal from the Nietzsche-Archive — which is bound to the Führer in hearty devotion — is supposed to be related to it. Now I know from personal experience that you have strongly endorsed our most treasured ideal.

> But it is precisely this which I find incomprehensible. Doesn't our beloved Führer offer the same ideal and values for the Third Reich which you expressed in your *Prussianism and Socialism*? Now what is it that caused your strong antipathy?[69]

Publicly, Spengler never spelled out his antipathies to National Socialism; privately, however, he jotted down his objections to the new regime and its policies. It became increasingly clear to the Nazi sympathizers that Spengler could not be enlisted in their cause. When Joseph Goebbels asked Spengler to contribute a propaganda piece for the fall elections of 1933, Spengler flatly refused.[70] Having regarded Spengler as a potential comrade-in-arms, the regime now turned against him by depriving him of his audience. The propaganda ministry simply forbade any mention of his name in the press. When his *Years of Decision* went to press, a number of influential Nazis tried to prevent its publication. The final decision rested with Hitler, to whom Spengler had sent a personal copy with the naive request to discuss the book at some future meeting.[71] Hitler finally gave his consent, although he personally found the book too pessimistic.

Hitler's reaction to Spengler was representative of the way the Germans now felt about the prophet of doom. Where Spengler offered "manly pessimism," Hitler promised the Germans a glorious future; where Spengler lamented the decline of the West, Hitler exalted the rise of a "Thousand Year Reich." The overwhelming majority of Germans opted for Hitler's optimistic vision. Albert Speer may serve as a case in point. In the 1920's, he reacted positively to Spengler, writing:

Spengler's *Decline of the West* had convinced me
that we were living in a period of decay strongly
similar to the late Roman Empire: inflation, decline
of morals, impotence of the German Reich. His
Essay "Prussianism and Socialism" excited me
especially because of the contempt for luxury and
comfort it expressed.[72]

Yet, after listening to Hitler, Speer was immediately
released from the pall that Spengler's shadow had cast over
him. Enthralled by Hitler's personality and by his optimistic
vision, Speer now wrote:

Here, it seemed to me, was hope. Here were new
ideals, a new understanding, new tasks. Even
Spengler's dark predictions seemed to me refuted,
and his prophecy of a new Roman emperor
simultaneously fulfilled. The peril of communism,
which seemed inexorable on its way, could be
checked, Hitler persuaded us, and instead of
hopeless unemployment, Germany could move
toward economic recovery.[73]

Spengler, the prophet of doom, now became a neglected
and forgotten figure. Many of his former friends, especially
those who belonged to the younger generation, deserted him
for the Nazi cause. Those who continued to share his views
either suffered his fate or experienced persecution by the
Nazis. During the Rohm purge of July 1934, a number of
Spengler's acquaintances were liquidated. His friends, fearing
for his life, recommended exile, but Spengler refused. His
hatred of the Hitler regime was an open secret; and had he
lived longer, Hitler's henchmen would probably have silenced
him.

Spengler's fear of isolation had become a reality. Sometimes he wondered out loud whether he belonged to his age: "I feel so estranged in it," he said, "that I sometimes get the feeling that the whole thing is none of my business."[74] On May 8, 1936, he died suddenly of a heart attack. Fate had spared him from experiencing the truth of his gloomy predictions.

FLAME: THE METAPHYSICS OF THE LIFE CYCLE

A. The History of an Idea

I

In 1904, Oswald Spengler, then a young aspiring doctoral candidate, wrote in his dissertation that "all creations of culture, state, society, custom, and contemplation are products of nature; they are subject to the same conditions of existence as are all remaining things — to the severe law that nothing endures and everything changes."[1] The young Spengler was grappling with the thought of the Greek philosopher Heraclitus, regarding the nature of change, transformation, decay, and the immutable life cycle. Although Spengler later asserted that men of different cultures could not understand each other, his own thought betrays a striking similarity to Heraclitus and Greek metaphysics. In fact, the underlying premises of Spengler's thought are Greek in origin and comprise the following ideas: the theory of physis (growth); the doctrine of cycles; the notions of degeneration, relativity, and contingency; and the idea of unity in multiplicity. Spengler became even more intimately acquainted with these Greek ideas by studying German philosophy. Indeed, the age of Goethe, to which Spengler was so closely tied, revitalized Greek metaphysics in a new historical setting. To understand Spengler we must, therefore, trace the threads which connect Heraclitus and Greek ideas of change with the German metaphysical tradition of the eighteenth and nineteenth centuries.

II

Fundamental to Greek metaphysics was the biological metaphor of growth, to which all living things, including man and his institutions, were subject. Robert Nisbet, who has traced the evolution of this metaphor in western thought, tells us that the Greeks were enchanted with all living things and never ceased to wonder about the miracle of the seed fructifying so many diverse forms of life.[2] Elaborate myths and rituals attended these wonders of nature. The myth of Demeter was perhaps the most important. Demeter was a seed-god who once brought calamity among men when his daughter Persephone was carried off into the underworld by Pluto — Lord of the Dead. Demeter was so disconsolate that he cursed the earth and withheld the seed which made things grow. Only Zeus' intervention saved the human race from certain destruction; Persephone was returned to her mother, as was the seed of life to man. Demeter taught man the secrets of life and the knowledge of its symbolism. "If we look closely at the myth of Demeter," Robert Nisbet observes, "all of the essential elements of conceptualization of growth are seen immediately: fecundity and sterility, of course, but also cyclical development and recurrence, potentiality, immanence, and telic purpose."[3]

The Greeks were preoccupied with the problem of "physis" or growth — with its underlying meaning, pattern, and law. From the analogy of biological growth, Greek thinkers deduced some of their most significant principles. The idea of the seed suggested the metamorphosis of living things: the acorn developing into the oak, the larva becoming an imago, winter giving way to spring, or families evolving into tribes and then states. The seed contained the future character of its mature nature in embryonic form. This suggested that all living things, including human institutions, undergo a definite and recognizable process of transformation, determined, in large part, by an inbuilt plan of development already embodied in their germinal forms. Thus, all living things possess certain predetermined potentialities which they seek to actualize in the course of their history. Aristotle (384 - 322 B.C.) made this idea of potentiality and actuality the cornerstone of his metaphysics.

Another philosophic implication of the doctrine of growth was the idea of cycles. The rhythm of nature appeared as a never-ending cycle of birth, growth, maturity, and decay. Why should the affairs of men be different? Thus, transferring the theory from nature to human affairs, Plato (427 – 347 B.C.), for example, showed that the wheel of generation traverses the successive stages of birth, youth, maturity, and old age. Plato also believed that the human cycle was itself only a part of a larger cosmic cycle, and that the course of history repeated itself every 72,000 years.[4] Similarly, Aristotle applied the idea of cycles to both natural and human events, holding – as Spengler did – that "the coming-to-be of anything, if it is absolutely necessary, must be cyclical – i.e., must return upon itself."[5] Aristotle also showed how politics obeyed the same cyclical pattern as do all living things. In his *Politics*, he demonstrated that all states experience the following evolutionary cycle: from monarchy to aristocracy, to oligarchy, to tryanny, to democracy, and back to monarchy.[6]

The presumption that the beginning phases of the life cycle are endowed with youthful instinct, good health, and vigor – an idea which figured so prominently in Spengler's *Decline of the West* — was a necessary consequence of the cyclical theory. Moreover, the first stage of the cycle was frequently associated with a Golden Age, a period to which the ancients of a more complex time looked back with romantic nostalgia. The Stoics, who wrote under the impact of the widespread cultural malaise of the late Empire, used the term "Spring" in describing a culture in the flower of its youth. Some historians, such as Florus (c. A.D. 125), anticipated Machiavelli and Spengler by likening the history of Rome to the age-phases of individual man — infancy, youth, manhood, and old age.[7] Hesiod, in his *Works and Days*, used the analogy of metals to refer to the age-phases of man's history, gold being first, then silver, next bronze, and finally iron.[8] As Robert Nisbet rightly insists, "this idea of continuous degeneration from some original point in the past was no more a universally Greek and Roman idea than it is a universal idea in our own day."[9]

The metaphor of growth, as Spengler and the Greeks envisioned it, also implied the evanescent nature of all things. If whirl was not necessarily king in Greek thought, many Greek philosophers did follow Heraclitus (530 - 470 B.C.) in his observation that "you cannot step twice into the same river, for other waters and yet others go ever flowing on."[10] Nature undulates as she changes. Man is caught by flux and his illusions about the permanence of his ideals or his institutions are crushed by the relentless waves of change. The problem of change, which figures so prominently in the thought of Heraclitus and other Greek philosophers, involved two fundamental aspects: on the other hand, there are states or conditions, on the other hand, that which enters successively into the different states, which is the basis of transformation. Thus, for Heraclitus, fire is the basis of the vast variety of things.

It is characteristic of some conditions to be mutually

exclusive. Water in the state of ice is not water in the state of vapor. If clarity of understanding involves separateness or discreteness in what is understood, then mutually exclusive states are more clearly understood than the relations which connect them in a process of development. There was a tendency in ancient thought which moved toward the emphasis of separateness. Zeno made use of this tendency when he referred to distinct positions or distinct steps, the assumption being that when one is in one position, or taking one step, one is not in another position nor taking the next step. Thus, there is a separation in space and a separation in time. This tendency had its culmination in atomism. There was also a countertendency in Greek thought which emphasized continuous becoming. This played a dominant role in the philosophy of Heraclitus, as it did in his modern disciple, Oswald Spengler.

In Heraclitus' conception of the world, everything flows and nothing remains. Change itself, however, is not chaotic: there is the common element, the order of change comprehended by the mind. This common element is not a state, but rather the order in the change of states. Heraclitus called this common element logos. In Greek philosophy, logos had many meanings — from oridinary expressions such as talk, conversation, telling a story, to more abstract notions signifying reasoning, taking full measure, perceiving relations, or recognizing general laws.[11] W. K. C. Guthrie informs us that Heraclitus used the word logos to draw attention to the common element in man — thought.[12] Since man perceives the world through thought, and organizes his experiences accordingly, logos also means the governing principle by which man explains the universe.[13] We all share logos in the sense that we are endowed with insight or intelligence.

Logos is not only thought; it is thought in a state of becoming. Heraclitus insisted that thinking is not a static activity, a view which followed logically from his idea that reality is flux. The mind does not apprehend petrified or static objects in the world. On the contrary, the perceiver and the perceived must be regarded in a setting of continuous change. This change, however, has a definite form or pattern. Some Greek thinkers perceived this pattern of change as a passage from some quality to its opposite, whereas others viewed it as a passage from one stage to another of a serial order.[14] Heraclitus made use of the first tendency by viewing change as an alternation from opposite to opposite. Thus, "cool things become warm, the warm grows cool; the moist dries, the parched becomes moist."[15] The mutual conversion of physical or intellectual elements by way of opposition suggests that change is cyclical. If cold things grow hot; and hot things, in turn, grow cold again, we have come full circle. As W. K. C. Guthrie remarks, Heraclitus believed that "what could apparently change into something else and then back into what it was before must have been the same all the time."[16] This was but another expression of the eternal circularity of time, based on recurrent seasonal changes. Although everything changes, the pattern of that change is identical because it is subject to the eternally recurring rhythm of the cycle. The symbol of change, which Heraclitus perceived more aesthetically than scientifically, is the everlasting fire. Although fire is the primary element of the vast variety of things, it is subject to change as are all other things in the world. Far from being an immutable substance, fire also obeys the cyclical process by changing to steam, to water, to earth, and then back to fire.

Like most Greek philosophers, Heraclitus transferred his conception of relativity and cyclical development to human affairs, holding that men, societies, or states rise and fall in accordance with the eternal rhythm of the life cycle. The motive force of change, both within nature and human

society, is strife — the father of all things.[17] Strife or war
arises not only because men are by nature wicked — a view
which Spengler shared with Heraclitus — but also because the
structure of the world is based on polarities. Change is
inconceivable without opposites. If strife would perish from
gods and men, Heraclitus said, then all things would cease to
exist.[18] The same would be true if one extreme triumphed
over its opposite: the good over the bad, the just over the
unjust, or the strong over the weak. The reason why there is
never a triumph of one extreme, Heraclitus argued, is due to a
balance of opposites. Heraclitus' idea about the identity of
opposites has led some thinkers to the conclusion that he was
the father of dialectics.[19] Spengler was by temperament
committed to the idea of static polarities and, therefore,
denied that Heraclitus advocated a kind of Hegelian
"permeation of opposites."

On the whole, Spengler took from Heraclitus and other
Greek thinkers whatever suited his own predilections. From
his dissertation, which contained much of his mature thought
in embryonic form, we can clearly see how much he owed to
Heraclitus. Spengler was enormously impressed by Heraclitus'
conception of change, which he called exceptional in ancient
thought. He believed that Heraclitus was the only Greek
thinker who viewed change as pure occurrence because all
other philosophers had posited a variety of unchanging
substances beyond the world of flux.[20] Spengler also
approved of Heraclitus' idea that change manifests itself in
cyclical form, and that eternal recurrence applied equally to
all the creations of man — to culture, state, society, customs,
and ideas. He even went so far as to honor Heraclitus with
the distinction of having discovered "the inner similarity
between culture and nature."[21]

Spengler frequently projected his own temperamental
biases into the thought of Heraclitus, to the point that his

dissertation revealed more about his own ideas than it did about the thought of Heraclitus. Thus, he lauded Heraclitus' bold speculative vision, his high sense of intuition, his daring synoptic approach, his stoic courage, and his aristocratic frame of mind. Heraclitus, we are told, always thought pictorially, never quantitatively.[22] This allowed him to view events in the broadest sense possible. According to Spengler, Heraclitus was a synoptic thinker who, by avoiding trifling details, always searched for deeper meanings. The collection of petty facts for its own sake was always abhorrent to him. Spengler also identified with Heraclitus' radical aristocratic spirit. When Heraclitus remarked that "one man is worth ten thousand if he is first-rate,"[23] he struck a responsive cord in Spengler's own heart. The assumption that the structure of the world is based on polarities, and that strife is the essence of life also appealed to Spengler's temperament. In Heraclitus' glorification of struggle, Spengler thought he saw the archetypal expression of Greek life.[24] As we shall see, Spengler used the idea of struggle as a key to his own philosophy of life.

From Heraclitus and other Greek thinkers, then, Spengler borrowed the idea of relativism, the principle of potentiality and actuality, the doctrine of degeneration, and — above all — the notion of cycles. These are concepts which he found ready-made in the thought of classical antiquity. Spengler often gave the misleading impression that he was the first to apply the cycle systematically to all aspects of culture. The Greeks, as we have seen, viewed natural as well as human events in cyclical terms, and so did numerous western thinkers before Spengler. It is true that the coming of Christianity meant a setback to the idea of eternal recurrence because Christian eschatology viewed development in a linear form.[25] In Christian thought, as we have seen, development traces a straight line from the Fall of Man to final Redemption. Christ died only once for our sins. This was a unique event which cannot be repeated. It follows that our destiny in life and in history is likewise played out only once.[26] History thus reveals a universal design that unfolds progressively in a straight line. Implicit in this Christian view was the universality of history and the doctrine of a shared destiny for all mankind. The Age of Enlightenment merely secularized the Christian view when it envisioned a common humanity moving ineluctably toward a progressive goal.

III

Still, the idea of cycles was held by a number of western thinkers long before Spengler. Niccolò Machiavelli (1487 - 1527) and other Renaissance thinkers were familiar with it, as was that lone genius Giambattista Vico (1668 - 1744) in the early eighteenth century. Although the idea of cycles had always been a powerful undercurrent in western thought, it was not really until the time of the Romantic Movement in Germany (1770 - 1830) that the cyclical theory was revitalized in a new context. Oswald Spengler was heir to the remarkable cultural renaissance which took place in the late eighteenth and early nineteenth century in Germany.[27] During this period, a new historical perception was created by such men as Johann Gottfried Herder (1744 - 1803), Johann Wolfgang von Goethe (1749 - 1832), or Wilhelm von Schelling (1775 - 1854). Summed up by Goethe's famous statement that "Individuum est ineffabile," the new historical outlook stressed the importance of the individual as a creative force in history.

The Enlightenment had searched for permanent forces in man's past in order to frame universal laws of history analogous to Newton's laws of physics. To most eighteenth century historians, singularity was only important as an instance of some general law. The historians of the Enlightenment not only deprecated singularity, they wrote history from a highly partisan point of view, evaluating the past in terms of their own biases. Exalting reason and science, the *philosophes* concentrated on those epochs which had been most "rational" or most "progressive." Voltaire, for example, insisted that mankind had only known four ages in which the arts and sciences had truly flourished: the Age of Pericles, the Age of Caesar and Alexander, the Age of the Renaissance, and the Age of Louis XIV.[28] The implication was clear enough: all other ages are of little consequence because they have been dominated by encrusted religious tradition. The *philosophes'* assault on encrusted tradition, epitomized by Voltaire's battlecry *ecrasez l'infame*, narrowed the historical horizon of the Enlightenment by making it difficult to appreciate other epochs sympathetically.[29]

Every age, of course, perceives the past in the light of its own biases, admiring those characteristics in it which are closest to its own cultural aspirations. The remarkable thing about the German Romantics was that they had a far clearer perception of historical reality because their appreciation of individuality tended to minimize the bias implicit in the partisanship of class, party, nation, or ideology. Since the Romantics, a true historical sense implies seeing merit in every age. As R. G. Collingwood has observed, "a truly historical view of human history sees everything in that history as having its own *raison d'etre* and coming into existence in order to serve the needs of the men whose minds have corporately created it."[30]

To the Romantics, then, every individual creature bears within itself the law of its own development. The Romantics derived this emphasis on singularity from the metaphysical doctrine which held that the transcendent fulfills itself in the flux of history. Leibniz, Lessing, and Goethe, for example, taught that the eternal did not exist apart from the world but was active within it, infusing the soul of every creature with the mark of his divinity. Since that spark of divinity manifests itself only gradually in the process of individual growth, it follows that we must study every individual thing in its historical development. This metaphysics gave rise in Germany to a new historicity *(Historismus)*, exercising a profound influence on European thought in the nineteenth and twentieth centuries.[31]

The immediate consequence of the new historical outlook was a loss of faith in the idea that history represented a unity. Those who exalted singularity could no longer accept the notion of humanity developing uniformly in a certain predetermined direction. This attack on linear development, initiated primarily by the German Romantics, prepared the way for a revival of historical cycles. Since the Romantics also revitalized the Greek conception of *physis* in the guise of "Naturphilosophie" (Philosophy of Nature), a few words must be said about their place in the spiritual heritage of Oswald Spengler.

Men such as Herder, Goethe, and Schelling denied both the Enlightenment and the Christian view of history as the linear progress of mankind. According to these thinkers, mankind as such does not exist; there are only individual men organized in various ‘cultural groupings. History is not the history of mankind; it is the story of unique peoples. More specifically, history is a showplace in which the cultures of unique peoples, each embodying a certain spirit *(Geist)*, grow and develop like biological organisms. If we truly want to understand history, these German thinkers urged, we must grasp the singularity of different peoples by imaginatively reconstructing in our own minds their unique cultural style. We can see that these philosophers revived the Greek idea of physis in a new historical setting.

The biological process of growth applies to history just as it does to nature. Thus, individuals, nations, and cultures define themselves in the process of their growth. To the German Romantics, the world of both man and nature was vital through and through. Far from being an inert ensemble of matter in mechanical motion, as the *philosophes* of the Enlightenment conceived it, nature is a gigantic organism teeming with life and vitality. The Romantics agreed with the Aristotelean doctrine that each being possessed an inbuilt plan of development already latent in its germinal form. Nature is thus replete with organic forms seeking to actualize their inner potentialities. In order to divine these purposive principles which are contained in every being, we must study nature in its evolution, in its ceaseless growth, and in its development from potentiality to actuality. The assumption that every organic form contains the future within its womb also indicated that we must study the internal rather than the external side of every being. Novalis was speaking for the whole Romantic movement when he observed that "the mysterious path leads us inward. Eternity and its worlds is in us or nowhere else."[32] This widespread concern with the inner life explains in large part the German tendency to concentrate on spiritual developments in history, art, literature, politics, and even in science. The metaphysical belief that the outward shell of a thing conceals a vital internal principle clearly implied that it is the internal rather than the external side of every being that needs to be explained. On the whole, the belief that the true essence of every being is revealed in its inner development, and that the present is, so to speak, pregnant with the future, had very fruitful consequences in such fields as history, psychology, literature, and art. It enabled investigators to probe behind the surface of events and to concentrate on inner motives. In sum, it focused attention on human behavior in its purposive aspects; and, in so doing, created a healthy counterpoise to the purely quantitative treatment of events by scientifically-trained historians.

Since Leibniz, German intellectuals have insisted that a good explanation in any field always involves two mental activities: a recognition of how things work and a corresponding apprehension of why they work that way. Scientific explanation should always be accompanied by metaphysical explication. The historian, for example, should proceed beyond the mere description of events to the meaning that is implied by them. In practice, this ideal was never fully approximated because the elucidation of spiritual factors in man's history was generally considered to be more important than the empirical collection of data or the framing of scientific laws. The Romantics were generally suspicious of the objective-scientific approach to human affairs because they felt that scientific explanation could not account for what was contradictory or nonrational in men's lives. Many things in human affairs, they believed, had to be emotionally or intuitively experienced rather than conceptually understood.

The Romantics were not opposed to science, only to its exclusivist pretension to knowledge. Metaphysical explication, they believed, must always follow scientific explanation. Moreover, they were deeply convinced that science was incapable of providing such a meaning. Since the Romantics, it has been common in Germany to separate the study of science from the study of the humanities. In history, this has taken the form of rescuing the humanities from the onslaught of the natural sciences and to delineate a "logic of history" which would be different from the logic of science.[33] In one way or another, many German historians and philosophers of the nineteenth century, including G. F. W. Hegel (1770 -

1831), Friedrich Wilhelm von Schelling (1775 - 1854), Johann Gustav Droysen (1808 - 1884), Wilhelm Dilthey (1833 - 1911), or Heinrich Rickert (1863 - 1936), sought to endow history with a logic of its own. Whatever the name of such a logic — dialectics, introspection, intuitive understanding, physiognomy, or ideographic science — the goal was generally the same: to comprehend human life in its purposive as well as in its reactive aspects.

IV

Of all the German thinkers who wrote under the dispensation of the new historical metaphysics between 1770 and 1830, it was Johann Wolfgang von Goethe (1749 - 1832) who exercised the most profound influence on Spengler. In fact, Spengler remarked several times that he owed everything to Goethe.[34] What did he mean by that unusual confession of indebtedness? He meant, for one thing, that he accepted Goethe's philosophy which exalted life as the irreducible phenomenon of existence. To Goethe, the only real thing that we know about is life experience. If we let life act upon us, we realize something else, namely, that life is pervaded by contradictions, paradoxes, and ultimate inexplicabilities. Only the professional scholar, whom Goethe hated, sees in life a rational plan. Life, however, does not obey the dictates of the syllogism. Those who exclusively rely upon logic will always find the portals to the deeper meaning of reality tightly shut in their faces. The scientist, priding himself on his rationalistic approach, distorts reality as soon as he insists that everything that cannot be logically ascertained is unknowable, nonexistent, or both. As a poet, Goethe know that reality was too rich for science. He knew that a great part of our experience could only become meaningful to us through poetic intuition.

When Goethe studied nature, he tried to feel its vital pulse and to glean its inner secrets from the way in which it creates life.[35] In line with the Romantics, he argued that we must study nature by examining the birth, growth, and decay of its organic forms. He also insisted that the logic of life was contained in each and every individual organism itself, and that, consequently, every living thing had to be studied on its own merit. The logic of life is the law of development of every individual organism. Applied to human nature, this principle of individuality obliges us to study man in the process of his becoming, to uncover the law by which this process is governed, and to explain what that process of growth means to every individual human life. We can see that Goethe tried to develop a logic as well as a metaphysics of life. The same was true of his disciple Oswald Spengler.

Goethe treated history as the life experience of past generations.[36] Spengler followed him in this, too. Goethe's equation of history with life required a special mode of cognition — one that could encompass all those variegated and complex actions by which men had expressed their lives in the past. The dissecting method of science, however, was not suited for this purpose because it could only explain outer uniformities, not inner meanings. Goethe admitted that poetry could not unravel the tangle of inner purposes in history, but he believed that it could uncover much that was inaccessible to the analytical understanding. In other words, the inside of events could only be apprehended, however inadequately, through imagination, metaphor, intuition — in short, poetic insight. How history was in itself Goethe conceded, will always be a conundrum. It is in this vein that Goethe's famous remark, "alles Vergängliche ist nur ein Gleichnis,"[37] must be understood.

Spengler was indebted to Goethe for three other important

ideas — the idea of the life cycle, the metamorphosis of plants, and the image of Faustian man. In many ways, Goethe revitalized the Greek idea of cycles in a new context by showing that eternal recurrence was a spiritual as much as a natural fact of life. Both nature and spirit, Goethe believed, obey the pendulum of the eternal systole and diastole of life. Everything can be conceived as a rhythmic beat analogous to the outward expansion and the inward contraction of the human heart. Like Heraclitus, Goethe felt that change occurs through opposition, though he was more insistent on the idea of the unification of opposites than was either Heraclitus or Spengler. In his *Dichtung and Wahrheit (Poetry and Truth)*, Goethe expressed the notion of recurrence as follows: "life is based on a regular recurrence of external things. The change of day and night, of the seasons, of blossoms and fruits, and of everything confronting us from epoch to epoch, . . . these are the essential motive forces of earthly life."[38]

Man's history, according to Goethe, is cyclical as well, exhibiting an eternal alteration of opposites. History neither presents a unity nor a linear progression towards a final preconceived goal. Goethe did not believe in inevitable progress. Every gain, he once said, always involves a corresponding loss. Unlike Spengler, however, he conceded the possibility of regeneration on the grounds that peoples or nations are always infused with new vital life. A nation may traverse the phases of a cycle and yet begin anew. Thus, a nation could conceivably experience several cycles without necessarily degenerating after having passed through only one of them.

Perhaps the most important idea which Spengler borrowed from Goethe was the metamorphosis of plants.[39] Since this theory determined Spengler's philosophy of culture and his physiognomic method, it will be treated at length in a later chapter. Here we will only adumbrate what Spengler did with

Goethe's insight. Briefly, Spengler transferred Goeth's metamorphosis of plants to history and culture. In his botanical studies, Goethe attempted to show that the life of plants could be explained both physically and spiritually. He felt that every organic form possessed an internal principle of development. As he beheld the amazing variety among plants, Goethe asked himself whether such variety possibly betrayed a common source of origin. This idea led him to posit a universal Primal Type (Urtypus) as the common ancestor of all plants. Only a century earlier, the same search for unity in variety had led Leibniz to the notion of a Primal Monad. A logical corollary to this notion of a transcendental type, from which all plant life originated, was the belief that the variety we see in nature has sprung from an original unity, and that there is a permanent Primal Type behind the diversity we behold in nature.

Spengler used this idea of a prime phenomenon in his explanation of cultures. He viewed cultures as the expression forms of certain underlying prime symbols. Thus, the variegated expressions of Faustian culture are the results of its prime symbol — the idea of infinite space. Spengler also borrowed Goethe's belief that every organic being possesses an inbuilt principle which is responsible for its peculiar growth and for its final form. Spengler applied this doctrine of "Gestaltung" to the life history of higher organisms which he called cultures.

Finally, Spengler borrowed from Goethe the vision of Faustian man portrayed in Goethe's immortal tragedy *Faust*. Spengler believed that the destiny of Faust was the destiny of western man. Faustian means a relentless striving to find the ultimate secrets of life. The motive concealed behind this quest is Faustian man's desire to make himself god-like. Spengler believed that the Faustian impulse was both spiritual — the search for complete self-knowledge — and physical —

the complete mastery over nature and other men.

When Goethe died in 1832, the Romantic impulse, which had sustained much of his thought, had been largely spent in Germany and the rest of Europe. Romanticism was radically aristocratic in spirit, fostering an aesthetic vision of culture which appeared incompatible with the values emerging from the industrialization of western Europe. The generation which grew to maturity at mid-century was more enchanted with the possibilities of machine technology than with the imaginative world of poetry, music, or art. The post-romantic generation believed that technology was more real, more vital, and — above all — more useful than the humanities. A series of exciting discoveries in science convinced most thinkers that society would one day be rendered fully rational, efficient, and perfect. Science applied to society, it was felt, would assure the future progress of mankind. This renewed faith in progress appeared increasingly justified by events, as Europe became wealthy at home and almost invincible abroad. When Mazzini cheerfully remarked around mid-century that Europe was the lever that moved the world, he expressed an obvious fact. Thanks to her advanced technology, Europe was about to subjugate the greater part of the world. The leading intellectuals throughout Europe celebrated the triumph of technology as proof positive that Western civilization was not only progressing, but progressing with inevitable necessity.

Thus, the idea of linear progress, which had been denigrated by the Romantics, reappeared greatly strengthened by the force of events. Progress also received the scientific imprimatur of Darwinian evolutionism and Marxian socialism. Only a small band of outsiders objected to the roseate visions which the prophets of progress projected into the future. Amidst the universal clamor of progress, there were a few faint voices preaching ·a profound historical pessimism. In Germany, the most persistent pessimists were Karl Friedrich

Vollgraff (1792 — 1863), Peter Ernst von Lasaulx (1815 — 1861), Jakob Burckhardt (1818 — 1897), Arthur Schopenhauer (1788 — 1860), and Friedrich Nietzsche (1844 — 1900). Recent scholarship has shown that Vollgraff and Lasaulx developed ideas which were remarkably similar to Spengler's theories in the *Decline of the West*.[40] However, there is no evidence that Spengler ever heard of either of them. Nor did Spengler know much, if anything, about the Swiss historian, Jakob Burckhardt. Although he read Schopenhauer, he never acknowledged him as a major source of influence. Nietzsche is another matter.

V

The apotheosis of Friedrich Nietzche by many young Germans, from the time of his insanity in 1889 to this very day, constitutes an important episode in German cultural history.[41] Most intellectuals of Spengler's generation were deeply touched by Nietzsche's visionary philosophy. Spengler always felt a very close kinship to Nietzsche, whose aristocratic outlook greatly resembled his own inner longings. In temperament, style of life, and literary expression, the two men were much alike. Both were taciturn and withdrawn personalities, preferring the life of isolation to the hectic pace of modern society. Both men suffered intensely from migraine headaches, a condition which was probably caused by extremely poor eyesight. The similarities do not end here. Spengler and Nietzsche had tried teaching but had abandoned it in favor of a life dedicated to contemplation and writing. Even the tenor and content of their writings are similar. Both thinkers, for example, chose the aphorism as their favorite means of expression. Most of Nietzsche's works, with the possible exception of the *Birth of Tragedy* (1872), were aphoristic in character. The same was true of Spengler's works. *The Decline of the West*, actually grew out of thousands of aphorisms.

It has often been observed that the aphorism is conducive to the problem thinker because no other literary device is capable of conveying moral paradox in quite the same way. The aphorism conceals double meanings, explodes platitudes and clichés, and convinces through clever turns of phrases. It is also the most pliable means of recording spontaneous and original thoughts. Historically, it is significant that the aphorism has generally predominated as a literary medium during periods of widespread uncertainties. Aphorisms are often reflections of an atomistic society in which values are in a state of dissolution.

Nietzsche and Spengler were outsiders in German society. Both believed that they were living in a decadent materialistic age, and that the superior man could only escape this decadence by creating from within his own soul a set of new values. Spengler also accepted Nietzsche's remedies, though he sometimes interpreted Nietzsche's ideas, especially the will to power and the overman, in highly un-Nietzschean terms.

Men who are strangers in their own times often look back nostalgically to some idealized past. This explains why both men were confirmed Grecophiles; and the man they admired most in Greek history was Heraclitus — the dark sage of Ephesus. With an obvious allusion to Heraclitus, Nietzsche at one point compared himself to an insatiable flame:

Ungesättigt gleich der Flamme
Glühe and verzehr ich mich
Licht wird alles was ich fasse,

Kohle alles was ich lasse:
Flamme bin ich sicherlich.
(Yes, I know from whence I came!
Insatiable as a flame
I glow and consume myself
Light will be what I seize
Coal all that I release:
Flame I am most certainly.)[42]

In this, as in so many other remarks, Nietzsche may be truly regarded as the link between Heraclitus and Spengler. Both men admired Heraclitus, especially his doctrine of strife and change. The glorification of the superior man, epitomized by Nietzsche's famous remark that "the goal of humanity cannot lie in the end but only in its highest specimens,"[43] was another idea which both Nietzsche and Spengler shared with Heraclitus. The two German philosophers agreed that Heraclitus' emphasis on struggle — the perpetual food of the soul, as Nietzsche called it — was the wellspring of Greek culture. Unlike Nietzsche, however, Spengler tended to see struggle far more in physical than in spiritual terms. In this, Spengler was committing an error common to most Germans at the time: intoxicated by the military prowess of the new Reich, he all too often viewed the will to power as smashing one's enemies rather than as the will to spiritual self-overcoming.

Another doctrine which Nietzsche and Spengler shared with Heraclitus was the idea of cycles. The idea of eternal recurrence is the key to both Nietzsche and Spengler's philosophy.[44] Nietzsche probably applied the idea of eternal recurrence far more consistently to his overall outlook than Spengler did. Spengler did not believe that a cycle, once it had unfolded, would ever return in the same form in the future. Once the Faustian culture had fulfilled its possibilities, it will have irrevocably perished. Nietzsche did not circumscribe the cycle in this way, nor did he regard cyclical development in wholly pessimistic terms. In point of fact, he celebrated eternal recurrence as a timeless solvent of decadence or sickness. In the *Gay Science* (1882), where he alluded to the idea of eternal recurrence for the first time, Nietzsche explicitly stressed the joyous element in the life cycle:

> What if a demon crept after you one day or night in your loneliest solitude and said to you: 'This life, as you live it now and have lived it, you will have to live again and again, times without number; and there will be nothing new in it, but every pain and every joy and every thought and sigh and all the unspeakably small and great in your life must return to you, and everything, in the same series and sequence — and in the same way this spider and this moonlight among the trees, and in the same way this moment and I myself. The eternal hourglass of existence will be turned again and again — and you with it, you dust of dust! '— Would you not throw yourself down and gnash your teeth and curse the demon who thus spoke? Or have you experienced a tremendous moment in which you would have answered him: 'You are a god and never did I hear anything more devine!'[45]

Near the end of Part III of *Zarathustra*, Nietzsche expressed the idea of eternal recurrence far more explicitly. The eagle and the serpent finally tell Zarathustra what eternal recurrence really means:

> ... your animals know well, O Zarathustra, who

you are and must become: behold, *you are the teacher of the eternal recurrence* — that is your destiny!

... 'Behold, we know what you teach: that all things recur eternally, and we ourselves too; and that we have already existed an eternal number of times, and all things with us. You teach that there is a great year of becoming, a monster of a great year, which must, like an hourglass, turn over again and again so that it may run down and run out again; and all these years are alike in what is greatest as in what is smallest; and we ourselves are alike in every great year, in what is greatest as in what is smallest.'[46]

These poetic images of eternal recurrence should not mislead us into thinking that Nietzsche viewed the cycle only in metaphorical terms. In fact, his interpretation differed from all previous accounts because it was couched in scientific terms. Nietzsche said that if we assume a finite amount of energy in a finite space and an infinite time, we cannot help but come to the conclusion that things in the universe would eventually rearrange themselves as before. In other words, if energy is finite, there must also be a finite number of configurations, so that the universe must reach a point at some future time which is identical to a previous state. As Nietzsche put it:

The amount of total force is limited, nothing "infinite"; let us avoid such vagaries of the concept. Hence, the number of states, changes, combinations, and developments of this force is tremendously large and practically "immeasurable," yet definite and not infinite. Time, however, in which the totality uses its force, is infinite — that is, is eternally the same and eternally active. Up to this moment, an infinity has passed — that is, all possible developments must have already *been there. Consequently,* the development of this moment must be a repetition and thus that development which gave birth to it, and that which originates from it, and thus on and on forward and backward.[47]

We do not have to inquire into the scientific validity of Nietzsche's theory, except to point out that his observations were not "the musings of a dilettante physicist."[48] The objection that eternal recurrence conflicts with the second law of thermodynamics misses the point because that law applies only to medium-sized systems, not to molecular or to the totality of phenomena.[49] Leaving aside the scientific implication of Nietzsche's theory, what was its historical significance?

The idea of eternal recurrence naturally squared ill with the assumption that history represents a unity. It also conflicted with the idea of progress. Nietzsche repeatedly mocked the proponents of progress by reminding them that "mankind does *not* represent a development toward something better or stronger or higher in the sense accepted today. 'Progress' is merely a modern idea, that is, a false idea."[50] Though eternal recurrence precludes linear progress, it does not necessarily preclude other kinds of progress. Nietzsche would have emphatically denied Spengler's deterministic verdict that cyclical development unfolds with inexorable movement from youth to maturity to old age. True, mankind does not move toward a predetermined pattern, but neither does it have a youth or old age. As

Nietzsche pointed out, "the layers cut through each other and lie above each other — and in a few millennia there may yet exist younger types of man than we can discover today. Decadence, on the other hand, belongs to all epochs of mankind . . ."[51] Even within cultures, Nietzsche believed, decadence is present at all times. Those who come at the end of a cultural tradition are not necessarily doomed to sterility, as the Greeks have so amply demonstrated. Coming at the end of a long cultural tradition, they fashioned a wholly new culture of their own.[52]

Nietzsche concluded that decadence was ubiquitous in Europe, but he would have denied Spengler's verdict that the West is inexorably doomed to an agonizing spiritual death. It was precisely his affirmation of eternal recurrence which precluded him from such an appalling pessimism. Unlike Spengler, Nietzsche did believe in the possibility of cultural regeneration. Hence, his transvaluation of values, his call for self-overcoming (the will to power), and his vision of the overman. Spengler, on the other hand, did not hold out any hope for renewal. He identified with Nietzsche's negative moods — his despair, suffering, loneliness, and apparent nihilism — while ignoring Nietzsche's constructive thought.

Spengler obviously chose from Nietzsche, as he did from other thinkers, whatever suited his own temperament. What has been said about Spengler's indebtedness to Heraclitus applies equally well to his indebtedness to Nietzsche: he encountered in the thought of these men feelings and ideas which resembled his own. Like every original thinker, however, he adapted ideas to his own convictions. It is, therefore, singularly *mal a propos* to admonish Spengler for not being Nietzschean. He took from Nietzsche whatever could be blended into his own thought. Obviously, this resulted in some theories which bore little relationship to the source from which he derived them. A case in point is

Spengler's use of "Apollonian" culture. He owed the concept to Nietzsche, who had used the term in his *Birth of Tragedy*. In this work, Nietzsche understood the art and history of Hellenic Greece in terms of the interplay of two hostile principles, which he baptized Apollonian and Dionysian. The Dionysian element he abstracted from the suffering Dionysus of the mysteries, for whom individuation, the development of the sense of self, is the eternal source of suffering. Dionysus, the god of wine, advocates the emancipation of the rational self and a return to an original sense of instinctual oneness. Apollo, god of the arts, teaches the diametrical opposite: moderation, self-knowledge, and the control of the instincts through reason. Nietzsche believed that the Appollonian principle of mature classicism, with its emphasis on *sophrosyne* (moderation and self-knowledge), was superimposed on the Dionysian principle of holism, the instinctual sense of completeness and oneness with nature and the divine. The brief historical moment in which these principles were held in balance saw, according to Nietzsche, the birth of the highest Greek tragedy, that of Aeschylus.

Spengler borrowed Nietzsche's concept "Apollonian" in describing Greco-Roman culture, but he conveniently ignored its opposite — the Dionysian. He only talked about the classical element in Greco-Roman culture because the admission of opposite trends would have detracted from his monistic view of culture. Spengler believed that a culture is an expression of a soul which strives to fulfill a distinct theme or plan. The diversity we see in culture, he believed, was the expression of a single unitary theme. He owed this view of culture to Nietzsche but amended it to fit Goethe's idea of the Prime Phenomenon. Nietzsche had said that culture is "the unity of the artistic style in all the expressions of the life of a people."[53] In saying this, he did not preclude variety from culture; nor did he imply that a culture was animated by only one theme. The unity of a culture is not given *a priori,* but arises from the interplay of different principles such as the Dionysian or the Appollonian. Spengler, on the other hand, lacked this fine dialectical sense which Nietzsche possessed to such an extraordinary degree. In Nietzsche, the unity of artistic style emerges only gradually in the course of a culture, whereas in Spengler, it exists as an innate disposition before anything has happened. Moreover, the development of a cultural style in Spengler does not occur through opposites. The Faustian theme does not define itself in a dialectical clash with the Apollonian; it merely actualizes its own inner potentialities.

Spengler, then, borrowed from Nietzsche, as he did from Heraclitus and Goethe, ideas which fitted his own philosophic vision. He owed to Nietzsche the concept of Apollonian culture, the aristocratic view of life, the mood of decadence and nihilism, and the idea that the will to power is man's basic drive. He also owed to Nietzsche the theory of eternal recurrence and the concept of culture as the unity of the artistic style, though he interpreted both in rather un-Nietzschean terms.

Every thinker, no matter how creative, is indebted to others for much of his own thoughts. This is why we may gain a glimmer into his mind by tracing his intellectual roots. In the final analysis, however, it is how a philosopher adapts that heritage to his own creative mind that needs to be explained. Let us see how Spengler applied the idea of the life cycle to the major premises of his own system: to the metaphysics of the life cycle, the morphology of culture, the physiognomic method, and the prophetic view of politics.

B. THE IDEA IN OSWALD SPENGLER

I

The major premises of Spengler's metaphysics, recurring time and again in the *Decline of the West* and elsewhere, are that the ultimate reality in the world is life, that life unfolds through opposites and cycles, and that this process is utterly and irremediably tragic. According to Spengler, we are little worlds in miniature, encased in the all-encompassing macrocosm.[54] Here is the first and the most fundamental polarity — that of microcosm and macrocosm. All that is cosmic, Spengler tells us, has periodicity or rhythm; all that is microcosmic has polarity or tension. By cosmic, Spengler meant the unalterable structure and processes of our known universe; by microcosmic, he understood all individual existence which defines itself in relation to the macrocosm. To the human eye, microcosm presents a showplace in which life pulsates in kaleidoscopic forms. Yet, life is subject to one great metaphysical principle: Polarity. Every conscious being, animal or human, perceives the world around it in discrete images; it defines itself in relation to something else. The world in which we live, the world of the microcosm, is dualistic through and through because clarity of understanding as well as physical survival demands that we make distinctions and perceive opposites. This way of perceiving, Spengler felt, permeates the world of nature and the world of history. Whether we know it or not, our lives are governed by polarities: self and others; ego and world; soul and body; space and time; past and future; becoming and the become.

The more complex organisms, Spengler tells us, have special organs which allow them to feel the cosmic beat and to be sensible to the microcosmic tensions. The blood system

106

and the sex organs are two cyclical organs of cosmic existence and express the plant-like or cosmic side of life, bearing the "mark of periodicity, beat, even to the extent of harmony with the great cycles of the stars, of relation between female nature and the moon, of this life generally to night, spring, warmth."[55] In addition, there are two differentiating organs of microcosmic mobility — the senses and the nerves. These organs bear the mark of "tensions, polarities of light and object illuminated, of cognition and that which is cognized, of wound and the weapon that has caused it."[56]

The symbol of life is blood — flowing, blazing, nourishing; its macrocosmic analogue is fire. Man's deep kinship to fire is revealed in every aspect of his existence: in his longing for the sunny south, in his fiery conflicts, in his tempestuous passions, and in the fire of his intellect.[57] It goes without saying that Spengler wants us to conceive fire intuitively, for as soon as we start thinking about it, we only find the process of oxidation! It is best, therefore, to let ourselves sink into its meaning by contemplating the sunset or the crackling flame of the fireplace.

Cosmic existence, symbolized on this earth by plant life, is being there (*Dasein*); whereas microcosmic existence, embodied most fully by animal and human life, is waking-consciousness (*Wachsein*). Though mobile animal life sometimes reverts to a plant-like state, as in sleep, its essence lies in its consciousness of polarity. Being is instinctual through and through; waking consciousness, on the other hand, is intellectual cognition, no matter how rudimentary such cognition may be. In man, waking consciousness implies differentiation, the perception of discrete things, and the recognition of subject and object. The instrument which discloses objects and their location in time and space to us is the eye. Of all the human organs, this one is the intellectual organ *par excellence* because it conveys the form world to the brain. "Man's thought," Spengler insisted again and again, "is visual thought, our concepts are derived from vision, and the whole fabric of our logic is a light-world in the imagination."[58] In man, the light world of the intellect intrudes upon his waking consciousness by intellectualizing his senses; and in so doing, introduces a permanent disunity in man, arrogating — as it does — too much importance in the ensemble of life.[59] Worse, thought, when it becomes interlocked with language and speech, makes life problematical because it trammels instinctive animal action. Thought and action become divorced in proportion to the complexity of man's culture — the higher the culture, the greater will be the gap between thought and action.[60]

Man may be a thinking being, Spengler observes, but it does not follow "that his being consists in thinking."[61] Like Goethe, Spengler proudly asserted that he never thought about thinking, which belongs to the realm of truth, but about life, which belongs to the realm of facts. Truths — and here Spengler introduces another polarity — belong to the world of causality rather than the world of history. The search for causal connection is the search for permanence in a world of ceaseless flux. Spengler never tired of applauding man's quest for knowledge and certainty, but at the same time he never ceased inveighing against the view that thought constitutes the essence of man. On the contrary, "life can exist without thought, but thought is only one mode of life."[62]

It is on this basic premise that Spengler's whole conception of man and history revolves. This planet, on which man is only a tiny fragment, is a compost heap of life teeming with tension, vitality, and struggle. The man who is cognizant of these facts, grasping his opportunities by sound instinct, will be the maker rather than the passive spectator of historical events; for in the last resort, as Spengler puts it, "only the active man, the man of destiny, lives in the *actual* world, the world of political, military, and economic decision, in which concepts and systems do not figure or count."[63] There is much truth in this observation, though not in such exaggerated form. Spengler was right when he said that "men of theory commit a huge mistake in believing that their place is at the head and not in the train of great events,"[64] wrong to imply that men of thought exercise *no* influence on great events. Spengler often had the disconcerting tendency to make his polarities absolute and to disregard life experiences in their interactions. The mingling of opposites, as we recall, was alien to his being. He thought in sharp polarities by dichotomizing the objects of his experience.

II

Another polarity which figures prominently in Spengler's thought is the distinction between becoming (*Werden*) and the become (*das Gewordene*). Strictly speaking, the distinction is tenuous because the become, which is supposed to denote the hard-set, is subject to change just as much as is the becoming — with the difference that the one changes while growing, the other while decaying. Spengler primarily used the distinction by juxtaposing the world of inert matter, in which there are only set-fast objects in motion, to the world of organic growth, in which living things grow, mature, and decay. At still other times, he applied the distinction to ideas, claiming that natural science thinking signifies the become, whereas historical thinking signifies becoming. Precisely why historical thinking grows, and natural science thinking does not, is left unexplained by Spengler. Presumably, this is because scientific formula expresses eternal truth, whereas historical thinking merely expresses "destiny" or deep-seated human significances. Yet, this would seem to be a vacuous distinction since Spengler informs us elsewhere that there are no eternal scientific formulas, and that scientific principles bear the same relativistic imprint of their specific cultures as do all other ideas. In any case, since Spengler made the dualism of becoming and the become one of the cornerstones of his metaphysics, we must try to comprehend its meaning, regardless of the inconsistencies involved. Spengler owed the distinction to Goethe, who argued that becoming not only precedes the become, but that it belongs to a different level of being. The become is vapid, inert, and dead; becoming on the other hand, is suffused with life and thus bears the mark of divinity:

> The Godhead is effective in the living and not in the dead, in the becoming and the changing, not in the become and the set-fast; and therefore, similarly, the reason (*Vernunft*) is concerned only to strive towards the divine through the becoming and the living, and the understanding (*Verstand*) only to make use of the become and the set-fast.[65]

According to both Goethe and Spengler, becoming belongs to the realm of life, whereas the become belongs to finished life, which already bears the mark of death. Spengler sometimes went so far as to equate the become with death. The significance of this dualism in Spengler's thought is the attempt to associate history with life or becoming and science with the become or set-fast. In other words, Spengler transferred the polarity between becoming and the become to culture and history. To draw such a sharp distinction is one thing, to prove it is another. Logically speaking, history is about past life not about life in the present. What exempts the past from the realm of the become, the hard-set, the dead? To show that the past belongs to becoming, Spengler would have to demonstrate how man's past is still alive in some sense. Nowhere does he come to grips with this problem, so that his relegation of history to life and science to death seems wholly arbitrary. Some philosophers, Dilthey or Collingwood come to mind, make the same distinction between science and history, but at least they tried to justify their assertions. Collingwood, for example, claimed that the act of re-experiencing a past thought was in some ways tantamount to reviving that thought in the present.[66] In other words, the past survives in the minds of those who live in the present. A philosophical treatise, a work of art, or a piece of music, though conceived ages ago, becomes revitalized when it is re-read, re-experienced, or replayed. Wandering through the stacks of a library, we are not walking through a mausoleum, because the books that have been preserved there are living symbols of the past, capable of changing our lives. We breathe life into the past by reading these books, no matter how old they may be. Dilthey and other idealist philosophers were right in emphasizing the fact that the past is always vital in the present, wrong to suggest that this vitality is somehow life-like. We should not confuse the metaphor with the thing it purports to describe. A portrait by Rembrandt may affect us deeply by speaking directly to our own experience, but this does not imply that Rembrandt's work is alive or vital. Even if it were possible to re-experience the emotions, the ideas, and the technical know-how it must have taken Rembrandt to paint the *Polish Rider*, the work of art we see in the museum still remains an inert object.

Spengler did not even grant the possibility of revitalizing the past in this sense. In fact, he emphatically denied that we could revitalize past works of art, particularly those artistic creations which have been produced by another culture.

"That the artistic masterpieces of all cultures are still living for us — 'immortal' as we say — is another . . . fancy."[67] Even in the case of our own Western culture, Spengler insisted, the men of today cannot fully comprehend the creations of the Renaissance or the Baroque: "All art is mortal, not merely the individual artifacts but the arts themselves. One day the last portrait of Rembrandt and the last bar of Mozart will have ceased to be — though possible a coloured canvas and a sheet of notes may remain . . ."[68] Spengler then clinches his argument against the vitality of the past by remarking that "every thought, faith, and science dies as soon as the spirits in whose worlds their 'eternal truths' were true and necessary are extinguished."[69] In what sense, then, is history alive or vital? Spengler does not tell us.

Having subsumed history under becoming and science under the become, Spengler then committed himself to several other daring dichotomies, the most prominent being the distinction between destiny and causality, a distinction which, in his view, involved the additional weighty problem of time and space. He attached particular importance to the distinction between destiny and causality, a distinction which, in his view, involved the additional weighty problem of time and space. He attached particular importance to the distinction between destiny and causality, holding that no one could possibly understand his philosophy if he did not grasp the meaning of "destiny" (*die Schicksalsidee*).[70] The idea of destiny, Spengler felt, denotes an habitual sense of anxiety that all men experience in the face of change. We may resort to various subterfuges to escape the meaning of relentless change by building monuments to eternity. Behind our illusions of permanence, however, there lurks the frightening awareness that we are growing older and increasingly estranged from our everchanging surroundings. This omnipresent (often suppressed) knowledge that change affects us with utter indifference to our wishes forces us to recognize that life obeys a different logic than thought. In the world of the systematic philosopher — the world of Aristotle or Kant — everything happens for a good reason. Life, however, cannot be put in the Procrustean bed of "reasons," "causes," "schemes," or "formulas." All rational schemes are at bottom nothing but revolts against the uncertain, tragic, and mysterious rhythm of life. The thinker in systems, Spengler observed, simply cannot admit that life is incomprehensible to rational thought. This is why he tries to escape from the uncertainty implicit in life by reducing human existence to a coherent scheme. As Spengler pointed out, "the abstract savant, the natural-science researcher, the thinker in systems, whose whole intellectual existence bases itself on the causality principle, are 'late' manifestations of an unconscious *hatred* of the powers of an incomprehensible Destiny."[7][1]

Spengler was never tired of repeating that life has nothing to do with the theoretical ideas of the ivory tower philosopher who has his head in the clouds. He felt that there are indeed more things in heaven and earth than are dreamed of in Aristotle or Kant's philosophy. The destiny idea is such an idea which the abstract thinker assiduously avoids or represses. Since Spengler held that destiny must be felt rather than rationally conceived, a certain amount of distortion is bound to result when we seek to put his idea on paper. We can only try — and probably fail — in conveying Spengler's highly mystical idea of destiny.

It is perhaps easier to describe how the idea of destiny suggests itself to the mind than to convey its content. A feeling of inexorable fate arises when we recognize that the grinding wheel of time shatters all human pretensions of permanence. This feeling of inevitable change, in turn, makes us acutely aware of time. Much has been written about man's sense of time; but most accounts of it, Spengler believed, missed the mark. The trouble lies in our inability to conceive time without space.[72] Philosophers have usually attempted to set spatial limits or boundaries to time, holding that time could not be measured if we did not set it in a spatial context. Spengler argued that the destiny idea could only be grasped once we got over the hurdle of thinking about time as though it were located in space. Let us stop asking what time is. Instead, let us ask what time means to the life of an individual man, a people, or a whole culture. Just like destiny, time has to do with concrete experiences of life. We may measure time, but we learn little about its meaning when we do so. The only way in which we can grasp the meaning of time is to feel its impact on our lives.

The man who feels time is led invariably to the recognition that there is a mysterious destiny which governs his life. A destiny suggests the secret process which governs human life. Spengler called it the organic logic of existence.[73] Unlike the logic of the inorganic, destiny cannot be measured or analyzed. In fact, the destiny of each and every one of us can only be vaguely adumbrated. Spengler said that the nature of causality could be conveyed through numbers or reasoned classification; the nature of destiny, on the other hand, could only be communicated artistically, as in metaphor, tragedy, or music.[74] We know what destiny is by letting ourselves sink into the meaning and sound of such words as fate, doom, chance, submission to providence, or predestination.[75] Each culture develops its own destiny idea and attempts to give it visible expression in its art, literature, music, religion, or philosophy. To know what is meant by providence, grace, or original sin is to know much about the Western soul. Similarly, we can gain a glimpse into other cultures by immersing ourselves in their destiny ideas — Moira, Ananke, Tyche, or Kismet.

Spengler's distinction between destiny and causality was

meant to underscore his deeply-felt conviction that life is not amenable to quantitative treatment. Life, as men actually live it, has no scientific logic. What it has is the inexplicable logic of destiny. As Spengler put it, "we can count, measure, dissect only the lifeless and so much of the living. Pure becoming, pure life, is in this sense incapable of being bounded. It lies beyond the domain of cause and effect, law and measure."[76] This verdict that life is at bottom a mystery flies in the face of civilized man who is imbued with the pretensions of science. Spengler was undoubtedly correct in pointing out the limits of scientific inquiry. He was also right in remainding us that life contains a large reservoir that cannot be logically bounded. At the same time, Spengler blunted his valuable insight by needless exaggeration. His relegation of science to the become, for example, seems highly arbitrary, because science, just like history, investigates not only inert objects in a world of dead matter but is equally concerned with the process of growth in the world of living organisms. Spengler would undoubtedly have replied that this is perfectly true, but that the kind of science he had in mind for the study of living organisms was historical rather than naturalistic. Spengler, like Goethe before him, was championing a life science which would operate according to methodological procedures different from those used in the natural sciences. Since very few scientists today consider this a viable issue, we can omit the Goethe/Newton controversy that raged in academic circles in Germany during the nineteenth century.

To summarize, Spengler's distinction between becoming and the become implied a condition of life and finished-life respectively. Ontologically speaking, becoming is endowed with the attribute of potentiality, whereas the become possesses actuality. Life is the "form in which the actualizing of the possible is accomplished."[78] Putting it another way,

Spengler explained that "soul is the still-to-be accomplished, world is accomplished, life is the accomplishing."[79] When asked what it is that gives direction to becoming or that sets becoming on a certain goal (as an opponent of natural science, Spengler refused to talk about the cause of becoming), he answered that becoming is urged on by the longing (*Sehnsucht*) of the soul to fulfill its inner potentialities in the outer world. All mobile life possesses this longing to give direction to becoming, to acutalize its genetic and spiritual inheritance. When Spengler spoke about the ego or the soul actualizing its potentialities, he only adumbrated the course of this development and remained silent about its precise content. Life, he reiterated, is at bottom a mystery, and the best we can do is to speak poetically or metaphorically about it. There is another caveat to be observed in discussing Spengler's metaphysics. Spengler's frequent use of the term soul should not mislead us into thinking that he was an idealist who spiritualized nature. Man and culture, to be sure, have a soul, but they also have a material form (body) which interacts and frequently influences the soul.[80] Spengler was never explicit on the body/soul relationship, but he was clearly not a Platonic idealist.

Driven on by a mysterious longing to actualize its potentiality, the soul encounters opposition in the form of other life, equally seeking to find its essence. The soul is also confronted by alien powers, most notably the inexplicable force of change and time. As life (becoming) moves on to its having become, the soul is filled with dread of the "irrevocable, the attained, the final."[81] All creatures, especially man, quiver in the presence of this dread. At the same time, as Spengler points out, man owes much of his creative potential to the fear that accompanies the recognition of what change has ultimately in store for him. Human beings cannot escape the thing become, though they never cease to search for solutions that might circumvent the inevitable destiny common to us all — death. It is in this relentless search for escaping the thing become that men rise to their greatest heights. They create magnificent monuments to eternity; they invent gods and an after-life; they produce lasting achievements in art, science, or philosophy that will live on after they have passed away; finally, they try to evade the thing become collectively by perpetuating the species and by building cultural traditions immune to change. All of it, of course, is to no avail because the wheel of time grinds on relentlessly, shattering all pretensions to permanence.

III

To Spengler, then, the structure of reality was permeated by polarities; the inorganic as well as the organic obeyed the eternal rhythm of opposites. Spengler underscored this theme again and again because he believed that it was an inherent part of the cosmos. In his notes, published posthumously under the title *Urfragen*, one heading bore the prominent title, "The Duality of the World." Since duality played such a major part in his outlook, this passage deserves to be quoted in full:

> The whole world is dualistic, and so are all the attempts to penetrate into its inner nature. The reason for this is that the nature of all mobile life is tension between microcosm and macrocosm, and that each world picture exists only for a mobile being.

> From the basic fact of polarity between microcosm and macrocosm, self and others, ego and world are derived all differences: feeling and sensing, soul and body, ego and world, space and time, noble and priest. We feel out of opposites, we think in contrarities, all concepts are formed in pairs of opposites.[82]

The logical conclusion of this juxtaposition of polar opposites, according to Spengler, is that life — animal or human — is determined by the rhythm of cosmic change and the specific form (war, strife, struggle) in which this change occurs.[83] Life is ceaseless change, but the pattern of it is the life cycle. The idea of life, Spengler argued, exhibits strict inner forms: conception, birth, growth, and decay. This is a cosmic destiny which encompasses the life of the lowliest protozoans to the mightiest cultures created by the hand of man.[84]

Although it is true that the cosmic cycle governs the process of change and transformation, it is far from the fact that most living beings ever experience all or even a few of its successive phases. Young birds may die when their mother is shot down by a bullet while seeking food for them. Young kittens may be torn to shreds by packs of dogs before reaching maturity. Similarly, famine, war, disease, or natural disasters may extinguish life in its infancy.

We are thus subject not only to the inexorable and inescapable destiny of the cosmic cycle, but also to the tension and strife implicit in it. From the beginning of life on this planet, Spengler believed, all species were conditioned by one primal experience: to perceive opposites and to maintain the self against the threat posed by the other alien beings. The consequence for Spengler, as for all "life philosophers," is that nature has and always will be red in tooth and claw; by implication, the same is true of man's history. "Life," Spengler asserted, "is endless murdering."[85] Man is a predatory animal similar in kind to other animals, except that he possesses the gift of invention which he owes to his superior brain and to his ambidextrous hands.[86] Man is by nature sly, predatory, cruel, and dominating; he is not the creature of sweet reasonableness depicted by the men of the Enlightenment.

Now Spengler believed firmly that man's fate or his existential condition was thoroughly tragic. This is not because man is a predatory animal. Spengler admired toughness and aggressiveness in man. He divided man into two groups, leaders and followers, and never ceased to praise the mer for their prowess and aggressive instincts. Man's tragedy does not lie in his war-like nature, but in peaceful impulses, derived in great part from the growing complexity of intellect and culture. This, again, is inherent in the life cycle, according to which the youthful phase signifies soundness of instinct and primitive strength. As soon as man begins to ruminate on the nature of life, living becomes problematical. Intellect is essentially negative and critical unless it serves the cause of instinct. Intellect is useful as a weapon, but as a mode of life, it is and always will be destructive of life.[87]

Thus, with the development of intellect and culture, man is alienated from his true essence. By opting for culture, man sacrifices more than he bargained for. Spengler, like Freud, conceived man's transition from primitiveness to culture as a revolution and a tragedy.[88] When man crossed the bridge leading from the life of primitive, individual acquisitiveness to the life of a regulated social community, he made a fateful decision. Freud and Spengler tell us that such a transition involved an enormous amount of libidinal sacrifice, a painful choice because man is motivated primarily by instinctual desires. In his primitive state, man followed his instincts, but at the same time he was exposed to the callous vicissitudes of nature. Security and fear drove man together into civil societies. In making this transition from the state of nature to civil society, however, man may have sacrificed too much of his former being. In the state of nature, man was a magnificent predatory animal following his sound instincts. Man may have been brutish in the parlance of civilized language, but at least he was psychologically whole — that is, his instincts were in harmony. In society, the pleasure and reality principle not only became differentiated but were brought in sharp conflict with each other. Man was forced to subordinate the greater part of his libidinal energy to the harsh demands of the reality principle — to unremitting toil, struggle, and the sublimation of his instinctual desires.

For Freud, as well as for Spengler, the implication is inescapable: culture is essentially alien to man. Culture means suffering for man because the tensions of existence are aggravated far beyond the limits prescribed by nature. In addition, culture implies increasing discrepance between thought and instincts. Spengler felt that culture imposed a second layer of being on the original or primitive personality, setting the primitive side in permanent opposition to the cultured side. We are consequently dealing here with another polarity, this one being deeply imbedded in human nature itself. Since man made his fateful transition to culture, he had to accept the burden of a second nature frequently — it not perennially — at odds with his original one. Thus, man himself is torn by polarity and the tension which inevitably results from it. Man's soul is a squabbling crowd of opposites, a battlefield of contradictory impulses. When we speak of "man," Spengler concluded, we must specify which man we are talking about. There is pre-culture man and culture man. The former is a universal type who exhibits elements common to all men: a reservoir of basic instincts, love, hate, hunger, fear, and aggression. This is the constant element in man. Culture can change its expression, but not its character. The variable element in man, of course, is that which is conditioned into him by his culture — the ·Freudian Superego. However strong it may be, the eternal primitive — the savage within — persists throughout changing cultural circumstances. Spengler never ceased to admire the eternal primitive in man because it represented his true essence; on the other hand, man's cultured side is always something artificial, no matter how magnificent it may manifest itself in man's works of art, religion, science, or philosophy. The highest cultural achievement, in fact, rests on the fact of man's primitiveness. As Spengler put it, every cultural symbol is merely a sublimation of the eternal primitive.[89]

As cultures grow and mature, the primitive side in man is increasingly stifled by civilized customs, especially in the cities, where the primitive becomes synonymous with savagery and retrogression. The cultured man of the city, according to Spengler, flatters himself on having outgrown his primitive heritage which explains why he so smugly depicts the primitive as ape-like, clumsy, coarse, superstitious, and stupid. This is a convenient image for the city man of late culture because it reinforces his prejudices by showing how far he has come from his ape-like beginnings.

In reality, Spengler observes, the primitive man (*Urmensch*) was a noble predatory animal like all other predatory animals.[90] It is, therefore, a tragedy that culture stifles man's primitiveness in proportion to his progress in the arts and sciences. Spengler agreed with Rousseau that culture has destroyed simplicity, virtue, and sound instincts in man. At the same time, he strongly disagreed with Rousseau that civilized man of the cosmopolis could recapture primitiveness within the context of his advanced technical civilization. He rejected this argument as the pipedream of alienated intellectuals who are out of touch with their instincts. Primitive vigor is not found in the later, but in the earlier phases of a culture. Vigor, youth, sureness of instinct, consciousness of race and blood — all these are symbols of the life cycle in its early phases. A mature culture which has already actualized its potentialities cannot revert to its beginnings. This is a patent absurdity. Spengler conceded that all mature cultures look back nostalgically when senility is about to overtake them. Rousseau's cry of a return to nature expresses the anguish of decadent culture man to be released from the crushing burden of civilization. It is the same with individual men when they become childlike in their old age. Tallyrand's pathetic remark. "Qui n'a pas vecu avant 1789 ne connait pas la couceur de vivre," is symptomatic of this longing for a more innocent, a sweeter age. The life cycle, however, grinds on relentlessly. Neither individual man nor the culture he creates is immune from its severe law that everything changes and nothing remains. Yet, the flame of the fire continues to blaze as life is created anew — vital, primitive, youthful.

AMOEBA AND MONAD: THE SOUL OF
PRIMITIVE AND HIGH CULTURES

I

In the life cycle, Spengler thought he had discovered the form language of human history. The problem now was how to apply the idea of cycles to history, which involved the further question, precisely what is in history that develops cyclically. We know that individual organisms undergo the phases of the cycle, but what units in history traverse the successive cycles? Clearly, since the cycle is inherent in the nature of things, it applies to all phenomena – to individuals, groups, peoples, and nations. Spengler's intuition, which was often remarkably sound, told him that history-in-the-round could only be meaningful if we studied the largest historical units: human cultures. According to Spengler, cultures are historical phenomena which encompass the common elements shared by particular individuals, groups, peoples, and nations at any given time in history.

Spengler believed that history was not a seamless web in time and space, but an unfolding of human destinies. Man's fate at any given time in history is embodied in the character of his culture. The proper study of history is, therefore, the study of culture. We cannot understand history properly if we study it microscopically; for in focusing exclusively on the trees, we lose sight of the forest. Nor can we grasp the course of history by dividing it into meaningless schemes such as "Ancient," "Medieval," or "Modern" – a scheme no more

123

accurate than Joachim Floris' division of history into the Age of the Father, the Age of the Son, and the Age of the Holy Ghost.[1] These categories are "jejune," as Spengler called them, because they distort by simplifying the complex expression that human life has assumed in the past. Besides, such schemes are invariably of West European origin; they confuse the pattern of western culture with the rest of the world, which is made to revolve around it. As Spengler put it, the scheme "Ancient," "Medieval," and "Modern" not only circumscribes the area of history, it rigs the stage. "The ground of West Europe," he went on to say, "is treated as a steady pole, a unique patch chosen on the surface of the sphere for no better reason, it seems, than because we live on it — and great histories of millenial duration and mighty faraway Cultures are made to revolve around this pole in all modesty."[2]

We also distort the course of history by relying exclusively on causal explanations — that is, by assuming a network of interrelated events in a specific spatio-temporal order. This is a useful method for disclosing certain outer uniformities, but it is woefully inadequate in explaining the real stuff of history: man's fears, aspirations, secret longings, or man's perennial search for meaning. The search for causes is the method of the bread and butter historian, who sees history as a "sort of tapeworm industriously adding on to itself one epoch after another."[3] Nor is it any more meaningful to read history as one would like it to be — a history of progress or a history of divine immanence. There is no ineluctable unfolding of reason or progress; there is no linear development of any sort; above all, there is no actualization of some divine plan in history. There is no "mankind," either progressing or regressing. "Mankind," Spengler wrote, "has no aim, no idea, no plan, any more than the family of butterflies or orchids."[4]

Yet, there is uniformity in historical variety. Among that bewildering mass of factual detail in history, the trained historian can discern a definitive rhythm and style, provided, of course, that he possesses the ability to perceive the forms (*Gestalten*) which lie concealed behind the welter of detail.[5] What is the form that human life has taken in the past? Spengler answered that history is a series of collective biographies in which past generations have recorded their innermost feelings about life, death, destiny, beauty, or truth. Although past generations have left their life histories, they have written vastly different stories. In surveying the past, we find that a chain of generations is bound by clearly recognizable ideals, by similar laws and institutions, by a common language, and by a shared vision of past, present, and future. These common elements or traits by which past generations expressed their lives constitute their cultures.

A culture, as Spengler defined it, is a living organism subject to the same laws of growth as any other living form. Cultures are organisms of the higest form, and "world-history is their collective biography."[6] Why they grow and flourish in certain peculiar ways will probably always remain a mystery. Spengler thought it best to stand back in silence and awe at the magnificent spectacle of cultural life. To be sure, we can describe the variegated expressions of a culture, but we can never penetrate into its ultimate secrets, specifically into the riddle of its growth.

If cultures are indeed living organisms, they must unfold according to the law of cycles. Every culture, Spengler tells us, "passes through the age-phases of the individual man. Each has its childhood, youth, manhood, and old age."[7] Moreover, a culture is endowed with certain potentialities which it tries to actualize in the course of its life history. When it has fulfilled its potentials, when the springs of its youthful creativity are dried up, it shrivels, and ultimately decays.

Putting it in more poetic language, Spengler observed:

> A culture is born in the moment when a great soul
> awakens out of the proto-spirituality (*dem
> urseelenhaften Zustande*) of ever-childish humanity,
> and detaches itself, a form from the formless, a
> bounded and mortal thing from the boundless and
> enduring. It blooms on the soil of an
> exactly-definable landscape, to which plant-wise it
> remains bound. It dies when this soul has actualized
> the full sum of its possibilities in the shape of
> peoples, languages, dogmas, arts, states, sciences,
> and reverts into the proto-soul...The aim once
> attained — the idea, the entire content of inner
> possibilities, fulfilled and made externally actual —
> the Culture suddenly hardens, it mortifies, its blood
> congeals, its force breaks down, and it becomes
> Civilization ... [8]

By civilization, Spengler meant the hard-set, the become,
the dead. He differed from most philosophers of history by
using civilization in a periodic sense, as "the *inevitable* destiny
of the Culture."[9] In other words, civilizations "are a
conclusion, the thing — become succeeding the thing —
becoming, death following life..."[10] Elsewhere, Spengler
referred to civilizations as decaying cultures;[11] or, even more
bluntly, as the mummies of erstwhile living cultures.[12]

Did Spengler really mean to equate cultures with biological
organisms? True, cultures may grow like organisms, but are
they really biological in essence? If we closely disentangle
some of Spengler's apparently contradictory statements, we
see that he made a distinction — perhaps philosophically ill
conceived — between the spiritual essence (soul) of a culture
and its outward organic shell. The fact clearly emerges that

Spengler only thought of cultures as organisms in regard to their development. In some sense, Spengler tells us, cultures are indeed living things, comparable to plants or animals. At the same time, they are obviously different because they are by nature spiritual. In one interesting passage, Spengler declared that cultures are life forms of the highest rank (*Lebewesen höchsten Ranges*) – a phrase which his English translator, Charles Francis Atkinson, erroneously rendered as "sublimated life-essences."[13] Oddly enough, the translator probably hit upon the real meaning of Spengler's idea of culture in this mistranslation! A culture, in Spengler's highly mystical conception, is indeed a sublimated life-essence, a form of spiritual life in which man's primitive drives have been transmuted into higher spiritual goals. But is it man who imparts life to culture by sublimating his impulses, or is it culture which makes use of man by fulfilling its own innate potentialities? Spengler seems to have vacillated between the two views. For the most part, he regarded cultures as organic human growths defining themselves in the process of their growth. At other times, however, he regarded culture as a kind of Leibnizean monad which fulfills its innate idea (Spengler's *Prime Symbol*) by descending into historical time and by using man for the actualization of its idea. Spengler probably would have rejected this Leibnizean interpretation by pointing out that his cultures are organic beings – not spiritual abstractions. Yet, his discussion of man's relationship to his culture reveals that Spengler's cultures often look suspiciously like reifications – that is, abstractions made into real life entities existing independently of man and, in a sense, determining his destiny. Culture, he observed, is not a being but a happening, fulfilling itself in and through men, who are elements of its expressions.[14] Spengler often spoke of people as mere instruments of a culture or being under its sway. "No people," he argued, "create culture, but is created by it."[15]

Again,

> World-history is the history of the great Cultures,
> and peoples are but the symbolic forms and vessels
> in which the men of these Cultures fulfil their
> Destinies.[16]

We have here a mixture of "life philosophy," as it was
advocated around the turn of the last century, and Leibnizean
idealism. A culture grows by virtue of its innate idea (theme,
prime symbol, plan) which it seeks to actualize in the course
of its life history. Cultures, then, *behave* like organisms, but
they are by nature spiritual substances. Spengler was always
anxious not to be mistaken for a Leibnizean idealist, to whom
change and transformation is always either an embarrassment
or an illusion. He wanted to endow his cultures with a soul,
but he also wanted to place that soul into historical flux for
the actualization of its idea.[17] In so doing, he often
confounded the idea of growth with the idea of spiritual
immanence, writing a metahistory replete with stunning
poetic insights but also ultimate scientific inexplicabilities.

II

Spengler distinguished two forms of culture — primitive
and high cultures. In the *Decline of the West*, he merely
touched on this distinction without much further elaboration.
After all, in the *Decline,* he was primarily concerned with
higher cultures — their growth, development, and decay. If we
only read the *Decline*, we would get a very misleading picture
of Spengler's cultural vision. The fact is that Spengler spent
the remaining years of his life after the *Decline of the West*
on prehistoric cultures, attempting — so to speak — to

continue the analysis of the *Decline* behind rather than beyond its starting point. In so doing, he was groping his way toward a vision of culture from the beginning of man to the present day.[18] As we have seen, it was an awesome plan which was even beyond the ken of Spengler's abilities. Though he continued to work on his theory of prehistoric cultures until his death, he never got beyond the note-taking stage. We are now fortunate to have these fragments in order to round out our picture of Spengler's vision, though we must be careful in using them because they were put together in a certain way by Spengler's heirs.[19]

Already in the *Decline of the West*, Spengler showed that there are two forms of culture — the primitive cultures, existing primarily in prehistoric times, and the high cultures, originating on the Nile and Euphrates about 3000 B.C.[20] Spengler conceded, especially after reading Leo Frobenius, that the primitive culture of Northwest Africa has endured since prehistoric times and is still alive today. Already in the *Decline of the West*, Spengler showed that primitive and high cultures, though structurally related by virtue of being organismic, are different in their expression forms. Moreover, the primitive cultures interact and influence each other, whereas the high cultures are monodological structures permitting no interaction. This is why Spengler chose the term amoeba to describe the expression form of some primitive cultures.

According to Spengler, man has traversed four major cultural phases in the course of his existence on this planet. He referred to these cultures by the alphabetic letters: *a, b, c,* and *d*. The first three are primitive, the fourth is a high culture. Sometimes Spengler used the symbols lava, crystal, and amoeba to explain their physiognomic character. Since his *d* culture is a self-sufficient entity, neither influenced nor influencing, we may liken it to the Leibnizean monad, to a soul without windows. Chronologically, lava approximately spans the years 100,000 — 20,000 B.C.; crystal comprises the years 20,000 to 8,000; and amoeba covers the period from 8,000 — 3,500. Spengler insisted that the life expectancies of cultures varied in proportion to their complexity. As usual, Spengler swam against the stream by equating primitiveness with vigor and a long life expectancy. Thus, higher forms of cultures such as amoeba and monad can expect a relatively short life span — 3,500 for amoeba (c) and 1,000 years for monad (d).

Spengler viewed man's prehistory in highly intuitive fashion; and most of his observations, scattered among the aphorisms and sketches of his posthumous writings, are boldly speculative in character. Given his penchant for abstract theorizing, we can readily see why prehistory, with its dearth of factual material, proved to be Spengler's great love. Here, he could give free reign to his intuitions. Specifically, he wanted to uncover the significance of those cosmic changes which took place between the beginning of the Ice Age and the emergence of the high cultures in Egypt and Babylon.[21] Man's destiny, he felt, must have been determined during these dark and forbidding times. How did man's soul lift itself above its animal origin? When and where did human history become tragic? In other words, Spengler looked to prehistory for an answer to his metaphysical queries. He wanted to trace, if possible, the evolution of the human soul from its obscure beginnings to its crystallization in the high cultures. In sum, Spengler wanted to write nothing short of an epic of the human soul.

Man's history, then, unfolds in four successive cultural phases, each in a sense representing a revolt against nature. Contrary to the Darwinians and their followers, man does not evolve from ape-like beginnings to homo sapiens, but he appears ready-made — the result, probably, of a great mutation. In fact, all profound historical changes are the result of mutations. The theory of a slow evolution from the ape to the man of today is a figment of late culture man. No doubt, it is a pleasing theory because it shows how far man has progressed over the ages. The real story, however, is quite different. As Spengler put it in his inimitable way:

A slow, phlegmatic evolution may correspond to the English temper, but not to that of nature. To uphold it, one threw around with millions of years, since nothing of the kind manifested itself in measurable times... We know nothing about the 'ancestors' of man, in spite of all the searching and anatomical comparisons. Ever since human skeletons surfaced, man has been what he is today. One sees the 'Neanderthal' in every public assembly. It is also quite impossible that the hand, the erect posture, bearing of the head and so on developed sequentially. All of it is there together and suddenly. World history proceeds onward from catastrophe to catastrophe, whether or not we can grasp or proof it. Since H. deVries, this is called 'mutation.'[22]

Quite mysteriously and quite suddenly, then, man appeared ready-made a hundred thousand years ago. Profound natural and human changes are always cataclysmic because nature does not evolve gradually in causing major developments. *Natura facit saltus:* each form, Spengler insisted, appears suddenly and ready-made. This is true of man, as it is of all other things of nature. The reason why Spengler did not accept the theory of evolution is obvious: it ran counter to his underlying assumptions about man and culture. Specifically, it was contrary to his metaphysical belief that everything is relative, and that there is cyclical but not linear development in history. Evolution would cut a path straight across Spengler's recurring cultural cycles, which made it a most embarrassing theory. The theory of mutation, on the other hand, fitted in readily with his idea of cycles. Being a doctrine of cataclysmic rather than evolutionary change, it posed no threat to what Spengler thought was the only legitimate theory of change — the theory of cycles.

Man, then, appears ready-made on this planet as a result of a mutation. Precisely why or even when this mutation occurred will always be shrouded in mystery. At first, man eked out a precarious existence on earth. In culture a, which Spengler likened to a blazing lava quickly solidifying, man was a predatory animal scattered across the earth in small groups. As yet, man was only dimly aware of the cosmic beat and the bearing it had on his life. The changes around him made relatively little impact on his thought, which was primarily "thinking by the hand." Whatever reflective abilities man may have had in this phase, he transmuted them into the creation of war-like instruments such as stone axes, wooden spears, flint hammerstones, or simply making use of unflaked pieces of stone with sharp edges. The ability to think by hand and to fashion tools expressive of the individual maker who produces them, is laden with momentous implications. Among all the animals, man alone possesses the ability of emancipating himself from the constraints placed upon him by his own species.[23] At this stage, or any other, individual man acted very much in accordance with the traits common to his species, but he already showed glimmers of self-expression.

In state b (crystal), of which we know as little as of stage a, the earth had changed perceptively. Man became more numerous and less scattered in isolated places. There were more frequent interactions between people who formerly lived in splendid isolation. The major development in culture *b* was that man learned to think visually, where he had only thought manually or practically in stage *a*. Spengler always likened reflective to visual thinking, holding that it formed the basis of all theoretical and critical acumen in man. To be sure, visual thinking at this stage was very rudimentary. Insofar as man thought at all, he did so by way of instinctive perception and dim surmises. Stage *b*, like stage *a*, was inorganic in nature because man's cultures were still too primitive and still too isolated to permit interaction. In both phases, man slowly, but steadily emerged out of his formless existence as a mere bird of prey, defining his instinct and his intelligence as he interacted with nature.

Cultures *a* and *b* comprise what archeologists would call Paleolithic and Neolithic times. Throughout his observations on primitive cultures, Spengler engaged in a prolonged polemic with archeologists because he believed that their criteria for classifying cultures were fallacious. To begin with, he thought that it was futile to divide prehistoric cultures on the basis of tools or metals found in museums.[24] Labels such as the Stone Age, the Bronze Age, or the Iron Age, Spengler declared, are wholly misleading ways of referring to primitive cultures. As more and more tools are uncovered, this scheme of classification will necessarily become more complex and more meaningless. Distinction between Châtelperronian, Aurignacian, Gravettian, Solutrean, or Magdalenian — all based on a wide variety of tools — may tell us something about craftsmanship, but it tells us nothing about the people who made them — unless, of course, we reconstruct intuitively and imaginatively what these tools disclose about the nature of their creators. It is this aspect of prehistory, Spengler felt, which should serve as a method of classification. Prehistory should describe the development of the primitive soul — not the evolution of stone axes, flint scrapers, knife blades, perforated batons, or the like. There is some justice to Spengler's challenge. Anthropology has been overly materialistic in its approach. At the same time, it so happens that prehistoric scholars must work with what they have, and that happens to be tools, tombs, death masks, vases, skeletons, weapons, or cave paintings. Prehistoric man simply did not leave his soul in written statements. Most prehistoric scholars, trained in careful scientific procedures, have been reticent in drawing conclusions which they feel are not warranted by the evidence. Spengler's brilliance as well as his shortcoming was that he developed intuitive conclusions from his evidence. It led him to embarrassing pitfalls as well as to highly novel insights.

As it turns out, Spengler tells us very little about the soul of primitive cultures, through we must temper this judgment by recalling that Spengler has left us only fragments on this matter. To continue our discussion of Spengler's primitive cultures, amoeba or culture a witnessed another mutation. Life in caves or under trees gave way about 6000 B.C. to life in domesticated settlements. Man became a domestic animal, and, by implication, a different creature. As he became tame and increasingly rationalistic, he also learned to communicate and to act in groups.[25] Psychologically, man now felt the full force of the ego as language taught him to differentiate between himself and the others around him. This is not to say that man had become a full-blown individualist free to make his own intellectual, religious, or political choices. Spengler merely wanted to show that the individual ego, formerly subservient to the instincts, had been awakened to perceive itself in relation to other egos. Spengler did not imply that some sort of individuation occurred in c culture. Not until the Greeks did the individual break the bonds of the social, political, or religious collectivity and feel himself as a free and autonomous being.

Most *c* cultures, Spengler continued, clustered on rivers such as the Indus, the Euphrates, and the Nile. Politcal life was as yet very rudimentary, manifesting itself largely in village or tribal form. Those who classify cultures by the way man makes a living would call this phase Mesolithic. In it, man made a transition from hunter, fisher, or keeper of small herds of animals to the regulated life of small scale agricultural communities. Spengler was right to call this a revolutionary step, though it is unlikely that it was caused by a catastrophic mutation. More likely, it was caused when men were forced to specialize in order to make a living and when they realized that this was only possible within the context of a well-regulated social community. The result was an economic revolution which shattered all earlier and more primitive social relationships. Thus, man changed from a purely acquisitive to a productive creature; where he had formerly gathered food, he now produced it by his own sweat and brow. A great deal of social cohesion was obviously required to raise crops and animals and to irrigate the fields. Rudimentary riparian bureaucracies made their appearance to meet these challenges, as did a professional class of priests to propitiate the gods who were seen to exercise sway over man's destiny.

A characteristic feature of all *c* cultures, Spengler believed, is that it is amoeba-like: expansive, mobile, and flowing. In other words, the *c* cultures interact and influence one another, thought the precise nature of these cross-cultural movements will probably always remain a mystery. In one of his early outlines on prehistoric cultures, Spengler discerned what he called three cultural circles: a primal nordic line, moving from Scandinavia to Korea and comprising primitive Indogermanic and Altayic groups; a south-east circle, beginning

in the middle of China and moving via Burma to Polynesia;
and a west circle, beginning in Northwest Africa and moving
toward Northeast Africa, the Nile, and even as far as the
Indus. Later, he baptized these circles *Turan, Kasch,* and
Atlantis, names he took from ancient legend and mythology.
In a highly imaginative vision, only vaguely adumbrated in his
fragments, he regarded these circles as expansive amoebas,
flowing into one another and ultimately laying the foundation
for the high cultures of the Ancient Near East and the
Classical World.

Atlantis and *Kasch,* Spengler insisted, are the two great
amoeba cultures which explain everything in the
Mediterranean.[26] *Atlantis* probably centered around Spain,
Tunesia, and Lybia — flowing as far as Crete, Cypress, Asia
Minor, and Egypt. A basic feature of *Atlantis* was its concrete
soul which expressed itself in megalithic architecture. The
basic social form was aristocracy; the original language
probably Hamitic. The religion of *Atlantis,* Spengler believed,
was polytheism, with a marked tendency toward animal forms
as the prime god symbol. *Kasch,* on the other hand, exhibited
quite different patterns. Its original home, Spengler suspected,
spanned the area of the Persian Gulf, Oman, Baluchistan, and
even Hyderabad. *Kasch* intereacted with *Atlantis* in its
movement from Southeast Africa to Northwest Africa. *Kasch*
was a priest-ridden culture and, therefore, far more
otherworldly in tenor. This is why Spengler described *Kasch*
as an abstract culture, governed primarily, if not wholly, by a
class of professional priests. Whereas *Atlantis* expressed its
concrete soul by erecting huge megaliths, *Kasch* expressed its
soul by building temples. Polytheism was again the major
religious belief, though in *Kasch* it took a slightly different
form. The gods were more abstractly conceived, either as
spirits or as heavenly forces. In both *Atlantis* and *Kasch*
immortality in some form was advocated.

Spengler believed that *Atlantis* (circa 4000 B.C.) was to *Kasch* (circa 5000 B.C.) what Occident is to the Orient. Moreover, he felt that the two cultures looked into each other's soul, interacted, and laid the basis of all subsequent high cultures in the Near East and the Classical World. Thus, in merging in about the middle of the fourth millennium, *Kasch* and *Atlantis* laid the foundation for the Babylonian and Egyptian high culture. The decline of Egypt and Babylon, together with the penetration of *Turan* in this area, resulted in the foundation of Classical, Indian, and Chinese culture.[27]

Spengler said very little about *Turan*, except that it fell into the northern circle. *Turan* seems to have been war-like in nature because horse and chariot had their home there. The basic features of *Turan* were: nomadic warriors, plunder, tent or possible primitive wood dwellings, nature mysticism, and a medley of Indogermanic-Altayic dialects. Although we know relatively little about *Turan*, we do know that it was here that the nomadic warriors who ravished the ancient world about 1500 B.C. originated. These "heroic" tribes suddenly moved south about 1500 B.C. and destroyed Egypt, Babylon, and the Minoan culture of Crete. In India, Aryan tribes invaded the World of the Dravidians, while China at the same time was about to enter the feudal period of the Chou. Thus, three new aristocractic cultures grew on older and more refined populations: (1) the Greco-Roman on the Minoan-Mycenaean; (2) the Aryan on the older Indus; and (3) the Chinese on as yet unknown groups.[28] We are on the threshold of the high cultures.

With the high cultures, to which we must now turn, cross-cultural influence came to an end, though Spengler's posthumous writing indicate that he was contemplating certain modifications. At any rate, he did conceive high cultures as hermetically sealed entities, each allotted a life-span of about one thousand years, each unfolding

according to the life cycle, and each developing the
potentialities inherent in its "prime symbol."

III

Every high culture, Spengler believed, is an independent
life form actualizing its inborn potentialities in the process of
its growth and development. The manner of this growth, we
need hardly reiterate, is cyclical. Spengler used the names of
the seasons — spring, summer, autumn, and winter — to
designate the various phases of cultural cycles. To date, eight
mighty cultures have shaped the histories of man on this
planet. These cultures, most of which have irrevocably
vanished, are "all of the same build, the same development,
and the same duration"[29] — a fact, Spengler believed, which
justifies us in looking at them comparatively. Spengler's eight
cultures are: the Egyptian (circa 3000 B.C.), the Babylonian
(circa 3000 B.C.), the Indian (after 1500 B.C.), the Chinese
(after 1500), the Classical or Apollonian, the Arabian or
Magian, the Mexican, and the Western or Faustian culture of
Europe and North America. All of these cultures, except the
Faustian, have either withered away or have lingered on like
giants of the primeval forest, thrusting their decaying branches
toward the sky, as in China, India, or the Islamic world.[30]

Spengler never specified why these cultures grow. No
intellectual answer, he felt, can ever solve such a question, so
that it is better to admit that all deeper questions of cultural
origin are conundrums. If we must talk about it, let us do so
poetically, which is the only way of conceiving the broad
sweep of history. Scanning the history of man, this is what
Spengler saw:

I see, in place of that empty figment of *one* linear

history which can only be kept up by shutting one's
eyes to the overwhelming multitude of the facts,
the drama of a *number* of mighty Cultures, each
springing with primitive strength from the soil of a
mother-region to which it remains firmly bound
throughout its whole lifecycle; each stamping its
material, its mankind, in *its own* image; each having
its own idea, *its own* passions, *its own* life, will and
feeling *its own* death.[31]

Each culture, then, stands on its own and fulfills the
destiny inherent in its soul. Each culture has a soul, but the
nature of that soul is vastly different. What determines that
difference? According to Spengler, cultures are qualitatively
different because their souls are animated by unique themes.
Spengler called this special theme which underlies every
culture a "prime symbol."

Each culture, Spengler believed, perceives the outer world
of extension from a different spatial perspective.[32] This
spatial perspective is the prime symbol of a culture. Although
Spengler talked a great deal about "space symbolism," he
never laid the proper epistemological foundation for his
assertion that different cultures perceive the world differently.
What he did accomplish, however, was to accentuate a very
real cultural difference by showing how it could be detected
in the art, architecture, music, and literature of the various
high cultures. What are the prime symbols of the various
cultures?

The prime symbol of Western Man is "endless space," that
of Classical (Greco-Roman) Man is "body and form."[33] It is
in his discussion of these two cultures that Spengler is at his
best. The classical soul, he argued, chose "the
sensuously-present individual body as the ideal type of the
extended."[34] From this it follows, according to Spengler, that

all classical works of art, literature, or philosophy must bear the imprint of this prime symbol. In a sense, the prime symbol is equivalent to the essence of a culture, for it imparts to it a specific style and historical form. Moreover, the prime symbol manifests itself in numerous derivatory sumbols in art, religion, science, philosophy, and politics. Such configurations of symbols in the classical world, all expressing the idea of the "sensuous present," are mechanical statics, the sensuous cult of the Olympian gods, the politically individual city-states of Greece, the doom of Oedipus and the Phallus symbol.[35] The classical prime symbol, Spengler observed elsewhere, means the attempt to

> tie down the meaning of things-become by means of the principle of *visible limits*; its taboo was focused upon the immediately-present and proximate alien. What was far away, invisible, was *ipso facto* 'not there'.[36]

In other words, the classical mind either felt ill at ease or denied the infinite. Whatever exceeded its visible horizon, inexorably bound up in the smallness of the city state, was nonexistent. The ancients, according to Spengler, were perpetually afraid to extend their horizon — to probe behind the tangible, to explore the world beyond the Pillars of Hercules, to go beyond the situation drama of the moment, or to abandon the small and the static — be it in vasepaining, fresco relief, the architecture of ranking columns, or the naked statue.

Spengler has been severely criticized for emphasizing only this one aspect of the classical soul.[37] No one denies that this static element was very real in the ancient world, but it was by no means the only one. Thus, the numerous data conflicting with Spengler's idea of the "sensuous present" cannot be ignored by calling them illusory. Spengler's idea of the prime symbol may or may not be a convenient instrument of reading the nature of a culture, but it loses its status as a convincing symbol of explanation when it precludes variety from its field of vision. The prime symbol, as Spengler used it, means one theme and one theme only. A logical corollary of this idea is that the different styles of a culture – the Romanesque, the Gothic, the Renaissance, or the Baroque – are all organically linked together by virtue of having grown out of the first style that bore the mark of the Faustian prime symbol – the Romanesque. Spengler's prime symbol implied a rigid monism, for there is only *one* style in art, literature, philosophy, or politics; variety, of course, is not denied *per se*, but is rather seen as an aspect of one and the same style.[38] This implies that different forms of expression are either illusory, nonexistent, or both.

Whereas the Apollonian prime symbol expresses the "sensuous present," the Faustian prime symbol implies "endless space."[39] This yearning for the infinite, epitomized by the legend of Faust, is embodied in the infinite universe of Copernicus, the Faustian striving for ultimate knowledge, the infinite space of tone emboidied in chamber-music, and the imperialistic impulse to expand in geographical space. The Faustian soul approximated its prime symbol most fully in Baroque science, architecture, and – above all – the Baroque music of Handel, Corelli, Vivaldi, or Bach. As Spengler asserted:

> Here our prime symbol of endless space is expressed as completely as the Spearman of Polycletus expresses that of intense bodiliness. When one of those ineffably yearning violin-melodies wanders through the spaces expanded around it by the orchestration of Tartini or Nardini, Haydn, Mozart

> or Beethoven, we know ourselves in the presence of
> an art beside which that of the Acropolis is alone
> worthy to be set.[40]

As we shall see later, Spengler insisted that prime symbols lie concealed behind man's artistic creations, and that it is futile to comprehend them intellectually. We either feel the presence of the Faustian spirit as we contemplate the broad sweep of Western culture or we do not. Thus, when we look at Western portraiture or Western science, we either intuit that inexplicable sense of striving or we do not. The man needs intellectual abstractions to understand historical events, Spengler conceded, will obviously dismiss such ideas as meaningless; and within the context of his world view, he would be right. All that Spengler asks in positing these highly imaginative symbols is to be met on the ground of intuition and poetic insight. All those who are trying to read his theories in purely analytical terms should remember this caveat, one that Spengler explicitly set forth in the preface to the *Decline*. In it, he stated that his work was "intuitive and depictive through and through, written in a language which seeks to present objects and relations illustratively instead of offering an army of ranked concepts."[41] Although Spengler cannot be immunized against analytical probing, he should be met half way; for otherwise, as Manfred Schroter has shown, all meaningful communication is at an end.

Returning to the idea of the prime symbol, Spengler said relatively little about the other six cultures and their inherent themes. He said nothing about the prime symbol of Mexican culture under the Mayas, and very little about the other five cultural themes. The prime symbol of Egypt, Spengler designated as "way,"[42] that of Babylon as "line and angle in space" (*Strecke and Winkel im Raum*),[43] that of Islam or Magian as "cavern,"[44] that of China as "aimless wandering,"[45] and that of Indian as "uncertain distance."[46] Each of these prime symbols expresses a depth-experience sensation expanded into the world, a unique way of perceiving the extended.[47] In the case of the Magian soul, this depth experience is symbolized by the cavern. Magian man needs the protective blanket of the cavern so that he can forget himself in the "pneumatic we" of a spiritual community. Magian roofing, which is expressive of this world feeling, covers in rather than opens out. This is why Hagia Sophia, in many ways the exemplar of the Magian soul, has been so aptly described as an "introverted Gothic striving under a closed outer casing."[48] According to Spengler, Magian are: algebra, astrology and alchemy, mosaics and arabesque, caliphates and mosques, and the sacraments and scriptures of the Persian, Jewish, Christian, Post-Classical and Manichaen religions.[49] Another characteristic feature of the Magian soul is its fairytale quality manifesting itself in amulets, mysterious events, secret letters, or the philosopher's stone.[50] The Magian, according to Spengler, "clothes his wall with sparkling, predominantly golden, mosaics and arabesques and so drowns his cavern in that unreal, fairy-tale light which for Northerners is always so seductive in Moorish art."[51] Finally, the Magian yearning for cavern-like expression forms reveals itself in the perception of dichotomies, especially that of black and white, light and darkness.

The only other prime symbols Spengler mentioned briefly are the Chinese and the Egyptian. From the Chinese penchant toward landscaping and gardening, he deduced the prime symbol of "aimless wandering."[52] The Chinese soul lacks an active force which would propel it straight to a goal. Instead, the soul and the world it inhabits obey the eternal rhythmic interplay between yang and yin. In the Chinese "waking-consciousness," therefore, becoming does not manifest itself as one-dimensional, but rather as multi-dimensional. Specifically, it appears as nondirectional because the Tao of man's soul is governed by the "unconstrained reciprocal working of ... the yang and yin ... "[53] The Chinese sees becoming or fulfillment in many directions, a fact which is clearly visible in his art and architecture. This explains, for example, why the landscape looms so large in Chinese art. Here, there is no direction, but innumerable details — all exemplifying the idea that units in nature are fashioned out of the interplay between yang yin. The emphasis is always on diversity, detail, and the relationships underlying them.

Whereas the Chinese wanders through his world, the Egyptian according to Spengler, treads ineluctably toward the end.[54] Obsessed by mortality, he conceived his life as a clearly defined path to death. "The Egyptian soul," Spengler believed, "saw itself as moving down a narrow and inexorably-prescribed life path to come at the end before the judges of the dead."[55] There is a "way" to death, and that way is along a "rhythmically ordered *sequence* of spaces," leading from "the gate-building on the Nile through passages, halls, arcaded courts and pillored rooms that grow ever narrower and narrower, to the chamber of the dead." According to Spengler, this explains the emphasis on extension, direction in depth, or *plane* effects; it explains, too, the need to express depth direction in the language of stone.

Spengler said next to nothing about the prime symbol of Babylon and India, probably because he knew little about them. In any case, it does not really matter because Spengler had explained the prime symbol which meant most to him — that of the Faustian West, whose decline he purported to chart. Let us, therefore, follow him in his discussion of the Faustian soul and its cyclical developments through the spring, summer, autumn, and winter of its life.

IV

The Faustian culture of the West, like every other culture, is a self-sustaining entity which is neither influenced nor influencing. In opposition to most historians, Spengler asserted that the West owes nothing to the classical world, except perhaps certain decorative fringes in order to embellish its own unique creations. The soul of the West is bound by its own charter,[56] defining itself in the process of its growth. The West was born about 900 A.D., following a lengthy period of embryonic growth, dating back to 500 A.D. Thus, Spengler insisted that the West did not grow within the womb of classical antiquity. If we designate 900 A.D. as the birth of the West, the age-phases of the Faustian soul would be roughly as follows: 900 − 1300 for spring, 1300 − 1600 for summer, 1600 − 1800 for autumn, and 1800 − 2000 for winter. These dates correspond roughly to the historical tables which Spengler appended to the *Decline of the West*.

Every springtime, be it Faustian, Apollonian, or Magian, begins with feudalism of one sort or another. In the West, the foundations of feudalism were laid by roving bands of heroic warriors, which crisscrossed Europe in the Dark Ages. These tribes not only laid the foundation of feudalism but gave first symbolic expression to the Faustian spirit. Of all these tribes, the Vikings represented the Faustian prime symbol of heroic striving after the infinite at its deepest level. Though the Vikings faded from the historical scene, their spirit continued to blaze in the Western soul.[57] The vitality of the Faustian soul was also exemplified by the landed nobility which had acquired its predominent position in society during the chaotic years following the fall of Rome. As centralized authority collapsed, power and influence gravitated into the hands of local strongmen, whose might was based on prowess and extensive landholding. It was to these mighty lords that many people turned for protection and order. But by submitting themselves to their authority, they lost their freedom. The common man, attached to the land and subject to his immediate overlord was, therefore, reduced to a state of serfdom. Feudalism implied legalized inequality, though its harshness was often mitigated by clearly defined rights and obligations between lord and serf.

Europe in the spring was a society without strong centralized authority. Power was exercised by local landlords in countless clusters of self-sufficient agricultural communities. There was no middle class and there were no markets. What was produced was consumed locally. Next to the nobility, Europe in the spring was dominated by the Church. Nobility and priesthood were tied to each other and to the feudal system. These two estates, according to Spengler, form the basis of every springtime culture. "All effectual history," he observed, "begins with the primary classes, nobility and priesthood, forming themselves and elevating themselves above the peasantry as such."[58] As to the peasant, he is historyless. In Spengler's judgment, he is,

> the eternal man, independent of every Culture that ensconces itself in the cities. He precedes it, he outlives it, a dumb creature propagating himself from generation to generation, limited to soil-bound callings and aptitudes, a mystical soul, a dry, shrewd understanding that sticks to practical matters, the origin and the ever-flowing source of the blood that makes world-history in the cities.[59]

Anchored to the soil, nobility and priesthood are deeply rooted, plant-like, and instinctive. Both estates possess good breeding and unshakable convictions. In marked contrast to the city man of a later time who needs to intellectualize every problem, the rural-aristocratic nobleman or priest acts instinctively whenever he perceives a threat to his chivalric-religious ideals.

The faith that sustains feudal estates is vital because it blooms in a natural-rural countryside. In other words, the creative foci in any culture rest on estates with breeding, exemplified at its highest by rural-intuitive aristocracies. The city is creative insofar as it develops the cultural mission that originates in the pre-urban countryside. The element of faith in a cultural theme is crucial. This is why the essence of every culture, according to Spengler, is religion.[60] Conversely, the essence of civilization is irreligion. Loss of faith implies not only the loss of a particular creed, but a profound disbelief in the cultural theme itself.

The springtime world was still sure of its faith and its instincts. For the West, that assurance leaps to the eye as we behold the archetypal features in the Faustian landscape — castle and cathedral. In Gothic architecture, with its stained glass windows, its vast interiors, and its heaven-bound steeples, Faustian man tried to reach out into the infinite. In the massive fortresses (the Burg), which dotted the landscape of Western Europe, he tried to give substance to his spiritual strivings. Gothic art, then, is an expression of the inner soul of the nascent Faustian culture. What it represents symbolically is rendered literally by scholastic theology with its stately procession of axiomatic truths.

Summertime means ripening. The Faustian soul became increasingly aware of its mission. Europe now expanded its horizons into two directions: horizontally and vertically. The horizontal expansion began with the Crusades, the rise of towns and the emergence of the middle class. Europe broke its shell of isolation and explored previously uncharted regions. The Crusades and the overseas explorations exercised a profound impact on the Faustian spirit. In Christopher Columbus or Henry the Navigator, Western man revealed his innermost secrets: to find the ultimate source of reality. The vertical expansion of knowledge was a necessary corollary, for it involved a similar quest to find the ultimate reality in the universe. Faustian man was about to shatter his conception of the cosmos, which led him from a geocentric view of the universe to a heliocentric one. In Copernicus, who appeared near the end of summer, Faustian man merely gave the scientific imprimatur to what had already been latent in the Vikings, the Crusaders, the Gothic cathedrals, or Christopher Columbus.

Summer also witnessed a gradual ripening of political forms. Out of feudal heterogeneity emerged the future nation states of Western Europe. The ideal was no longer a decentralized state administration preserving considerable measure of local or regional variety, but strong centralized control at all levels. The feudal aristocracy, intimately tied to the former system, desperately tried to stem the tide of royal absolutism in a series of Frondes. It was to no avail because the monarchy had fashioned new political alliances with the middle class. The new monarchs, who equated themselves with the state, basically wanted the same thing as the middle class: centralization, rationalization, and efficiency. Summer, then, witnessed a new style of politics: royal absolutism based on middle class consent. Hand in hand with these developments, we find that the spirit of the countryside gradually gave way to the intellectualism of the city. The style of politics, as of art and religion, became increasingly secular. These changes, of course, were not smooth. The encrusted traditions of springtime linger on precariously and never cease to hold their attraction. Thus, in the Reformation and the ensuing wars of religion, the old and the new were intertwined as the last flickers of spring asserted their ideals.

Autumn means the fulfillment of possibilities. The grand style of autumn aspired to transcend space. This is why instrumental music became the ruling art. It is as though music now wanted to provide visible, imaginative expression to its yearning for spatial transcendence by using "the characteristic tone-colours of the instruments, and the contrasts of string and wind, human voices and instrumental voices, as means wherewith to *paint*."[61] In autumn, therefore, painting and music complemented one another in making the transcendental vision concrete in the sensory dimension. Painting became polyphonic, picturesque, and infinite-seeking; its colors resembled the tones of the cantata and the madrigal.[62] Music sought to parallel the great masters from Titian to Velasquez and Rembrandt. As Spengler suggests, music makes pictures in the sonatas of Corelli, in the pastoral cantatas or the lines of melodies in Monteverde's *Lament of Ariandne*.[63] This great autumn style reached its culmination in the bodiless dynamic of chamber music. The symbol in music, as in science, was the fugue. What Corelli, Handel, Bach, or Vivaldi expressed in the art of the fugue was paralleled in science by the infinitesimal Calculus of Newton and Leibniz. The symbolism of the *Principia Mathematica* was a music of the heavenly spheres, expressing Faustian man's never-ending search to discover the infinite and to bring it under the rule of scientific law.

Intellect triumphed over instinct in late autumn. All aspects of life fell under the dispensation of reason. In politics it was the bourgeoisie, reared on rational calculation for several centuries, which made its bid for power. Spengler equated the business spirit with the English and their pursuit of selfishness, individualism, money politics, and utilitarian morality.[64] He argued that the English temper triumphed over French culture in late autumn; and in so doing, laid the foundation of the winter phase, dominated by Anglo-American materialism. Politically, power now gravitated into the hands of the bourgeois, who equated politics with party or class interests. According to Spengler, this is the philosophy of negative government which would haunt Europe for the next two centuries. On the ruins of liberalism, with its lack of purpose and principle, a new idea of mass allegiance would ultimately emerge. Politically, the end of autumn coincided with the French Revolution, Napoleon, and the rise of the English business spirit born of the Industrial Revolution. The old Europe withered away under the impact of science, commercial capitalism and *raison d'etat*. The traditional culture patterns, comprising a divinely sanctioned monarchy, a privileged state-supported church, and a privileged nobility, were replaced by megapolitan civilization.

Spengler dated the Decline of the West as early as 1800, the onset of the winter period. Decline in any culture occurs when there is a widespread feeling that the existing institutions and ideals are no longer viable. In the life history of every culture, there comes a point when its original vitality has been dissipated — when it is experiencing either a profound "failure of nerve" or bureaucratic decadence. This "failure of nerve" manifests itself as a loss of faith and instinct, as intellectualism pure and simple. In a declining culture, Spengler observes, "the brain rules because the soul abdicates."[65] The nineteenth century, Spengler felt, was materialistic through and through. In the growing megapolitan centers, where life became exclusively located, intellect and money ruled supreme. The trouble with intellect, Spengler believed, is that it makes life problematical. The city man of the late civilization feeds on criticism and doubt, and he spreads his poison of negativity throughout the general population. Criticism, uncertainty, and endless analysis kill the instinct for action. A culture is healthy when its members act intuitively or on faith. Spengler often likened a healthy culture to sports, calling it "being in form."[66] In the nineteenth and twentieth centuries, the West was no longer in form. This means that the West will either disintegrate from within or that it will be absorbed by another culture. True, the West expanded throughout the civilized world in the nineteenth century; but far from being healthy, this imperialistic impuse actually portends incipient decline. Imperialism, we recall, led to the internal exhaustion of European powers and to internacine world wars. There is, then, in all cultures, according to Spengler, this tendency toward internal decay. Such internal exhaustion is analogous to the principle of entropy in physics: there is a growing inability of a civilization to satisfy the instinctual needs of its members because its source of energy has dried up. Spengler followed Henry Adams in applying the Second Law of Thermodynamics (the degradation of energy) to late civilization.[67] According to this theory, the West shares the inevitable destiny of our solar system: the sun will ultimately cool down, the tides will immobilize the revolutions of the earth, and the universe will die as its energy reaches equilibrium.

As Spengler watched the West while he was writing the *Decline*, he saw numerous signs of the impending doom. In politics, decline coincides with the coming of the masses, the growth of party politics, and the rule of money. Nothing is more disastrous to good politics, Spengler believed, than the pre-eminence of economics in politics. When the ship of state is seized by moneyed interests, nothing can stay its internal collapse or its conquest by primitive foreign powers. The ship of state must be run by the captain and his crew, not by the businessman who owns the cargo.[68] Good politics requires men of breeding who stand above the *canaille* and above plutocratic interests. Parliamentary democracy, which Spengler despised, is a symbol of decline, because it preaches disreputable or hypocritical ideals such as *"enrichissez-vous,"* "progress," material comfort, happiness. Democracy is the triumph of mediocrity, the revolt of the peasant turned city dweller against breeding, good taste, and all higher spiritual values.

The waking consciousness of these decadent men of civilization is spent in the cosmopolis with its artificiality, its sham, and its barbarism. Spengler argued that the final drama which will destroy the West will be enacted in gigantic cities:

> The stone Colossus 'Cosmopolis' stands at the end of the life's course of every great Culture. The Culture-man whom the land has spiritually formed is seized and possessed by his own creation, the City, and is made into its creature, its executive organ, and finally its victim. This stony mass is the *absolute* city. Its image, as it appears with all its grandiose beauty in the light-world of the human eye, contains the whole noble death-symbolism of the definitive thing-become. The spirit-pervaded stone of Gothic buildings, after a millennium of style-evolution, has become the soulless material of this daemonic stone-desert.[69]

The pulse of the decaying cosmopolis is tension, agitation, violence. No one can retreat into the tranquility of privacy because the rhythm of existence has been accelerated to the point of madness. The keynote of the cosmopolis is sterility, as reflected in the gaudy architecture, the pulp magazines, and the meaningless superspectacles conducted for the excitement of the masses. "Cinema, Expressionism, Theosophy, boxing contests, nigger dances, poker, and racing – one can find it all in Rome."[70] As in declining Rome, genuine creativity is replaced by fake or modish art, philosophy, or religion. Occultist and theosophic frauds, Spengler observed, multiply in all decaying cultures to bring temporary solace to a spiritually dying population. Though late culture man invents countless slogans to rekindle the lost vitality, the fire has burned out. Exhortations to go back to Nature are meaningless in the setting of the cosmopolis. What we see now, according to Spengler, "is just a toying with myths that no one really believes, a tasting of cults that it is hoped might fill the inner void."[7][1]

The tragedy of it all is that late culture man is rarely, if ever, cognizant of his destiny. Parades of intellectuals will continue to preach progress to the masses to the very end. Only a few solitary thinkers, with a keen eye for historical realities, know that the "progress-mongers" are wrong. Unfortunately, no one heeds the voice of these Cassandras, to whom Spengler felt a deep kinship. To the very end, men of the winter phase believe that they are progressing, and that their accomplishments tower miles high above the past. Spengler dealt harshly with such "fakers," especially those who claimed that the latest innovation was *ipso facto* the "best." He never ceased ranting against the fake art of his time, whose unhistorical pretensions he abhorred. Art, he claimed, becomes risky, meticulous, and diseased as good form and proportion are thrown to the wind.[7][2] Modern art, Spengler exclaimed, is impotence and falsehood:

> What do we possess to-day as 'art'? A faked music, filled with artificial noisiness of massed instruments; a faked painting, full of idiotic, exotic and showcard effects, that every ten years or so concocts out of the form-wealth of millennia some new 'style,'...[7][3]

What we see in the art galleries or hear in the concert halls, Spengler continued, is the work of "industrious cobblers and noisy fools, who delight to produce something for the market, something that will 'catch on' with a public for whom art and music and drama have long ceased to be spiritual necessities."[74]

What form does cultural decline take? Does a culture collapse under the weight of its rotten values or its crumbling institutions; or is it pushed into collapse by outside forces? Who can predict, Spengler would reply. The West may indeed consume itself in a series of annihilation wars initiated by future Caesars. Cataclysmic decline, if it comes, might be precipitated by class warfare from within and barbarian onslaughts from without. Other races with the vigor of youth on their side might gradually doubt the superiority of the white man. Having learned his technology, they may turn on him with a vengeance. Decline could also be a gradual process. Spengler warned that the term "decline" should not be confused with the image of a sinking ocean liner.[75] From the decline of other cultures, we know that it has taken centuries. Spengler did not write, nor did he want to write, a doomsday scenario. He did insist, however, that decline involved a breakdown of central institutions, a second Vikingism, and a return to formlessness. The state of "being in form" passes from nations to bands and retinues of adventurers, self-styled Caesars, or barbarian kings.[76]

With this phase, man has come full cycle. In Spengler's poetic image, man "becomes a plant again, adhering to the soil, dumb and enduring. The timeless village and the 'eternal' peasant reappear, begetting children and burying seed in Mother Earth."[77]

The precise events which propel a culture through its successive phases are unique and will never recur. Analogous to all cultures, however, are shared forms of events.[78]

Feudalism and priesthood dominate all spring phases, and so do feudal forms of artistic, literary, or religious expressions. Similarly, Buddhism, Stoicism, and Socialism are forms of late civilization. Spengler plotted the destiny of Faustian culture in great detail, but he also showed how other cultures unfold and why they do so in uniform ways. Although every culture may have a unique prime symbol, the manner of its growth is shared by other cultures. In sum, every culture has similar expression forms relating to its place in a given stage of its development. We can study these forms, Spengler believed, by the method of morphology. Spengler not only sketched a history but also a comparative study of culture. Having observed Spengler the metaphysician and the historian of culture, it is now time to take a look at Spengler the philosopher of history.

MORPHOLOGY AND PHYSIOGNOMIC TACT

I

Each culture, Spengler had shown, is a unique organism which grows and develops in accordance with the rhythmic beat of the life cycle. Each culture also fulfills its innate character in the process of its historical growth. The resemblence of Spengler's cultures to Leibniz's monads has been alluded to in the last chapter. The monodological analogy not only colored Spengler's study of culture, but also his philosophy of history. For this reason, a brief description of Spengler's indebtedness to Leibniz might be helpful in illuminating the problems which the acceptance of the monodological view entailed for Oswald Spengler.

Spengler's cultures are monads because they strive to fulfill a spiritual theme in the course of their life history. Leibniz, we remember, conceived reality as populated by myriads of monads or spiritual atoms.[1] These monads, like Spengler's cultures, are wholly self-sufficient and hermetically sealed from the world of matter. The monad is a simple substance; it is unextended, indivisible, formless, and indestructible. We may liken the Leibnizian monad to a kind of spiritual force-center. Although it exists behind the material world, it gives form and substance to the world as it appears in our sense experience. Leibniz believed that monads are vital through and through, and that they possess an inbuilt principle which they seek to acutalize in the course of their life history. Since the life of a monad is the life of its ideas,

156

we must envision this process of development in mental terms. Some monads, it is true, are incapable of ideas, although they do possess varying degrees of consciousness. The Leibnizian world was thus populated by an infinite variety of unique and self-contained substances, all striving to fulfill their potentialities in order to emulate the perfection of the primal monad — God.

In the preface to the *Decline of the West*, Spengler paid brief homage to Leibniz. This is hardly surprising because Spengler's most admired hero, Goethe, owed much of his thought to Leibniz. What Spengler chose from Goethe, he borrowed indirectly from Leibniz; and the most important concept he owed to both thinkers was the notion of entelechy or spiritual substance. The idea of entelechy, as so many other ideas, dates back to Greek metaphysics and denotes the inner nature of anything.[2] Every entelechy possesses an innate trait which it seeks to fulfill in the process of its growth. The monads of Leibniz are entelechies, as are Spengler's cultures. Although Leibniz and Spengler were preoccupied by fundamentally different concerns, they shared this metaphysical belief in spiritual substances. Both men illustrated this metaphysical vision by an impressive array of learning and scholarship. The broad similarities do not end here. In order to maintain the thesis of self-sustained entities, both were beset by serious epistemological difficulties. In Leibniz's case, the problem revolved around the issue of perception and interaction.[3] If nothing enters the monad from without, how can it perceive the world; let alone interact with other monads? Leibniz answered that no monad ever perceives the world directly, but only through the mediation of God, who has programmed the world in such a way that each monad perceives exactly the same film as every other monad. God is the immediate external object of our thoughts; and it is through his mediation that we perceive all things. We are all monads or little worlds in miniature encased in our mental world. The external world of things exists only in the imagination of our minds. Although mind and matter are different realms, they are synchronized by God so that they may function in perfect rhythm and harmony.

Spengler faced similar epistemological problems because his cultures are also monodological structures. Did he try to resolve the dilemma by the same *deus ex machina* approach as Leibniz? Two particularly acute difficulties assailed Spengler: first, the issue of cross-cultural influence, and secondly, the problem of deliniating the common elements in different cultures. Only if we know what is common to cultures can we develop methods to study or compare them.

Spengler was uncompromising in his insistence that each culture has its own mathematics, its own morality, its own law, its own art, or its own religion.[4] Needless to say, this "relativistic" argument excludes any kind of cross-cultural influence. If cultures are self-contained and develop the theme inherent in their prime symbols, it follows logically that action at a distance is impossible. We have seen that Spengler conceded the possibility of interaction among primitive cultures, (a, b, c), but he denied similar interaction among the high cultures. As long as his high cultures are separated in time and in space, there is no particular problem. But when cultures are conterminous, as in the case of the Magian to the Apollonian, the Faustian to the Apollonian, the Chinese to the Japanese, or the Mayan to the Toltec-Aztec, Spengler's rigid monodological view is obviously much harder to maintain.[5] What is Spengler to do with the ancient Near East, where the Classical and the Magian culture confronted each other? Similarly, what is he to do with the persistence of classical antiquity in Western Europe, especially in the Renaissance? Spengler tried to meet these objections in several ways. He argued that, on closer inspection, cross-cultural influences always turn out to be either superficial or illusory. Even in cases where cultures coexist in time and place, as in the Hellenistic Near East, cross-cultural influence is not what it appears to be. Spengler could not deny that Greco-Roman culture affected the Ancient Near East; the facts were too overwhelming. In order to extricate himself from this embarrassing situation, he tried at once to admit and deny that the Apollonian culture influenced the Magian. He did this by altering the word influence, making it read "paralysis." By a kind of legerdemain, he argued that the Apollonian culture paralyzed the Magian soul, preventing it from fulfilling its potentialities. The Apollonian soul did not impart its cultural ideals to the nascent Magian soul. The only way in which it affected the Magian soul was to stunt its growth.[6] One soul, Spengler believed, could not determine the shape or destiny of another. What it can do, however, is to inhibit the growth of another soul. Spengler called this domination of one culture by another culture a pseudomorphosis — a term he borrowed from minerology:

> By the term 'historical pseudomorphosis', I propose to designate those cases in which an older alien Culture lies so massively over the land that a young Culture, born in this land, cannot get its breath and fails not only to achieve pure and specific expression forms, but even to develop fully its own self-consciousness.[7]

According to the logic of Spengler's system, the Magian soul should have prevailed in its clash with the Apollonian soul. At the time of its growth, the Magian soul confronted an already sterile and sclerotic Apollonian civilization. It follows that the youthful and vigorous Magian culture should have triumphed against its senile enemy. The reverse, of course, took place. In a rather amusing passage, Spengler sadly acknowledged this fact. At Actium (31 B.C.), Spengler observed, Antony, fighting on behalf of the nascent Magian soul, should have defeated Octavian, the representative of late Roman civilization![8] The issue at Actium was whether the Roman principate or the Magian caliphate would determine the future course of history in the Mediterranean. Antony's victory, according to Spengler, would have freed the Magian soul; his defeat, however, drew over the Near East the hard sheets of the Roman Imperium.[9] Worse yet, the senile Roman giant went on to new creative heights as Octavian ushered in the golden age of the Antonines!

Spengler, then, was forced to admit the triumph of the Apollonian soul, but he stubbornly refused to acknowledge the reality of cultural diffusion. The triumph of Rome was not the triumph of its cultural ideals. The only form in which Rome affected the Magian soul was to stunt its growth. Spengler's stubbornness to maintain a theory in face of all the facts is somewhat reminiscent of those medieval astronomers who tried to sustain the Ptolemaic theory of celestial motion. The theory of perfect circular motion, which was one of the cornerstones of Ptolemaic astronomy, was upheld long after it had been shown that the planets did not move in perfect figures. Spengler's pseudomorphosis was a similar attempt to sustain the monodological character of cultures, even though the evidence showed that cultures do in fact interact.

Critics of Spengler have eagerly seized upon his rigid monodological view to prove the unsoundness of his overall approach to culture. They forget that his concept of culture is not necessarily invalidated just because it is monodological. The cultures which Spengler delineated are real historical units; they are not abstractions inaccessible to empirical evidence. Moreover, what Spengler designated as the style in the life of a culture has been confirmed in large part by historical and anthropological research.[10] It is only his exaggerated view that cultures cannot interact which is open to serious objection. Even so, his monodological argument has been very beneficial because it has caused many historians to reconsider what they mean by cross-cultural influence. Spengler's monodological view of culture, for all its shortcomings, has served as a valuable corrective to some exaggerated ideas of cultural diffusion.

For example, historians often write textbooks in which Western civilization is made to encompass the Babylonians, the Egyptians, the Jews, the Greeks, the Romans, and the various nationalities of Western Europe. This creates the impression as though everything has been slowly leading up to "our own time." Western civilization is presented as a unique blend of Greco-Roman and Judeo-Christian ideas. Such simple-minded history-writing, which still dominates our schools, was roundly denounced by Spengler. Western culture, Spengler insisted, cannot be "traced back" to the pyramids, to the Greek polis, or to the Roman senate. Every culture has its own style, a style that owes nothing substantial to other cultures. Spengler conceded that certain elements of the Greco-Roman past have been accepted by the Faustian West, but only because these elements reinforced what had already grown on the soil of the West. The ideas of one culture are always altered in the setting of another. Platonic ideas in the West, Spengler argued, bear little resemblence to Plato, who would not have recognized his own ideas in their western garb. The same is true of Aristotle. I wish, Spengler once said, that somebody would finally write the history of the three Aristotles — the Greek, the Arabian, and the Gothic![11] If a Chinese converts to Christianity, Spengler said, his new belief would not be Christian, but Taoism in Christian garb.[12] In other words, all men carry the egg shells of their cultural heritage with them to the very end, no matter what they may imbibe from alien sources. A man's own cultural milieu is primary; everything else is secondary.

II

If cultures are monodological structures with their own unique souls, how can we compare them? To compare several entities, we must be able to identify what is common to them. Spengler has ruled out cross-cultural influence as a criterion for making comparisons. What remains? According to Spengler, cultures are organic forms which resemble other biological systems because they possess a definite structure and pattern of growth. In other words, cultures, like biological organisms, are natural systems that can be studied by identifying, classifying, and comparing the organisms which exist in them. Biologists have recognized for a long time that different life forms are related because they share similar organic structures. The science which compares the form of living organisms under all manners of changes or transformations is called morphology. The word "morphology" comes from two Greek words: *morphe* (meaning "form") and *logos* (meaning "doctrine"). Hence, morphology is the doctrine of forms.

The first thinker in modern times who tried to develop a systematic science of living forms was Goethe. As we have seen, in his *Metamorphosis of Plants* (1790), Goethe tried to elucidate the process by which living organisms assumed their peculiar form. The formative process (*Gestaltung*) captivated most of his interest, as did the question of constancy in change. Goethe asked himself whether there was a common structure, a type, which underlies every organism. Among the infinite variety of plants, for example, Goethe discerned a primal plant (*Urpflanze*) out of which nature had developed the multiplicity of plant life. Goethe also asked himself whether there was a common element underlying organisms of different types. In other words, are there general principles which account for the differences in structure among living things? Are the skeletons of man and other mammals constructed on the same principles? Goethe answered this question in the affirmative because he firmly believed in a common primal type from which every living thing was abstracted. This belief in a common type led him to the discovery of the intermaxillary bone in the human skull. Scientists before Goethe had denied that man possessed an intermaxillary bone, and they had made that denial the basis for their belief that man and animals were different. Goethe proved that there was such a bone, that it was located between the two main sections of the upper jaw, and that it proved the homogeneity of biological organization.[13]

Goethe's botanical and anatomical studies, for all their shortcomings, for the first time opened the possibility for an exact study of organic forms. Goethe launched morphology on its scientific career by defining its tasks and by developing its techniques. Students of nature had always been aware that different types such as insects or vertebrate animals could be compared because they possessed certain structural similarities, but it was not until Goethe that reliable principles of comparing different organic forms were developed. Goethe was one of the first to develop the study of homology or the comparative study of organic structures in different animals. As we shall see, this idea was to have a profound influence on Oswald Spengler.

Goethe has been severely reproached for his idealistic approach to morphology. There is some justice to this criticism, for Goethe tended to view living things largely from the perspective of transcendental principles. When he talked about form, he did so only in its ideal aspects.[14] Moreover, he all too often conceived the process of growth itself in spiritual terms as the unfolding of a specific purpose; and in so doing, he lost sight of the importance of the material aspects of growth. As a poet, he envisaged growth more in aesthetic than in scientific terms, a widespread practice among the Romantics. Goethe believed that life could not be grasped in mechanistic or quantitative terms, but had to be contemplated as a work of art — as a purposive, creative, and spiritual process. Samuel Taylor Coleridge (1772–1834), Goethe's greatest admirer in England, stated the Romantic distinction between the organic and the inorganic better than anyone else:

> The form is mechanic when on any given material we impress a pre-determined form, not necessarily arising out of the properties of the material, as when to a mass of wet clay we give whatever shape we wish it to retain when hardened. The organic form, on the other hand, is innate; it shapes as it develops itself from within, and the fullness of its development is one and the same with the perfection of its outward form. Such is the life, such the form. Nature, the prime genial artist, inexhaustible in diverse powers, is equally inexhaustible in forms. Each exterior is the physiognomy of the being within, its true image reflected and thrown out from the concave mirror.[15]

It was this idealistic aspect of Goethe's scientific approach which appealed strongly to Spengler. When Spengler transferred morphology from biology to culture, it was the transcendental kind of morphology of Goethe, Lorenz Oken

(1778–1851), or Geoffroy St. Hillaire (1772–1844) that he accepted as the only method of cultural explanation.[16] The major assumption of transcendental morphology, clearly visible in Spengler's approach to cultural organisms, is that the whole is primary and precedes the differentiation of its parts.[17] As the organism develops, it assimilates elements from without to its own substance. This implies that the internal processes of a living organism determine the outside processes rather than vice versa. Finally, the transcendental morphologists insisted on the interdependence of the living parts, implying that the absence or destruction of a part would sever the original unity of the whole. These organicist premises figured prominently in German biology from Goethe to Hans Driesch (1867–1941). Spengler was heir to that tradition and used its concepts to describe the behavior of cultural organisms.

Oswald Spengler believed that morphology, being the science of growth and transformation, was particularly suited to history. The physical scientist, he claimed, could not do justice to life and history because his subject matter dealt with inert objects in mechanical motion. His attempt to comprehend objects causally by describing them in the form of universal empirical laws is entirely legitimate as long as he limits himself to the world of inert matter. The form of life, however, is not amenable to such treatment. As Spengler put it, "the means whereby to identify dead forms is Mathematical Law. The means whereby to understand living forms is Analogy."[18]

The task for historians of the future, as Spengler conceived it, was to search out analogical techniques by which the living forms of culture could be explained and compared. These techniques, he said, had already been discovered by biologists and only needed to be transferred to the study of cultures: "If we want to learn to recognize inward forms that constantly and everywhere repeat themselves, the comparative morphology of plants and animals has long ago given us the methods."[19] In a footnote, he hastened to add that the kind of morphology he had in mind for the study of culture was "not the dissecting morphology of the Darwinian's pragmatic zoology with its hunt for causal connexions, but the seeing and overseeing morphology of Goethe."[20]

The technique which is used in morphology to identify the structure of related organisms is called homology.[21] A homological correlation is based on the place which a particular organ occupies in different animals and on the importance it has in it. Organs can be homologous even if they differ in shape and function. The following would be considered homologous: the wing of a bat and the foreleg of a mouse; the lung of mammals and the air bladder of fish; the human arm and the wing of a bird; or the knee of a horse and the wrist of a man. It should be noted that such homological correlations are not as valid as equivalent concepts in logic or mathematics. The reason for this is that homology does not deal with mathematical structures, but with relations that have been abstracted from a living context. Still, this does not diminish their usefulness in biology and other disciplines. Homology is a simple identification, a comparison between two magnitudes: $a = b$. The identity between a and b, of course, cannot be verified experimentally by simply exchanging magnitudes. In homology, identity is inferential. Moreover, homological similarity does not mean absolute identity, as in mathematics. Organisms may be related to each other and still exhibit external differences. According to recent scholars, homology is a perfectly legitimate technique for making comparisons in many disciplines, such as linguistics, prehistory, sociology, or cultural history. We all know homological words in related languages: *mère-mater; aqua-eau, hundert-centum.*[22] The same is true of related grammatical constructions in different languages. Anthropologists use homology in comparing different prehistoric vases, while cultural historians make use of homology in comparing various artistic styles in different cultures.

In Spengler's day, homological criteria were still rather loose. Since he cited Goethe and Sir Richard Owen, we must assume that he made use of their criteria in making cultural homologies.[23] This is revealed in the following passage:

> ... for every part of the bone-structure of the human head an exactly corresponding part is found in all vertebrated animals right down to the fish, and that the pectoral fins of fish and the feet, wings and hands of terrestrial vertebrates are homologous organs, even though they have lost every trace of similarity. The lungs of terrestrial, and the swim-bladders of aquatic animals are homologous, while lungs and gills on the other hand are analogous — that is, similar in point of use.[24]

We can see that Spengler had a clear understanding of contemporary criteria of homology, and that he was fully aware of Owen's important distinction between homology and analogy, the former denoting morphological equivalence, the latter functional equivalence. Analogy refers to an organ or part which has the same function in one animal as another part or organ has in a different animal. Homology refers to the same organ in different animals under all manner of form changes and functions.

Transferred to culture, the principle of homology was meant to investigate similar institutions or forms of expression in different cultures. According to Spengler, homologies are:

classical sculpture and West European orchestration; Indian
Buddhism and Roman Stoicism.[25] These are similar organic
structures, even though their outward form is quite different.
Classical sculpture and East European orchestration are similar
means of expressing the major aesthetic needs in two different
cultures, while pyramids and cathedrals are similar forms of
expressing a religious impulse in two different cultures. The
homological criterion here is a specific quality shared by two
structures, a quality reckoned in aesthetic or religious terms.
Other homologous forms are: the periods of the Punic Wars;
the age of Pericles and the age of the Ommayads; the epochs
of the Rigveda, of Plotinus, and of Dante.[26] Notice that these
homological forms deal with periods rather than structures.
Spengler did not specify why periods are homological, though
we can guess that it had to do with the criterion of
"topographical location" — a principle first enunciated by
Goethe. According to this criterion, two similar organic
structures in different animals must be situated
topographically in similar location.[27] Spengler transferred this
idea of location from space into historical time — a dubious
procedure, at best. Within the context of cultural cycles, the
periods of the contending states in China, the Hyksos, and the
Punic Wars are similar because they are all located at the
beginning of the winter phase in each culture. On the other
hand, the hymns of Rigveda, and the works of Plotinus and
Dante betoken the youthful vigor of spring. In the hymns,
prayers and magical spells of the Rigveda we witness an
exuberant Aryan culture that expresses its longings in a highly
intuitive-mystical fashion. The same is true of the age of
Dante and Plotinus in the Faustian and Magian soul.

From these homological procedures Spengler deduced the
idea of "contemporaneous" events in different cultures,
denoting by this term two or more "historical facts that occur
in exactly the same — relative — positions in their respective

cultures."[28] In science, Pythagoras was the contemporary of Descartes, Archytas of Laplace, and Archimedes of Gauss. The same is true of all expression forms in different cultures, which grow, mature, and die down contemporaneously in all the cultures.[29] Spengler expected extraordinary things from this procedure, for he believed that any age could get its "correct" cultural bearing by locating its analogical state in other cultures. On a chart, we could presumably plot even our future destiny. Here Spengler's positivism asserted itself at its most rigid and uncompromising. Repeating the claim advanced in the very opening passage of the *Decline*, Spengler argued that morphology, properly applied, for the first time opened the possibility of:

> Overpassing the present as a research-limit, and predetermining the spiritual form, duration, rhythm, meaning and product of the *still unaccomplished* stages of our western history; and reconstructing long-vanished and unknown epochs, even whole Cultures of the past, by means of morphological connexions, in much the same way as modern paleontology deduces far-reaching and trustworthy conclusions as to skeletal structure and species from a single unearthed skull-fragment.[30]

There are two major claims which Spengler made as a morphologist of history: first, that cultures, though unique, possess similar forms of expression; and, secondly, that the knowledge we derive from past expression forms allows us to predict future history. Thus, despite his denigration of science, Spengler tried to apply procedures to history which were not too disimilar from those of the natural sciences. He believed that historical events obeyed the life cycle, that they recurred in a few limited shapes (bearing the mark of childhood, youth, manhood, or old age), and, consequently, that they exhibited a uniform pattern which would enable the historian to identify, compare, and even predict them. The nature of a typical scientific explanation, of course, is somewhat different, since it deals with causal statements. At the same time, Spengler aspired, consciously or unconsciously, to the same ideal that the natural scientist accepts in his research — to render predictable what is explained by subsuming it under a universal law. As we shall see, Spengler repeatedly rejected natural science procedures because, in his judgment, they are only applicable to the world of inert matter. History, he said, could not be explained scientifically because its subject matter was purposive human life that unfolds in unique rhythms. As such, it is not amenable to causal treatment; yet, Spengler's much vaunted relativism is deceptive. The fact is that Spengler was only a relativist when it suited him. Historical occurrences, he often observed, are unique and incapable of being repeated. This is why "law and the domain of law are anti-historical."[31] Yet, the very first statement of the *Decline* reads as follows: "In this book is attempted for the first time the venture of predetermining history."[32] Now predetermining means predicting and predicting generally means drawing conclusions from a set of regular relations in the past. The scientist predicts an event by showing that it stands in a certain regular relation to another or antecedent event. Thus, a particular occurrence e is only intelligible when we specify the relationship between e and certain other occurrences usually referred to collectively as antecedent conditions. Whenever there are certain sufficient conditions of the kind $C_1, \ldots, C_n$, the scientist claims then an instance of a kind E occurs in a specific spatio-temporal relationship to $C_1, \ldots, C_n$. Spengler would agree that natural science connects events in causal patterns and makes predictions based on regularity of behavior. But prediction in history, he seems to have felt, is not of this kind. As it turns out, however, events in history, according to Spengler, are repetitive in certain uniform ways and thus predictable.

On page two of the *Decline*, Spengler tried to show that history could be predetermined because the expression forms of world history are limited in number, and because the eras, epochs, situations, and persons are ever repeating themselves true to type. True to what type? Presumably, the specific way in which an event unfolds is unique, but not the general form. Caesars are common types in all cultures, though they may appear in different guises. It is precisely this type of uniformity, Spengler believed, which enables us to generalize and make predictions. But is this really different from prediction in the natural sciences? Spengler had the disconcerting tendency to insist on the sharp differentiation between history and science, while at the same time mingling elements of both in his explanations. Before discussing Spengler's own physiognomic method, which is supposed to have been free of the taint of the natural sciences, we should briefly examine his distinction between history and science.

III

In Spengler's treatment of history, one theme recurs time and again, namely, that events in time must be studied differently than events in space. There is a logic of time and a logic of space, the former belonging to history, the latter to nature. Spengler insisted with the greatest possible force that nature and history belonged to two different realms of experience — the world of the become (the hard-set) and the world of becoming (life).[33] Since these are two different modes of being, we need different methods to study them.

History is an affair of life and exhibits problems which are beyond the reach of ordinary scientific methods. Why history is not amenable to scientific treatment can be answered in two ways: first, the process of history, unlike that of nature, is not really intelligible in causal terms. To the superficial observer, Spengler conceded, events do indeed appear to unfold causally because natural science bias has taught him to regard events as though they were linked in a network of interrelated causes. The fact is that, just because one event precedes another, there is no logical ground for assuming that it must cause or even relate to the event which follows it.

Let us always remember, Spengler insisted, that history possesses no causal logic because its subject matter is human life. Only shallowness and distortion ensue when we treat past life as a sequence of "states" of a mechanical type and handle it like a physical experiment.[34] Life is not reducible to a mechanical state which obeys the rules of formal logic. Let us not be deceived by the claims of the scientists that the only explanation worthy of the name must be couched in causal form. It is perfectly legitimate, Spengler said, to explain something without naming its cause. To subsume an event under a causal law is merely one way of explaining it.

Much ink has been spilled by philosophers on the problem of causation. Unfortunately, this has not always resulted in clarity but in obfuscation. Spengler contributed his share in spreading confusion because he insisted on equating the concept of cause with a state of things in nature. Spengler failed to realize that causation not only describes a process of nature, but also a state of mind. One of the ways in which the human mind explains events is by casting them into some form of causal sequence. In other words, we cannot dispense with causality because this is one of the ways in which our minds work. The precise form in which causal analysis is cast may be open to discussion, but not the fact that we think causally. Had Spengler appreciated the significance of this psychological fact, he might have been more charitable to causal thinking in history. The man who thinks about history does not think wholly differently than the man who thinks about natural events. Historical thinking may differ in some ways from scientific thinking, but it is not an intrinsically different *kind* of thinking, as Spengler would like us to believe.

Now, historical thinking, like any other kind of thinking, cannot dispense with the concept of causality because the historian has to explain a present situation by going back to some event in the past which caused it. The historian wants to find out how something in history became what it was at any given stage. In other words, he seeks an answer to the perennial human question: What is the cause or origin of this or that event? To ask for the origins of something is already tantamount to asking for its cause; and when the historian elucidates the cause or causes of an historical event, his explanation resembles similar causal explanations in the natural sciences. The only difference, as Carl Hempel has shown, is that causal explanations in history lack the precision and the predictive value of scientific explanations.[35] Still, the purpose of explanation is similar in both cases: the historian, like his colleague in the natural sciences, tries to show that an event is not a matter of "chance," but was to be expected in view of certain antecedent conditions. Whether he admits it or not, every historian does in fact explain the origins of events in causal terms.

At the same time, Spengler was right to insist that explanation by cause is merely one way of explaining something. An historian not only describes the origins of an event, but also its nature; and as soon as he deals with the nature of something — be it the nature of an idea, a movement, or an institution — he is beyond the pale of causation. Explanation by cause must yield to other explanations. An operational definition of a thing (the planets are kept in their orbits by gravity) discloses nothing about the nature of that thing or process (gravity). Nor does the account of a thing's historical development necessarily tell us anything about its nature. As Sidney Hook has observed,

> a detailed account of a thing's development cannot serve as a substitute for an analysis of its *nature*. Not that knowledge of a thing's development does not contribute to our understanding of its nature, but rather that such knowledge of the past serves at best as a suggestive aid to the experimental determination in the present of what the thing really is.[36]

Explanation by genetic origin cannot explain the meaning of an event, nor the effect it had on the minds of the people who were affected by it. The manner in which people react to events is not comparable to how one billiard ball reacts when it is struck by another. Billiard balls do not think or feel, but humans do. Spengler accentuated this difference between human and mechanical reaction to change time and again. Although he often exaggerated this difference, he did show that a fact or statement about human life is often different from a fact about a natural occurrence. Events in nature can be quantitatively ascertained and brought under universal laws; but the behavior of human beings, which is frequently irrational, cannot be apprehended in the same way. Those who treat man's history in causal-scientific terms by showing that everything happens for a good reason are welcome to their explanations. Spengler was not dogmatic on this point. If certain people are satisfied by scientific explanations, well and good; but his whole being rebelled against the presumption that the physical sciences possess the *only* true method of explanation. At bottom, he was convinced that there are no "true" methods of explanation, and that the truth or falsity of an explanation depended not on the logic which sustained it, but on its power to persuade men. Spengler believed that people believe something when they are persuaded, a process which is as much emotional as it is logical. One thing people would never be persuaded to believe was that their history and their lives could be treated in the same spirit in which the scientist treats inanimate objects in nature.

An explanation, then, is that which satisfies or persuades people. There is no single correct mode of explaining anything — be it a natural or a human event. Personally, Spengler believed that the scientific way of explaining history was shallow because the past is always grossly distorted whenever we impose a logical scheme on it. The arrangement of historical events into neat sequences of cause and effect may disclose certain superficial uniformities, but it is conspicuously unsuccessful in reconstructing the past in all its richness, complexity, and detail. Spengler repeatedly warned that events in the past are not *meaningful* if they are subsumed under a causal law. Again, he repeated his original objection to causal analysis: to know the causes of an event, no matter how intimately, is not equivalent to knowing the event itself. We may pride ourselves on collecting numerous long-term or short-term causes of the French Revolution, but what have we really proven? To name the causes or "forces" that have led to the French Revolution tells us nothing about the inner meaning of the Revolution itself.[37] Everyone can name causes, that is child's play. But to penetrate into the real meaning of an event, and to show its impact on man's lives, that is quite another matter.

Perhaps a more fruitful approach to the past, Spengler

suggested, is to rely on intuitive, symbolic, and psychological approaches. History, after all, deals with man's accomplishments in the past, and man acts in ways which are notoriously inappropriate to scientific treatment. Real historical vision, he went on to explain, does not belong to the sphere of law, but to the realm of meaning and value. The history of man has to do not so much with events connected according to causal laws in time and space, but with man's longings, aspirations, dreams, or hopes. Events are only the outward skeleton of history; they are merely points of orientation. The core of history is about man's quest for meaning. Clearly, this part of history is not accessible to scientific probing, but must be felt and intuited. Science cannot help us here, for how are we to treat fears, hopes, dreams, or aspirations in scientific form? As Spengler observed:

> ... at bottom the wish to write history *scientifically* involves a contradiction. True science reaches just as far as the notions of truth and falsity have validity: this applies to mathematics and it applies also to the science of historical spade-work, viz., the collection, ordering and sifting of material. But real historical vision (which only *begins* at this point) belongs to the domain of significances, in which the crucial words are not 'correct' and 'erroneous,' but 'deep' and 'shallow' ... Nature is to be handled scientifically, History poetically.[38]

As with all of Spengler's deeply-felt convictions, this one is full of wisdom as well as exaggeration. Anyone who has been afflicted with history in our schools can sympathize with Spengler's attack on dates and causal thinking. Students are still trained to subsume historical events under law, to search for "determining" economic or political forces, to lay bare the causes of events, and to commit "facts" to memory. Spengler was clearly right in reminding us that this is pure rote memorization which explains the external portions of events, but does not penetrate to the underlying significance of things. If history writing becomes an abstract interplay between impersonal forces — as it certainly has become under the dispensation of the scientific outlook — then the real drama of human clashes and ideas is bound to be lost in the shuffle. Spengler was right in reminding us that we have forgotten how man truly expressed himself in the past, how he perceived his environment, and how he expressed his innermost feelings.

On the other hand, Spengler's categorical denial that past events cannot be submitted to causal treatment is obviously fallacious. Sometimes Spengler did not state his case in quite such an extreme form, conceding that it is possible, though meaningless, to arrange events in causal patterns. Strictly speaking, we should not ask what caused an event but what that event meant to a particular people at any given stage in its culture. Yet, both questions are intimately related, the one usually suggesting the other. We shall examine later on how Spengler explained the meaning or significance of historical events; in the meantime, let us see whether Spengler can explain the "how" of events without resorting to causal analysis. It is all well and good to talk about the insignificance of causality, but what does one put in its place as a viable alternative?

If causality is dismissed as a meaningful method of explanation, how does the historian account for change and development? In other words, how do events happen in Spengler's system? Spengler answered that events do not become what they are because they are caused by antecedent events. An event is not caused; it grows. To avoid the foibles of causality, Spengler proposed to substitute the biological model of morphology for the mechanical model of causality. In history, events must be regarded as living organisms which grow and change organically. If this is so, the question as to what causes a living organism to grow is irrelevant because the fact of growth is fully explicable in terms of its own biological laws. Morphology, Spengler observed, is not a causal science, but comparative typology.[39] A biological or historical type is not caused by another type but grows by virtue of its own law of becoming. A type, of course, has its variants. In morphology, however, the relationship between a type and its variant is not a causal one: the type contains within itself all the single cases.

Within limitation, Spengler might have been able to maintain this morphological theory. There is nothing illegitimate in applying a biological model to history. The only trouble was that Spengler did not perceive the limitations of his model. He could only apply it to self-enclosed substantial types. Moreover, his model precluded him from explaining events in the process of interaction. As long as individuals, classes, nations, or cultures are considered like flowers in the field — an analogy that is itself fraught with potential distortions — the historian does not have to resort to causal analysis. History, however, is not a showplace of monodological entities, for men and events are in a constant process of interaction. One man causes or compels another man to do certain things; one class forces another class to accept its whims; similarly, one nation interacts with another in countless different ways. If history were merely the story of self-sustained biographies, we could then dispense with causality, for each organism would be explicable in terms of its own biological laws.

Spengler could account for the growth of historical types, but he could not account for the interaction of those types.[40] A type is not explicable by itself because it interacts with other types. Spengler's historical typology was, therefore, beset by serious limitations. These limitations, it should be noted, do not detract from the usefulness of his general model because it is perfectly legitimate to view epochs in history typologically. Cultural historians do it all the time, especially when they seek to explain the evolution of a style, an idea, or a political tradition. As one method of explanation, it is useful; as the only mode of explanation, it is dangerous. Again, this is because influence or interaction between types cannot be accounted for within the morphological model. There are other dangers. The very act of abstracting an historical type from the welter of happenings implies a certain arbitrariness. When that type is seen in spiritual terms, as in Spengler's analysis of culture, the dangers are multiplied. Spengler's historical typology was constantly threatened by the following pitfalls: the very act of abstracting a spiritual type implied that he had dichotomized an age into a spiritual and material side. Secondly, by designating an epoch as spiritual, he often tacitly assumed that its material side was explicable only in spiritual terms. Having done so, this misled him into hypostatizing the spiritual and then launching it on an illusory path of growth, maturity, and decay. Spengler often fell into the pitfalls implicit in his biological model. Since he never laid the proper epistemological foundations for that model, he was often unaware of the practical difficulties. As it stands, his morphological model is a suggestive aid rather than a systematic paradigm of historical explanation. This is not to say that it could not become a scientific paradigm. The only reason why it has not been taken up by philosophers or historians is because biology has never replaced physics as an exemplar of scientific explanation.

Spengler, then, wanted to replace causality with

morphology. If he had to write history morphologically, how would he do it? Let us suppose that Spengler had to explain the French Revolution. How would he go about it? One thing is certain: his morphological approach would preclude him from looking at it causally. The average historian, on the other hand, would start precisely at this point. He would show that the Revolution was caused by a set of sufficient conditions, probably comprising the following: cumulative change in the social structure of the ancien regime, profound economic changes, the financial straits of the government, the survival of feudalism within a nascent capitalistic society, the clash between nobility and middle class, the dearth of good leadership, or the desertion of the intellectuals. These factors, he would say, collectively (not singly) provided the setting for a revolutionary situation. Now it is hard to see how Spengler could have avoided such an analysis had he been commissioned to write a history of the French Revolution. The fact is that Spengler never wrote a narrative history; for if he had written one, he could not have avoided this kind of causal analysis. As it was, Spengler only wrote grand cultural history in which he treated events such as the French Revolution as an instance of change in a late cultural period. According to him, the French Revolution is a typical example of the clash between bourgeoisie and nobility in late autumn, signifying the victory of money, intellectualism, and party politics over landed property and estate politics. Such revolutions, Spengler would claim, can be found contemporaneously in all cultures. There is nothing unique about them. The business of the historian would be lightened considerably if he followed Spengler! All he would have to do is to consult his cultural charts and the answer would be found. Alas, this is not the way to do justice to historical complexities. Spengler's procedure is easy and simple, but is it really a viable alternative to causal analysis? Many historians would probably concede to Spengler the point that the meaning or significance of historical events cannot be explained in causal terms, but few, if any, practicing historians would eschew causal analysis to explain the "how" of events.

The only way of disclosing the inner meaning of events in history, Spengler asserted, is by way of "physiognomic tact." To understand what he meant by physiognomic, it might be helpful to recall that Spengler believed that the configuration of historical events was form-like. Cultures, we remember, are forms with a definite feature.[41] The same is true of individual events in a culture. Since these events have distinct features or physiognomies, the historian should penetrate to the character concealed behind them. To do this, however, he must know how to practice character analysis.

IV

A physiognomist attempts to discover the inner character of a man by interpreting its outward form of expression. Character manifests itself in such visible forms as facial feature, physical characteristics, or emotional expressions. The greater part of a physiognomist's work, Spengler admitted, is intuitive, for a good physiognomist does not dissect or analyze a given form, but intuits its character. The physiognomic approach, however, is not based on intuition alone. After all, intuitions are only as sound as the wisdom which sustains them. A good judge of character is a man of wide experience, a man who knows the vicissitudes of life. All successful diplomats or politicians, Spengler suggested, are good physiognomists because they have learned through experience how to size up men and how to form sound judgments. Horse trainers should serve as a model for sound physiognomic insight because they can tell us in a glance which horse possesses good breeding and which does not. We can never discover whether a man has good breeding simply by probing his intelligence or by giving him IQ tests. Only men of pure reason, reared in the city of the intellect, size up people in analytic terms. This is why scientific psychology, according to Spengler, has "always been the shallowest and most worthless discipline of philosophy."[42] In deriding intuition and empathetic feeling, the scientific psychologist falsely believes that the mind behaves like a machine, and that he can submit it to quantitative analysis. To transmute the non-extended into the extended, to mistake a system of cause for something that only manifests itself physiognomically, and to believe that this system represents the structure of the soul is a typical example of misplaced intellectualism. This way of looking at man, Spengler warned, is to learn the superficialities of his behavior but not the character of his soul. Only by penetrating behind the physiognomy of the face to its inner character can we learn something about man.

Physiognomic tact is not just intuitive flair. Quite often, we do indeed size up men intuitively, as by first impressions. When we come upon a new face, we often associate its features or expressions with past semblances; and as we do so, we form a provisional judgment as to its character. This is physiognomic flair or immediate certainty given by various intutitions, illuminations, and life experiences. The emphasis in physiognomic tact is not so much on the intuitive flash, as it is on the wisdom that can only come from life experience. Again, the sapient diplomat possesses physiognomic tact, as does the born leader of men. Destiny men or men of action are always better judges of character than causality men or men of thought.[43] This does not mean, however, that men of thought cannot be sound physiognomists. The great poets, dramatists, musicians, or painters were superb physiognomists because they gave artistic expression to real life experiences. Men who have suffered and wrestled with life such as Shakespeare, Michelangelo, Da Vinci, Goethe, La Rouchefoucauld, Machiavelli, or Nietzsche are far better psychologists than any arm-chair philosopher who spins out theories which have nothing to do with life. An historian has physiognomic tact when he possesses the ability to visualize the underlying forms which sustain the welter of external events. Only then can he read the innermost character of a culture. Now, the historian reads the character of a culture by studying its expressions in literature, art, politics, religion, and music. Spengler reiterated his warning that the character of a culture cannot be recreated causally, but must be reconstructed imaginatively from the many and apparently unconnected fragments of man's variegated cultural life. The cultural historian, in Spengler's view, creates a physiognomy (form) out of the heterogeneous elements which he encounters in the past. Unlike the causal historian, who dissects events into their component parts, the cultural historian combines the apparently unrelated parts into a synthetic whole. In other words, the cultural historian, working with the aid of empathy, metaphor, imagination, and analogy, has the advantage of perceiving interconnections, relations, and hidden analogies. The causal historian is prevented by his approach to perceive the relationships which inwardly bind together *all* branches of a culture. As Spengler justly put it:

> who amongst them realizes that between the Differential Calculus and the dynastic principle of politics in the age of Louis XIV, between the Classical city-state and the Euclidean geometry, between the space-perspective of Western

oil-painting and the conquest of space by railroad, telephone and long-range weapon, between contrapuntal music and credit economics, there are deep uniformities?[44]

Spengler's physiognomic approach, then, involves the study of cultural expressions, the perception of interrelationships which bind these expressions together, and the elucidation of the underlying unity which governs all cultural activities. The unity in cultural variety is represented by what Spengler calls "cultural forms." These forms or holisms, though delineated by the cultural historian, are objectively present in history; they are not arbitrary creations by the subjective mind of the historian.

The best way to perceive and study these cultural forms, Spengler believed, was to study their artistic, literary, or political "styles." The style betrays the man. Each form, Spengler said, has a physiognomy and each physiognomy, in turn, is but a confession of a soul. It takes "physiognomic tact" to uncover the artistic styles which are embodied in the expression forms of a culture. Once we have discovered what that style is, we have also rediscovered that it obeys the organic rhythm of the life cycle. In other words, each style bears the mark of childhood, youth, manhood, and old age.

In his discussion of style, Spengler reiterated a theme he had raised earlier, namely, that Faustian man — guided by his unique prime symbol — perceives the world differently than Apollonian man. To the objection that all men possess the same sense organs and, therefore, perceive the world in similar form, Spengler would have replied that perception is as much a cultural as it is a physiological process. We see the world in and through the symbols of our culture, symbols which are so deeply embedded in our unconscious that we are scarcely cognizant how much they actually determine the way in which we perceive objects and people around us. Consciously or unconsciously, we interpose the ideals or beliefs of our culture between our innermost being and the external world. In other words, basic motivations, needs, expectations, beliefs, and values strongly influence sensory experience. Spengler's insight has been fully corroborated by recent psychologists who argue that perception depends in large part on our "perceptual readiness" to see what we are ready to see.[45]

Spengler illustrated this point by contrasting the way in which Faustian and Apollonian men perceive and depict the world. After long and careful study of various art forms in both classical and western culture, he came to the conclusion that Faustian man had a more developed "internal sense" than Apollonian man. The cultivation of a sense of self is largely absent in Greco-Roman culture, which — in Spengler's judgment — accounts for the lack of autobiographies, diaries, character dramas, portraitures, and the need for auricular confessions in the classical world. Unlike Apollonian man, who always tried to relate the private to the public life, Faustian man has been conditioned by his culture to listen to his inner voice and to perceive himself as an autonomous ego vis-a-vis other equally independent egos. Faustian man experiences the world of sense subjectively as a private experience, not objectively as a realistic apprehension of objects in space. The reader will notice that Spengler's portrait of Faustian man comprises characteristics which we would call distinctly romantic. Indeed, Spengler's Faustian man is the Romantic man of feeling, of restless striving, and of inexhaustible energy. He is the egomaniac par excellence; and though he may parade in public under the guise of "classical order," he can never conceal his true romantic nature. Faustian man does not wholly reject the classical preference for order, rationality, clarity of form and expression, and the rule of law so long as it is related to the inner life. The romantic always seeks to relate the external order to the inner life. This attitude is perhaps best summed up by Ludwig Tieck when he said that "I do not want to describe these particular plants or mountains, but my own emotions (*Gemüth*), my own temperamental mood which governs me at this moment; it is this which I would like to single out."[46] Tieck and other Faustian-Romantic souls always appeal from the outer senses to the inner, to the power of imagination.

Aesthetically, this "inner bias" of Faustian man manifests itself in all aspects of the arts as "a will to spatial transcendence," as a mighty effort to express a spiritual theme in the material work of art. Faustian architecture, for example, always conceals an interior motive behind its outer facade. The reverse is true for Apollonian architecture with its marked preference for representing a theme by accentuating the exterior structure of its buildings. In Faustian architecture, according to Spengler, the outer form of a building — be it a castle, a cathedral, or a simple dwelling place — is always "brought into relation with the meaning that governs the arrangement of the interior, a meaning undisclosed in the mosque and non-existent in the temple."[47]

In western art, Spengler tells us, the prime symbol manifests itself as a collective and largely unconscious endeavor by every generation of artists to "transcend space." Western art is, therefore, all of a piece; it is a mighty epic in which each generation carries on the work of the preceding one. Consequently, there is only one style — the style of the culture. As Spengler put it, "Romanesque, Gothic, Renaissance, or Baroque are only *stages of one and the same style.*"[48] One theme runs through all these styles: the quest for spatial transcendence. This story leads us from the polyphony of human voices to the chorus of instruments, of wind, and of string; from Gothic music, which is vocal and architectural to Baroque music, which is pictorial and instrumental; from the art of the sense-perceptible foreground to the art of the indeterminate and indefinable background; from the art of fresco and sculpture, which defines and narrates the material, to the art of oil painting, which interprets and transcends space.

The physiognomic approach to western art, as Spengler envisioned it, would be roughly as follows. The Faustian soul, as we have seen, stirred for the first time in 900 A.D., a period of uncertainty and groping for identity. Artistically, Europe's sense of anxiety is best represented in Romanesque church buildings with their thick and massive walls, their heavy and closely spaced piers, and their semicircular barrel vaults. During this phase of western art, Spengler asserted, the Faustian spirit was still uncertain of its destiny, an uncertainty that is most strikingly demonstrated by the famous building of Bishop Bernward's at Hildesheim. But the coming of spring witnessed a great renaissance. Everywhere and quite suddenly, a farrago of new forms was conceived. Between the Seine and the Scheldt, the motherland of the high Gothic, Europe's first and only "Renaissance" took place. The West expanded into rustic spring as it formulated a new God-feeling, a new vision of the cosmos. Artistically, the symbols of rustic spring are: counterpoint, flying buttress, glass-painting, stone vaultings, and the coordinates of Oresme. The first cycle of western art, therefore, ended with the magnificent Gothic cathedrals, the stately castles, the illuminated manuscripts, and the metaphysical systems of the schoolmen.

However, doubts appeared as youth came to an end. In both the Renaissance and the Reformation art was subject to a tug-of-war between contending impulses. The Renaissance was enveloped in a "dream-state" of classical antiquity. Spengler rigorously stood his ground in denying that the

Renaissance owed anything substantial to classical antiquity, and that even when Renaissance artists thought they were creating in the classical spirit, they actually produced works of art which were wholly unclassical.[49] Western portraiture, for example, is completely different as an art form from the classical because it expresses personality rather than attitude. The classical artist sought to portray a fixed moment, a static pose; and he tried to convey this by concentrating on the sense-perceptible foreground and by placing his figures and groups separately, deliberately avoiding space and time relations in the plane of representation. As Spengler observed, classical art is the apotheosis of the bodily phenomenon — "the rhythmic proportioning of limbs and harmoniously built muscles."[50] The classical *form ideal*, Spengler said, was the "Act"; and the technique of representing it consisted in accentuating the exterior structure of the work of art. Western art — and that includes the Renaissance — has a wholly different *form ideal:* the "Portrait"; and the technique of representing the art of portraiture is to reveal an inner meaning behind the exterior surface.[51] Thus, a portrait by Rembrandt, Holbein, or Titian is a biography, a life history. It is a representation of a dynamic ego with a history. Spengler conceded that Leonardo, Michelangelo, and Raphael attempted to emulate classical antiquity, but none of these giants succeeded in recreating the classical. Despite all their efforts to substitute proportion for relation, drawing for light-and-air effects, Euclidean body for pure space, the Renaissance painters and sculptors did not even approximate the classical ideal. Spengler thought it a tragedy that so many Renaissance artists attempted to subordinate their creative Faustian energy to the shackles of fixed classical rules. This conflict was particularly marked in Michelangelo, who strained the resources of marble to their utmost; and, in so doing, created works of art which bore only the slightest resemblence to the works of Phidias and Praxiteles. Michelangelo also epitomizes the impossibility of the Faustian spirit to revive the classical. His classical soul utilized every resource of fresco and marble to liberate the paganism of the high-Renaissance; but his second soul — that of the Gothic and the Christian — was pulling in the opposite direction.[52] In Michelangelo, as in Leonardo and Raphael, the Gothic soul ultimately asserted itself against a temporary enchantment with the classical. All three Renaissance giants anticipated the musical arts of the Baroque in their unconscious striving towards movement, distance, and depth.[53]

It is in this fashion, then, that Spengler disposes of the problem of Renaissance classicism. Again, there is much sense in what Spengler said; but again, there is also much exaggeration in the way he said it. The argument that the Renaissance was a genuine revival of classical antiquity is now regarded as intellectually bankrupt. Spengler was right in arguing that no art is ever reborn in the setting of a different culture, but he was wrong in minimizing the powerful attraction which classical antiquity exercised on the western mind for many centuries. This love affair with classical-antiquity cannot be written off as a simple detour or, worse, a "dream state." The denial of cross-cultural influences, as we have seen, obliged Spengler to play fast and loose when the body of facts became overwhelming. Spengler generally exorcized the ghost of cross-cultural influence either by calling it superficial, as in the case of the Renaissance, or as pseudo-metamorphic, as in the case of Islam or Russian culture.

The Renaissance and the Reformation, artistically as well as politically, were opposition movements to the springtime forms, seeking either to resist or to destroy the youthful synthesis of the thirteenth century. Yet, the style of dynamic space, born in the Romanesque, continued to thrive even though it had left its home in the countryside. The manhood of a style occurred when the city began to dominate the country. It was at this stage in all cultures that style became suffused with intellectualism, and that the primitive faith of the pre-urban countryside, which had determined art in the springtime, surrendered to urban secularism. A logical consequence of this stylistic development was the disappearance of sacred symbolism. Artists became acutely conscious of having been severed from the mystical umbilical cord. Detached and cut off from the old mysteries, the artist now had to wrestle with new forms. Michelangelo did so and the result was something new, as seen in the Dome of St. Peter's. Michelangelo, Da Vinci, or Raphael recreated the prime symbol in its urban setting; and, in so doing, laid the foundation for the school of the great masters — Rembrandt, Vermeer, Bernini, Titian, or Rubens. Here, in the Baroque, the Faustian prime symbol had actualized its potentialities, for everything that followed was a mere working out of already defined expression forms. Autumn was, therefore, the fulfillment of artistic, as of political, economic, or scientific potentialities. In the Baroque and the Rococo, the possibilities of the Faustian soul were actualized in a series of stunning accomplishments. These ranged in music from the Baroque concerto to the symphonies of Beethoven; in politics, from the cabinet diplomacy of Richelieu to the enlightened rule of Frederick the Great; in science, from Newton's *Principia Mathematica* to Kant's *Critique of Pure Reason*; and in art, from the Baroque splendor of Versailles to the Rococo sweetness of Watteau, Dresden porcelain, and the "frozen music" of stone at Potsdam, Vienna, or Würzburg.

Old age portends incipient decline, manifesting itself in senile classicism of one sort or another.[54] Art became excessively ornamental, a sure sign of decay. There was endless experimentation with various arsenals of forms. Art was no longer truly imitational but ornamental; it no longer exhalted love, song, riot, or dance, but fell prey to risky experimentation. The megalopolis of today consumes the grand style either by destroying it, as in the formlessness of expressionism, or by wildly distorting it, as in the American skyscraper. The grand style of Western culture that rose out of the pre-urban countryside and was carried through in the cities has now reached its finale in the cosmopolis, where it shrivels up and dies. There can be no renascences. This is the fate of Western art as it is of all other arts.

Such a brief sketch cannot do justice to the wealth of dazzling observations Spengler made on the arts of form. As with everything he wrote, his discussion of the arts is animated by unshakeable convictions, usually stated in uncompromising terms. This is not the place to ponder the rightness or wrongness of Spengler's judgment, but to examine his physiognomic approach. Spengler is telling us that the soul of a culture is revealed in its artistic expressions, and that we can interpret these expressions physiognomically. His belief that physiognomic flair enables the historian to read a whole life in a face or to sum up whole peoples from the picture of an epoch was basically sound and can teach us a great deal. Spengler's recommendation that historians should work with the aid of analogy, empathetic understanding, or intuitive flair should also merit serious consideration. The spirit of an age, Spengler insisted again and again, cannot be recaptured by ordinary methods of social science. Only insight and imagination, balanced, to be sure, by the experience of life, will be of use in disclosing the *Zeitgeist* of an age. After all, a culture expresses its innermost character through its archetypal forms. These forms must be felt since they embody something that cannot be analyzed — a culture's shared attitude toward life, death, destiny, or eternity. We can describe these deeper cultural attitudes, as they are reflected in a work of art, but we cannot fully grasp their meaning analytically. The task of the historian, according to Spengler, is not to convince the reader by marshalling facts or causes, but to move him emotionally by recreating a sense of past life. The Baroque, for example, will only come to life when the historian recaptures in the mind of his readers such typical Baroque symbols as the flowing wig, the sweeping staircase, contrapuntal music, cabinet politics, or the excessive ornamentation in the style of art and life. Again, what better way is there than to portray some of the emotional attitudes of Baroque man. One thinks of such attitudes as the exaggerated sense of honor, the ceaseless pursuit of glory, the compulsive need to reconcile faith and reason, or the contradictory, and perhaps perverse, quest for blending gross sensuality with self-denying asceticism. Again, what better way is there than to examine the typical figures behind such poses. Through admired heroes, Spengler suggested, we often meet a glimpse into the innermost character of a culture.[55] Every culture worships a certain image of man and designates distinct individuals as heroic examples. Thus, to know what is meant by the hero as artist, is to know much about Quattrocento Italy, and to know much about the self-made Yankee in the Gilded Age is to know much about the American character. We capture much of the spirit of late civilization by studying the life and career of one single man — Cecil Rhodes. Here, again, physiognomic flair will be of immeasurable help, since it discloses the character of a man by studying his stature, his bearing, his air, his stride, or his way of speaking and writing.[56]

In summarizing Spengler's method of studying history, we are struck by the wealth of suggestive insights. His admonition to probe beneath the superficialities of chronology or causal relationships in history was fully justified, as was his equally forceful caveat that scientific methods could never reconstruct the richness of historical events. The past will always be a memory picture in our imagination; and only imaginative history-writing can bring it to life. History is not a neutral description of what happened; no one, Spengler believed, can ever know *"wie es eigentlich gewesen"* (how it actually was). The historian should not ask what actually happened, but what might have happened. He should reconstruct how things might have been; and to do so, he must be a poet, not a scientist. Under the dispensation of the scientific method, the historical imagination necessarily wilted because it was not allowed to soar above bland factuality. The good scientific historian is urged to stifle his imagination and to keep his intuition in strict abeyance.[57] Spengler conceded that this approach has its proper place, but he attacked the reductionist argument that this is the only avenue to the past. To transmute the objective spirit of describing "facts" into a methodological principle, he felt, was to narrow our historical perception. Historians should describe the facts, such as they are known, but they should not torture themselves by clothing their interpretation of the facts in neutral scientific terminology. Again, this is because it is impossible *on principle* to describe how things actually were. In history, we can only describe how things might have been. It follows that history-writing is creation, is poetry in the highest sense.[58]

Although Spengler's insights were often sound and valuable, he had the disconcerting habit to mar them by needless exaggeration. Good history is good literature, but it is not poetry. Good history-writing does require physiognomic insight, but it also demands painstaking causal analysis. Spengler often pontificated from his theoretical heights without testing his theories in practice. Had he been a practicing historian, he might have conceivably recognized some of the limitations or pitfalls of his theories. As it was, he never tested the practical applications of his morphological approach. This is not to say that Spengler's methodology does not have its merits. In fact, the beguiling thing about his historical methodology is the persuasive rhetoric which sustains it. We are enthralled by its basic premises less because they are logically demonstrated, but because they seem to "ring true." There is something profound about the idea of the life cycle and the methodological principles by which Spengler claimed to comprehend it. True, Spengler did not "prove" in what sense history was about life; nor did he "prove" the universal applicability of his biological model. What he did, however, was to perform a valuable corrective to the social science approach to history: he made us think about history biologically. If history, as he believed, is about past life, why should it not be explained in biological terms? This was Spengler's most profound insight. Future historians would do well to keep this vision alive.

THE VOICE OF CASSANDRA:
THE PROPHET IN POLITICS

I

Cassandra, daughter of the Trojan king Priam, received the gift of prophecy from the god Apollo, who had fallen in love with her. When she did not return Apollo's love, he put a curse on her: no one was to believe in her prophecies. When Cassandra prophesied the decline of Troy, and even predicted its fall by a wooden horse, it came to pass that no one believed her. Cassandra's fate was that her prophecies were true, but that no one heeded them. Spengler also believed that he possessed the gift of prophecy, though unlike Cassandra, he felt that his prophecies would come to pass — even if people believed in them. What can such a man contribute to the political issues of the day? When the severe prophet of the West entered the realm of political debate, he found himself enmeshed in a seemingly insoluble dilemma: how could he move men when he knew that the West was doomed?

The idea that the West was in the throes of incipient decline determined everything Spengler wrote about politics. This was not just a vague feeling on his part, but the corollary of his philosophy of history. Spengler affirmed this belief in the inevitable decline of the West and stoically accepted the consequences. Nothing can stay our inevitable destiny because it is written in history. Unlike most prophets of doom, Spengler had at least the honesty of his convictions, for he vehemently denied the possibility of renascences. We will not muddle through somehow and recapture our former youth; on

195

the contrary, we will share the fate of all living things — death. His personal life, as we have seen, was weighed down by this oppressive conviction. One wintry day, his biographer tells us, Spengler and Professor Manfred Schroter listened to music in a Munich coffee house. Schroter pointed to the window and the whirling snow beyond and asked whether this was a sign of our cultural phase. "Yes," Spengler answered after some reflection, "but it is a winter that will never be followed by spring."[1] No other episode can capture Spengler's tragic sense of life quite as poignantly as this one.

If there are no more springs, what can we do? Spengler answered that we must face our destiny honestly, avoiding the blandishments of sweet illusions. Writing to Oscar Lang shortly before the end of the First World War, Spengler observed that one could take three approaches to the world in wintertime: that of the Romantic, who rejects its materialism and seeks to recapture a lost vitality; that of the idéologue, who tries to shape the future in accordance with his utopian plans; and that of the Realist, who recognizes that the present, with all its faults, is unalterable and must be accepted stoically.[2] Needless to say, Spengler chose the third approach. Escape into the past may give us some solace but it is the coward's way out; the same is true, Spengler argued, of the escape into an ideal future. This is the route taken by all "progress-mongers," whom he despised so much. Both the romantic and the idéologue display an appalling ignorance of world history. Had they studied history realistically, they would have recognized that peace, universal brotherhood, progress, or the perfectibility of man are projections of their own desires, not objective historical happenings. Historical reality, sad to say, does not confirm the existence or even the possibility of such ideals.

We may disagree with Spengler's negative judgment, but we can only applaud his ruthless unmasking of historical illusions.

After decades of self-deception, Spengler's brutal frankness
was a welcome relief. With an honesty that is at once startling
and exhilerating, he stripped man of his ideological
pretensions and exposed the unsettling truths which lay
concealed behind the facade of such catch words as
"progress," "reason," or "perfectibility." Such men, of
course, are not loved either by their contemporaries or by
posterity. The price of ruthless honesty, as Spengler well
knew, is often the universal hatred and disapprobation of
one's fellow man. Indeed, it was precisely this radical
unmasking of illusions, this categorical denial of future
progress, which brought such a shower of denunciation on
Spengler's head.[3]

Pessimism as a philosophy of life squares ill with the
Western tradition of the last two centuries. Since the
Enlightenment, politicians have been preaching that things are
always getting better, and that the West is headed —
inescapably and ineluctably — into one sort of utopia or
another.[4] Spengler preached the exact opposite: we are not
marching into utopia, he said, but we will share the fate of
our Roman, Chinese, Egyptian, or Babylonian predecessors —
inevitable decline. Spengler delighted in pointing out that only
politicians talk about "mankind" following some goal. "As to
a 'goal of mankind'," he said, "I am a thorough-going and
decided pessimist. For me, mankind is a zoological expression.
I see no progress, no goal or path for mankind, except in the
heads of western progress-mongers."[5]

Spengler, however, tempered this apparently hopeless
pessimism by adding that he was not a fatalist who allowed
himself to be paralyzed by events because he envisioned no
more tasks. Let us recognize reality and adjust our lives
accordingly. For us, reality means that we are now living in
the winter or senescent phase of western history. This, in
turn, implies that our destiny is unalterably determined by

events common to all late civilizations — mass politics, Caesarism, competing ideologies, imperialism, and crass materialism. These are the facts; let us make the best of them. It follows that certain goals are no longer viable. Romantic poetry, idealistic philosophy, or other-worldly religion are passé. The coming events, Spengler predicted, will demand discipline of the most rigorous sort:

Severity, Roman severity is now beginning in the world. Soon there will be hardly room for anything else. Art, yes; but art in concrete and steel; poetry, yes; but from men with iron nerves and uncompromising depth of vision; religion, yes; but take up your missal, not your Confucius on hand-made paper, and then go to church; politics, yes; but from statesmen and not world improvers. Anything else is out of the question. And we must never forget what lies behind and ahead of us citizens of this century. We Germans will never again produce a Goethe, but indeed a Caesar.[6]

Political reality, past or present, implies the acceptance of martial qualities, the cultivation of Prussian *Realpolitik* pure and simple. Christian virtues such as humility, self-effacement, or submissiveness, however, admirable in themselves, have no place in the scheme of world history.[7] Every successful statesman knows that world history has always revolved around power: its acquisition, use, expansion, and loss. Spengler agreed with Machiavelli that power is its own source of appeal, and that reason of state must override all religious codes of ethics. If men were good and reasonable, amoral power politics would be unnecessary; but since men are basically aggressive, there is no other viable rationale for political action. Man is thrown into a world of strife and friction in which the strong always devour the weak. What is true of individuals is equally true of states: the strong conquer the weak. Spengler believed that the nuts and bolts of history were in the shape of wars or political struggles. The grand events − the ones that really count − are in the nature of cosmic upheavals: revolutions, great diplomatic or military alliances, and world wars. In studying these events, Spengler urged, we should concentrate primarily on the "why" and "how" of success because "the fact-world of history knows only the success which turns the law of the stronger into the law of all."[8] Ideas are irrelevant unless men turn them into levers for action. The world of history is red in tooth and claw; it is a seething cauldron of tension and struggle, involving individuals, classes, or nations. Only those survive who are "in form" − that is, who know how to fight by instinct.

Spengler would have agreed with Karl Marx that the history of all hitherto existing societies was the history of struggle, though he would have added that such struggles are political rather than economic. Life is always a struggle for power. The generating force of this struggle, however, is not a conscious motive rooted in economic consideration. Quite the contrary, man fights, he competes, he dominates because he is aggressive through and through. To define struggle in terms other than biological, is to misunderstand what life is all about. Spengler always insisted that life does not obey the rules of logic. When we thirst for power, we do so because it is in our nature. Later, of course, we may shroud our primitive impulses in idealistic formulations to prove what noble creatures we really are.

Intuitively, every man knows he is an aggressive animal, though he may not consciously admit it. Nations also know it because their inner constitutions always aim at being "in condition" for the outer fight.[9] According to Spengler, it follows that individual or collective survival depends on "being in form." Now, a nation is in form when power is firmly rooted and exercised by men of good breeding. When power becomes either diffused or a moral problem, a nation is no longer in form. History shows that nations are in form when they are governed by capable minorities. The western nations, for example, were in condition as long as they were governed by a self-perpetuating elite which was conscious of its duty and its destiny. In this respect, Spengler never ceased to admire the English aristocracy because, in his view, it was always conscious of its duty to king and country.[10] At Eton, Harrow, Oxford, or Cambridge, generations of gifted public servants, reared on the idea of state service, were taught to make England great at home and abroad.

As long as a nation is cognizant of political realities, it does not matter exactly how power is exercised in it. The English, in Spengler's judgment, were relatively safe from attack and could, therefore, approach the exercise of power in more or less individualistic terms. To the English, centralized power was always obnoxious, whereas to the Germans, less favored by geography, power was inconceivable except in centralized form. Actually, power always belongs to the state, though the idea of the state may vary considerably from country to country.[11] In England, Spengler felt, the nation was in form under the class and not under the state regime, as in France or Prussia.[12] As long as power is exercised resolutely and according to a common goal, the state will be in form. Conversely, when power is shared, as in modern parliamentary democracies, then the state is out of form, destined to disintegrate from within, or to be conquered from without by another healthy state.

These are the political realities Spengler wanted to impress upon his readers. The question is, can a late civilization be in form? Having predicted political formlessness and incipient decline, Spengler was hard put to affirm real political vigor in our winter phase. What then can we do? Spengler answered in rather dramatic tone by saying that the "alternatives now are to stand fast or to go under — there is no middle course. The only moral that the logic of things permits to us now is that of the climber on the face of the crag — a moment's weakness and all is over."[13] We must stand fast, he urged his countrymen, but how is this possible when everything inexorably changes for the worst? We should be in condition, Spengler urged; but in a declining culture, nothing can be in condition! Rigorously propounded, a philosophic system often has the tendency to circumscribe our options. This was certainly true in Spengler's case; for in his system, the West was entering a period of political formlessness — do what we will. Our age, he often said, is an age of mass politics, dominated by party systems, elections, the press, and ideological slogans of one sort or another. In fact, Spengler advised prospective politicians to work within the present system because it represents the mainstream of our cultural epoch. "The means of the present," he predicted, "are, and will be for many years, parliamentary."[14]

Yet, by temperament, Spengler despised democracy and all it stood for in his mind — the rule of the *canaille*, the domination of money, the cheap infighting among political factions, and — worst of all — the triumph of mediocrity. According to the logic of his system, all these hideous trends are unavoidable. Yet, according to the logic of his passions, all of these events must be avoided!

Spengler, therefore, found himself in a rather ambiguous position as he entered the world of politics. As we have previously seen, he was by temperament and conviction a Prussian royalist, a conservative in a world which saw no need for tradition. Spengler's pronouncements on political questions must be seen in the light of this dilemma. Politically, he was a conservative who glorified the Prussian past; culturally, he was a relativist who knew full well that the tradition he admired was bound to succumb to the flux of change. What tension it must have created in his mind!

In his discussion of Spengler's politics, Klemens von Klemperer observes that "Spengler was confused and he spread confusion,"[15] a judgment which is partly true. The source of Spengler's confusion was the attempt to blend the Prussian tradition, rooted in a feudal-aristocratic experience, with the politics of a modern technocratic society. Specifically, Spengler's ambiguity lay in his attempt to fuse Prussianism and socialism. Spengler did indeed advocate a kind of "National Socialism," though it bore little relationship to the Nazi tyranny of the Thirties. The center of his political vision can be found in this ambitious attempt to free socialism from Karl Marx and merge it with the Prussian style of life. Since Spengler's Prussian socialism grew out of his political experiences during the Weimar Republic, we should take a closer look at his attitude toward Weimar democracy.

II

The Weimar Republic was the product of defeat. In the eyes of Spengler and many other Germans, Weimar democracy was tainted by the surrender of 1918 and the humiliation of Versailles. Born amidst the chaos and defeat of the post-war period, liberal democracy always had to wrestle with the stigma of Versailles. This is one reason why democracy failed in Germany. Another reason, which Spengler was never tired of pointing out, was that the German people were neither historically nor psychologically prepared to accept such a sharp break in their political heritage. The new government, its opponents argued, represented an abrupt break with tradition. Since it was not rooted in the past, it had no chance of growing on German soil. This argument was a typical conservative objection to Weimar. What does not grow naturally, according to this Burkean argument, is condemned to wither on the vine. Spengler denounced the government because it was a theoretical model conceived in the minds of liberal professors who had no sense for political realities. Constructed under extreme pressure, and mainly to please the western powers, Weimar democracy was alien to the German spirit. As it turned out, of course, the Western powers did not reward the Germans for establishing a democratic regime. In their eyes, the Germans did not expiate their past sins just because they built a liberal-democratic regime. This brings us to another failure of Weimar: the allies did much to undermine its work. Time and again, the parties loyal to Weimar — the Democrats, the Social Democrats, or the Center Party — were forced to accept harsh terms by the allies. In doing so, they were branded as traitors by the proliferating right-wing parties. Thus, added to the pressure from without — the vindictiveness of the allies — was added the pressure from within — the chorus of right-wing denunciation of democracy. Oswald Spengler joined that chorus, and his voice grew shriller as Germany's problems multiplied under the impact of reparations, inflation, widespread violence, and foreign intervention.[16] Hardly had the Republic been formed, when it was threatened by inflation and Putsches from within and foreign intervention from without. From 1919 to 1923, the very time when Spengler entered the political field, the new Republic was fighting for its life. These years witnessed the Kapp and Hitler Putsches, the growth of extremism, communist attempts to seize power, the invasion of the Ruhr, and catastrophic inflation.

The *Decline of the West* made a spectacular impact on these apocalyptical times. No wonder that a public so disoriented by events was eager to hear more pronouncements from the oracle of the *Decline*. Spengler did not disappoint his audience: in pamphlets, books, and a number of speeches, he addressed himself to political questions, delighting the conservatives and outraging the liberals. Although Spengler never aligned himself with any party, his sympathies were with the extreme right-wing groups such as the German People's Party, the German National People's Party, and several paramilitary groups.[17] As long as a politician displayed a strong sense of nationalism, he generally supported him. Some of his close friends and associates were scattered across several parties, including the German People's Party, the German National People's Party, the Bavarian People's Party, the Center, and even the Social Democratic Party.[18]

As we have seen, Spengler's first entrance into politics came in 1920, when he accepted an invitation by the famous conservative *June Club* to discuss his ideas with Moeller van den Bruck.[19] Spengler found that he shared many ideas with Moeller, whose book *The Third Reich* (1923) became almost as sensational as Spengler's *Decline of the West*. Moeller's concept of a *Third Reich* captivated the imagination of many Germans weary of political rancor, liberal indecisiveness, and class divisions. Moeller championed a traditional German order in which the keynote was on state service, consciousness of race, political equilibrium, and spiritual regeneration. Spengler was in broad agreement with Moeller's theories. The members of the *June Club*, we are told, were so moved by Spengler and Moeller's views, that they solemnly swore to devote their lives to the realiztion of their visions.[20]

Actually, the ideas of the *June Club* were nothing new. The anti-liberal and anti-parliamentarian views which were in vogue among the members of the *June Club* date back to pre-war times, especially to the various irrationalist movements associated with Friedrich Nietzsche, Stefan George, Paul de Lagarde, and the powerful youth organizations. But perhaps the culmination of these developments is summed up by "the ideas of 1914," a term coined by Johann Plenge, professor of sociology at the University of Münster.[21] A whole roster of famous men pledged their allegiance to the ideas of 1914, among them being Ernst Troeltsch, Thomas Mann, Friedrich Meinecke, Walter Rathenau, Max Scheler, Werner Sombart, or Friedrich Naumann. All of these men were in substantial agreement that Anglo-American liberalism, with its lack of principle and moral vision, was a menace to German culture. In place of bourgeois liberalism and its crass materialistic approach to life, they hoped to establish a national community based on tradition, honor, love of country, and consciousness of the German past. Socially, their ideal was an organic community without class divisions, a society in which each individual or group performed its duty for the sake of the common good — the state. Werner Sombart, Max Weber, and Ernst Troeltsch never ceased inveighing against the English spirit of laissez-faire individualism. To impose the capitalistic business spirit on politics, they argued, was to soil political behavior and to corrupt all higher moral values. These ideas also figured prominently in Thomas Mann's novels and essays.[22] Mann believed that the liberal values of 1789 had been corrupted by bourgeois materialism and were now utterly destructive of good politics and all higher spiritual values. Perhaps the most influential voice was that of Friedrich Naumann, who called for a supernational order in Central Europe under the political and spiritual aegis of Germany. In his highly influential book, *Mitteleuropa* (1915), Naumann provided the most articulate statement of Germany's professed aims in the First World War. He envisioned a loose economic union between Germany and the nationalities of the Habsburg monarchy, a union he believed which would bring political and economic stability to this troubled part of Europe. Germany, of course, would play a dominant role, seeing to it that order and freedom would prevail in Central Europe.

All of the "men of 1914" were acutely conscious of the social question. Like Bismarck, they realized that socialism was a force to be reckoned with in politics. For this reason, they tried to build bridges to the working classes, whose peaceful participation in politics could no longer be avoided. The men of 1914 were revisionary socialists who placed emphasis on gradual change and peaceful cooperation among all social classes. To a man, they wanted to exorcize the specter of Marx from political theory in general and socialism in particular.[23] Marxism they felt, was a destructive social theory because it revelled in sanguinary images and set one class against another for no better reason, it seemed, than narrow class interests. Class warfare was utterly destructive of political life according to these intellectuals. Thus, in order to avoid the rancor of class divisions, they favored the incorporation of the working classes in the body politic. The best way to do so, they thought, was to win the working classes over to the monarchy and the nation. There was much talk in those days of a "National Socialism" in order to avert social disruption, national weakness, and alienation among classes. The industrialist Walther Rathenau, with whom Spengler corresponded after the war, made special efforts to unite the classes, to alleviate the condition of the workers, and to lessen some of the odious results of late nineteenth century technology.[24]

Spengler was a firm believer in the "ideas of 1914." Like many German intellectuals during the war, he thought that these ideals were worth fighting for. Since Germany lost the war, Anglo-American historians have found it easy to sneer at these ideals – all the more so after World War II, because the ideas of 1914 were later wildly distorted by the Nazis. Time, however, has a tendency to put things in perspective, allowing us to disentangle the ideals of the German intellectual community before World War I from those of the Nazis. Moreover, with catastrophe breathing down on our necks after decades of social strife, political corruption, and lack of spiritual values, we can sympathize more readily with the men of 1914, who honestly – if sometimes erroneously – tried to cope with an unknown social-political reality.

In any case, Spengler believed that the ideas of 1914 were still relevant after the war, and so did the conservative thinkers with whom he exchanged ideas during the Weimar period. The post-war Revolution and the ensuing class warfare in Germany convinced Spengler that only a strong authoritarian regime could stem the tide of anarchy. When the tenor of parliamentary politics became clear, his worst suspicions of liberal-democracy were confirmed. To a man like Spengler, who had always cherished an elitist view of culture, Weimar democracy must have seemed an unmitigated disaster. Indeed, Spengler's critique of Weimar culture must rank among one of the most negative. Where others saw an outpouring of liberated artistic impulses, Spengler only perceived anarchy and decadence; where others saw democratic freedom, he saw nihilism and the dissolution of all higher values. True, there was much that was seamy and trashy in Weimar culture; true, the tenor of politics was mediocre and often sordid. At the same time, it must be admitted that Weimar released some long repressed, pent-up energies; and in so doing, made possible some great artistic, literary, and scientific achievements.[25] Although artistic or literary works often reflected the anarchism of the times, who can say whether ten or twenty additional years of Weimar might not have provided mature form to that initial outburst of creative anarchy?

Spengler flatly denied the possibility that democracy was compatible with higher culture. In this, he was supported by most German intellectuals. No wonder that Weimar culture was stillborn, for it lacked the support of those who create culture — men of vision and genius. Even those intellectuals who gave their guarded approval of Weimar — men such as Gustav Stresemann, Berthold Brecht, Max Weber, or Friedrich Meinecke — could never reconcile themselves to its democratic spirit. Both the left-wing and the right-wing intellectuals disliked Weimar. The liberals disliked it because the Social Democratic regime allowed itself to be guided by reactionary pre-war institutions — the military, the courts, the bureaucracy — whereas the right-wing thinkers hated Weimar because it spelled democratic anarchy. Ludwig Marcuse summed up the moderate view when he said that "I don't remember if I voted in those years — and certainly not for whom."[26] For men like Marcuse or Thomas Mann, politics was a danger to culture because it profaned the world of the spirit with the corruption of politics. Disdain or insouciance marked the attitude of the moderates, who would have agreed with Heinrich Mann's outburst: "I hate politics and the belief in politics, because it makes men arrogant, doctrinaire, obstinate, and inhuman."[27] Spengler and the conservative intellectuals, on the other hand, did not hate politics per se, though they certainly hated Weimar politics. While the moderates stayed aloof, the conservatives did their best to participate in politics in order to realize their plans. Both groups contributed in destroying Weimar and in helping to create something they really did not want — Nazi Totalitarianism.

Spengler's critique of Weimar democracy was

uncompromising in its negativity. The whole range of democratic forms — constitutions, parties, elections — was anathema to him. Government for and by the people, he felt, was fatal to viable government because an amorphous mass cannot define goals and set policies. Democratic theory, according to Spengler, is based on the mistaken assumption that all men are created equal, a noble theory which is neither borne out by experience nor by history. The fact is that every society in the past, even when it was ostensibly based on equality, was founded on the inequality of man. Equal rights, Spengler asserted, are against nature, which knows no equality.[28] Elitism is a fact of life; equality is a dream. There will always be elites, even in democracies, where they generally appear in plutocratic form. "The fundamental right of the mass to choose its own representatives," Spengler said, "remains pure theory, for in actuality every developed organization recruits itself."[29]

To Spengler, democracy was nihilistic because it dissolved all higher spiritual values; it was anarchistic because it encouraged factionalism based on political or economic self-interest; and it was mediocre because equality always levels rather than elevates the quality of culture. Finally, liberal democracy is destructive of traditional culture because it creates a type of man who only knows how to destroy faith — the liberal intellectual. According to Spengler, the liberal is the gravedigger of traditional culture because he only knows how to tear down but does not know how to build up, except by way of unrealistic utopias. Priding himself on his open mind and his willingness to examine all issues, he is notoriously incapable of ever reaching deeply-felt convictions. He cannot stand firmly on any principle, except the principle of tolerating all views. His analytical attitude is a sharp edge of criticism, but it is an ineffectual tool for creating lasting values. Citing Pascal, Spengler observed that the understanding

— unaided by faith or the passions — is only capable of discovering errors. When this liberal attitude pervades politics, he felt, only doubts and uncertainties reign supreme. The liberal in politics sows the seeds of negativity under the guise of reason, toleration, and the rights of the individual. Moreover, liberalism creates factionalism because it demands diversity of interests.

Looking at European history in general and German history in particular, Spengler blamed liberal democracy for tearing apart the very fabric of tradition. The trouble in Germany began under Bismarck, who unconsciously fed the liberal syndrome by encouraging factional interests, which he thought he could play against one another. Already during his chancellorship, German politics was polluted by narrow factions — all placing their self-interests above the common good. Bismarck not only tolerated this situation, but he perpetuated it, for he neither educated the Germans in practical politics, nor imbued them with real principles. Under Bismarck and his successors, parliament was excluded from decision-making and, consequently, became nothing more than a grumbling pit (*Nörgelgrube*) of impotent orators.[30] This political tenor was reflected across the length and breadth of the nation in thousands of beer halls, where all the excluded groups thundered away at the government. In this way grew up a host of divisive ideas — all of them inimical to the good of the state. Weimar, Spengler lamented, had aggravated this divisiveness a thousandfold. To Spengler, Weimar had made anarchy habitual. What we witness today, he said, referring to the early years of Weimar, is the pathetic spectacle of parties turned into business organizations for the sole purpose of enriching themselves. When elements of this sort attain political power, the national interest is lost. He contemptuously referred to the Republican experiment in 1924 as a five-year orgy of incompetence, cowardice, and vulgarity.[31]

This bill of particulars was a commonplace among right-wing conservatives. For the conservatives, criticism was cheap. Since they were out of power, they could indulge themselves in vituperative exercises; but in so doing, they undercut the honest efforts of the government to cope with the staggering problems of the post-war years. When Chancellor Josef Wirth pointed his finger at the conservative wing in the Reichstag after the assassination of Walther Rathenau and warned that "the enemy is on the right," he was not being melodramatic. Right-wing groups had done their share in humiliating Germany. As we recall, they had a leading hand in conducting and losing the war; but in losing, they gingerly stepped aside to let others take the blame for it. The socialists and liberals may have weakened the war effort, but the generals lost it! Suppose the conservative forces had been charged with political leadership after the war? What could they have done vis-a-vis the victorious allies that the democratic parties did not do? In the irrational exchange of hysterical views between right and left — to which Spengler contributed his share — no side won. Spengler and others did much to destroy the moderate-liberal government in Germany.[32] The irony was that, when the Nazis assumed power, Spengler and his conservative friends looked aghast at the alternative!

What, we may ask, was Spengler's political alternative to decadent Weimar liberalism? In a series of books and pamphlets, written between 1920 and 1933, he repeatedly advocated one remedy — Prussian Socialism. What did he mean by that apparently self-contradictory term?

III

Spengler, we recall, was basically a nineteenth century monarchist who glorified the Bismarckian power state (*Machtstaat*). In his eyes, the nation should be like a superb athlete, ever vigilant and ever prepared to face the eternal struggle between competing states. To be strong for the outer fight presupposed two things: absolute power at the top and internal peace among all social classes. Spengler believed that domestic tranquility would be difficult to maintain because the Industrial Revolution had sown deep seeds of hostility into the body politic. The solution to the dilemma of social conflict, however, had already been discovered by the Hohenzollerns. A brief glance at Prussian history, Spengler claimed, would confirm this judgement. The Hohenzollerns had generally displayed an uncanny intuitive sense of political realities. Far from exploiting their subjects, the Hohenzollerns had always been magnificent higher civil servants. Frederick the Great, for example, envisioned himself as a supreme moral and political arbiter, whose task it was to rise above petty interests and to conduct the country's business for the good of all. His famous maxim, "I am the first servant of the State," implied that he viewed his role as a monarch in a far different sense than did Louis XIV, whose saying "I am the state" implied the effective exclusion of all other groups from power and responsibility. According to Spengler, Frederick did not place himself in a position of splendid regal authority, but saw his role more modestly as the first servant of the State. To be sure, first servant meant a special responsiblity — that of giving visible expression to the general will. The Hohenzollerns believed that the function of monarchy was the preservation of the common good, and that such a task involved the maintenance of social harmony, the suppression of selfish interests, and the promotion of enlightened social policies. From Frederick William I right up to the Kaiser, the Hohenzollerns had always pursued a paternalistic social policy — as is evidenced by the fact that Germany under Bismarck was the first European country to institute a broad program of Social Security, unemployment benefits, old age pensions, and medical care for its citizens.

This is why Spengler argued that Prussianism had always meant a kind of socialism. To be sure, it was not the kind of socialism that Marx advocated, for it did not mean the pursuit of selfish class-interests and the incitement to class warfare. Prussian socialism, Spengler contended, is both a social theory and a political style of life. Politically, it is a view of the State in which the individual is always subordinate. Prussianism means service to the highest moral and political authority — the State. Unlike English liberalism, Prussianism means that the individual derives meaning and purpose only in and through the state. Spengler claimed that Prussianism demanded that every individual should become a civil servant who must sacrifice his private interest to the good of the state.[33] The state, however, is not identical with the ruler; the monarch is only the first servant of the state.

Spengler argued that every late civilization witnesses the coming of socialism in one form or another. In the West, there are basically two kinds of socialism: one manifests itself as resignation philosophy and the will of the masses, the other as the spirit of order and discipline. The first is Marxian or English, the second is Prussian or German. One is megalopolitan, formless and violent; the other is summed up by the idea of obedience and duty to the State. The motto for Germans should be "travailler pour le roi de Prusse."[34] Since many Germans have been polluted by English socialism, the urgent task is to free socialism from the fetters of Marx.

Spengler's criticism of Marx was often incisive, sometimes

brilliant, and never dull. According to Spengler, Marx went astray by confusing socialism with an economic system, and by compounding this error in accepting the economic premises of English liberalism. The fact is that socialism is an instinct, not an economic theory. Specifically, it is a kind of herd instinct which prompts the group to seek power and possession for itself. Like every other ideology, Socialism is first and foremost an instinct for power. Had Marx read European history correctly, he would have realized that Western history was not a history of economic class struggles, but a history of two antagonistic power instincts. Struggle, yes; but struggle between two Faustian instincts — the Viking spirit and the spirit of the Teutonic knights.[35] Both were originally German, but differentiated in time as one group of Germans roamed the seas and the other settled the continent. Scandinavia and the British Isles nourished a free-roving predatory instinct, whereas the rest of the continent nourished a more communal spirit. Rooted in the soil, the Germanic knights developed a sense of community in which the will of the individual had to be subordinated to the will of all. This was far less the case in England or Scandinavia, where individual exploits and initiative, based on the experience of the sea, were highly prized. As the centuries advanced, Spengler argued, the Viking spirit became transmuted in England and later in America into a laissez-faire style of life. To the question, is the state or the individual supreme, the Anglo-American naturally responds by saying that the individual is pre-eminent; the German, on the contrary, would answer that the state is supreme.

Although Spengler's historical analysis of these two instincts is sometimes strained, he was quite accurate in delineating what H. G. Wells called a community of will and a community of obedience. Spengler, however, would have denied H. G. Wells' further distinction that one is essentially passive, the other aggressive. Both communities, according to Spengler, are aggressive through and through because they are bearers of the Faustian spirit. The only difference is that, in one community, the will to power is individual; in the other — it is collective. The German community binds each member to every other member. Everyone for himself, Spengler claimed, is English; one for all and all for one is German.[36] Stated in such exaggerated fashion, the original insight of two different cultural communities is largely fanciful.

In the Viking community, Spengler continued, the spirit of rugged individualism leads to sharp social distinctions which are primarily reckoned in economic terms. There are, consequently, those who have enriched themselves and those who have not. To divide the members of society into the rich and the poor, the exploiters and the exploited, is true as long as we are talking about England or America, but it is certainly false in the case of Germany. Marx made this mistake and distorted not only European but world history. The truth is that social distinctions in Germany are based on the relative position a man occupies in the communal hierarchy. In Germany, Spengler claimed, a man is not judged by the amount of money he has but by his contribution to the state. The Prussian instinct is to turn everyone into a civil servant so that he has a real stake in the community.[37] In England, on the other hand, a man is what he is by virtue of his wealth. This is why the British government has always resembled a kind of joint stock company, in which its members invest their money in order to receive emoluments and profits. The rich, of course, serve the nation, but they do so primarily to serve themselves. The English, Spengler claimed, have never shed the origin of their Viking ancestors, for the lust of booty is still their basic goal. To be sure, the predatory instinct no longer manifests itself in its original primitive form; it now appears in the form of cut-throat competition in trade or commerce. As Spengler pointed out, however, what is trade if not a "cultivated form of robbery."[38]

Spengler concluded his analysis by saying that the West must choose which cultural community it wants to emulate, the laissez-faire spirit of England and America or the civil servant spirit of Prussia. Are there no other alternatives? What about France? The French, or any other nation, has dissipated its vitality completely and cannot serve as a leader of the West. According to Spengler, the French nation has dissolved itself into two parts: the majority, consisting of placid bourgeois Girondins; and the minority, comprising an ever-shrinking Jacobin element. The majority is tired in spirit and dreams of a secure *rentier* existence. Although there is still a small remnant of chauvinists, a tiny group who advocates a revival of *le grand nation*, its political fortunes are desperate.[39] The facts are inescapable: the West will fall under the dispensation of the Prussian or the English spirit. Between the two, there can be no compromise because both Germans and Anglo-Americans are Faustian natures who recognize no compromises and no boundaries.

If the West falls under Anglo-American hegemony, what will it be like? One thing is certain, Spengler thought: the world will be ravaged and exploited by rapacious plutocrats. These men will not rest until every section of the world has been industrialized for profit and money. Spengler thought that this process would probably be carried out by Americans because they possessed a far larger reservoir of industrial might. Whatever group ultimately develops the world — English or American — the result will be the same — the rule of materialism in its most frightening form. The goal of the Viking instinct will be the creation of private wealth; the elimination of competition; and the exploitation of the public through advertising, monetary politics, stimulation of false needs, and control of supply and demand.[40]

If the Prussian instinct wins — and Spengler was far from convinced that it would — the world will be organized according to the rigor of a well-trained army. Presumably, everyone will do his duty for the common good rather than for his own selfish interests. The Prussian goal is to create a civil service community, in which men will be measured by performance, talent, and loyalty to the state. Spengler did not elaborate upon the aims of the Prussian system; nor did he specify precisely what role Germany would play in a world that had become Germanic in spirit. It is unlikely that Spengler fostered the illusion that Germany would conquer Europe, let alone the world: what he wanted to see was not the military triumph of Germany, but the acceptance of the Germanic-Prussian rather than the Anglo-American spirit. Little did he suspect that the issue would be decided sooner than he thought. The Caesars of the West have not turned out to be diligent civil servants of the Prussian type, but corporate millionaires in charge of a supra-national network of corporations. Perhaps this outcome is preferable to Spengler's solution, for we have seen that Prussianism in practice under Hitler was a far more sinister affair.

For most of his political opinions, Spengler was a man of the old pre-war order. While he always spurned ideals, he really wanted to see the re-establishment of the Hohenzollern monarchy. As anachronistic as it may sound, Spengler was a socialist and a monarchist. Monarchy symbolized good order, leadership, and tradition; socialism meant equality of service to the state, whose highest embodiment was the figure of the monarch. If one could somehow instill this "correct" kind of socialism in the working people, strife and social disruption would disappear. This is why Marxism must be destroyed because it is a cancerous growth on the body politic. Marxian socialism, Spengler argued, is not only devoid of all higher spiritual values, but it represents the tyranny of the lower classes. Gross materialism and mob tyranny — these are the twin evils of Marxism. Though the lower classes have become envious and dangerous, the fault lies not with them but with their leaders.[41] The aim of the lower class demagogues and their intellectual dupes is to destroy tradition through revolution. This cannot be tolerated. Nor can we tolerate crippling strikes and wage extortion on the part of the workers. Spengler would have discipline and self-denial among the workers! The more we pamper the worker, he seems to have felt, the more he will demand and the less he will produce. If we do not stop coddling the worker, we will pay a heavy price. The black and yellow races, still unspoiled by luxury, will take our place and be masters of the world. This is another reason why we need Prussian rigor. Addressing himself to young Germans, Spengler admonished and exorted them to become men of iron:

> I am appealing to youth. I am calling on all those who have marrow in their bones and blood in their veins. Educate yourselves! Become men! We no longer need any idéologues, no palaver about intellect and cosmopolitanism and the spiritual mission of Germans. We need hardness; we need a courageous skepticism; we need a class of socialistic conquerors. Once again: socialism means power, power and again power. Thoughts and schemes are nothing without power. The road to power has already been mapped: the valuable element of German labor in union with the best representatives of the old Prussian state idea, both determined to build a strictly socialistic state . . . [42]

This statement, as so many Spenglerian pronouncements on politics, could have been written or delivered as a stump speech by Adolf Hitler. All the elements of National Socialism are there: the courting of youth, the call to discipline and toughness, the glorification of the Prussian style of life, and the appeal to the working classes. Was Spengler a National Socialist? Yes and no. Yes, in the sense that he did embrace a philosophy that gloried in war, struggle, and rigorous discipline. Yes, in the sense that he advocated a militant nationalism sustained by a peculiar sort of socialism. No, because the kind of national socialism that was finally established under Hitler did not meet his approval. As we have seen, Spengler had nothing but scorn for the Nazis, whom he depicted as infantile romantics intoxicated by goostepping, parades, and wholly illusory goals. Nor did he approve of their racial policies. Spengler was not a racist. In fact, he felt that racial mixture was a healthy thing. As he put it in unmistakeable terms: "racial mixture has always and everywhere been a fact. Climate or position always forge new types. Only racial inferiors preach race."[43]

If Spengler was not a national socialist in the Hitlerian sense, he did much to pave the way for the Nazis. Again and again, he called for goals which were not too dissimilar from those of the National Socialists. For example, his demand that Germany must breed an iron-willed elite animated by a love for struggle and hardness sounded like the Hitlerian call for breeding a master race. The belief in a great leader was another favorite idea of Spengler. Our times, he said in 1924, demand a great leader who can inspire confidence in people. "The best Germans," Spengler insisted, "are waiting for the appearance of a great man to whom the destiny of the nation can be entrusted."[44] When that man arrived in 1933, Spengler was at first skeptical and then downright disdainful. Spengler had predicted National Socialism and Caesarism, but when both arrived, he was shocked by what he saw!

Spengler died in 1936, before the holocaust of the Second

World War. Although he did not live to see the outcome, he predicted its coming. In his last work entitled *Years of Decision* (1933), he made some interesting comments on future developments. How prophetic were these last predictions of Oswald Spengler?

IV

Spengler's last book was avowedly prophetic. In the very opening passages, he announced self-confidently that he saw farther than others, and that his observations should be given the most serious consideration. Writing just before the Nazi seizure of power, he warned that Germany should not drown itself in the Wagnerian clamor of parades, dazzling uniforms, or stirring marching songs.[45] A second world war, he indicated, is just around the corner; let us be prepared for it. Spengler also prophesied several other impending catastrophies — continuing racial and class warfare, the coming of Caesarism, the despoliation of the world by industry, and the demise of the white man.

The *Years of Decision* bears such ominous chapter headings as "World Wars and World Powers," "The White World Revolution," and "The Colored World Revolution." The premise of Spengler's book is that the white race of Europe and America has dissipated its energy, and that it will probably have to surrender its power to other and more healthy races — unless it comes to its senses before it is too late. Here is that Spenglerian ambiguity again. Strictly speaking, the Faustian West cannot come to its senses, as Spengler knew full well. What he really meant to say was that we should go down with the ship while the band is playing on deck. In other words, we should accept our destiny stoically

and face the impending catastrophies with dignity, honor, and
— above all — a sense of style! He advocated as much in a
previous work, entitled *Man and Technics* (1931), in which he
advised his readers to face the inevitable doom in the manner
of the Roman guard who stood watch at Pompey during the
eruption of Mount Vesuvius. The soldier was standing guard
as the blazing lava enveloped him; he could have shirked his
duty by running away. As a Roman, however, he knew that
he could not leave his post because he had not been
relieved.[46]

Such an appalling fatalism squared ill even with many
Germans, who were intoxicated at this time by the roseate
visions of National Socialism. This is why Spengler moderated
his fatalism by conceding the possibility that Germany might
somehow stem or at least delay the incipient decline of the
West.[47] Actually, Spengler did not believe anything of the
kind, especially after seeing the Nazis in action. He probably
sensed that Germany, far from stemming the tide of decline,
would probably accelerate it. The book leaves no doubt that
he envisioned a terrifying future. Why was the future so dark?

We need hardly recall that this is because the Faustian
West was well into its winter phase. World War I, Spengler
believed, was the turning point. The old Europe died in that
holocaust. Specifically, it was the old ruling elite which was
defeated by the war. Four major empires collapsed, and with
them, the old symbols of authority which had provided
permanence and stability to the social fabric. World War I,
however, only sealed a development which had begun with
the French Revolution — the first assault on traditional
Europe. The nineteenth century represented one continuous
attack on tradition by such forces as liberalism and socialism.
Spengler referred to this process as the Revolution from
below against tradition.[48] Much of the blame rests on the
ruling elites themselves. Riddled by liberal guilt, unsure of

their heritage, and uncertain of their goals, the traditional power elites simply made too many concessions to the classes below. Thus, the New England gentry in America, the Tories in England, and the landed aristocrats in Germany or France have effectively surrendered their political preeminence to the *nouveaux riches*, the intellectuals, or the working classes. The sad fact is that there is nothing to take the place of the old elites — except a materialistic mob of half embourgoisized serfs. Spengler would have fully agreed with Ortega y Gasset in calling this political phase "The Revolt of the Masses." There was only one direction in which it could lead — the triumph of Caesarism.

If the elites have lost mastery over their former servants at home, they have also lost grip on their colonial subjects abroad. Having taught the colored races the secrets of Faustian technology, it will not be too long until the former servants will turn that technology on their master.[49] The European habit of authority, once respected without question, is now openly mocked throughout the world. Again, World War I was a turning point in this respect. In World War I, the colored races witnessed the white man's weaknesses as he slaughtered his own kind. In Russia and Japan, Spengler thought he saw the potential gravediggers of the West.

What will the future portend and what will it demand of Faustian man? The coming times, Spengler predicted, will demand utmost discipline, Prussian rigor pure and simple. The lazy pre-war years, filled with deceptive calm and unprecedented material comfort, will not return again.[50] The rest of the century will see terrible things — annihilation wars, Caesarism, racial wars, class warfare, and many other frightening events. We will soften the impact of some of these events if we squarely face the facts. Happy ends, Spengler warned, are for the movies but not for life. The coming times will demand men of iron will, not romantic dreamers or tender souls. During World War I, we have been brought face to face with the savage from within. He is always there below the facade of polite culture and he will rear his head again, sweeping away the weak, the romantic, the bookworm, and the starry-eyed world improver.

The West, according to Spengler, has entered the period of the World Wars. From a cultural perspective, the past analogue of these events was the time between Cannae and Actium. The eventual result will be the same as in Rome. Who will take the place of Europe? Spengler believed that Russia, having recaptured its Asiatic heritage, might challenge Europe's former position. He did not rule out the possibility that a new vigorous culture could rise out of the Russian landscape. In fact, he already designated "endless distance" as the prime symbol of Russia.[51] If Russia ever expects to develop a viable culture of its own, it must extirpate its Western heritage. To a large extent, Spengler thought, Russia had already done so. To be sure, the Soviet regime seems to follow the dictates of Marxism — a decadent western ideology. However, this "western" aspect of Russia is deceptive. The Soviet Union is not a Marxist state; it is far closer to the old Tartar absolutism than to any western model. Spengler was intrigued by the Soviet Union and spoke respectfully of its authoritarian bureaucracy. The destiny of Europe may well lie in the hands of Russia.

If Spengler was intrigued by the Russians, he was puzzled by the Americans. He often referred to America as a pale replica of the West. The trouble with America is that it did not participate in the vitality of the West but only in its decadent or senile phase. What America has learned from the West is its materialism — nothing else. Moreover, the native landscape, ripe for plunder and spoliation, has reinforced this materialistic impulse a thousandfold. The hordes of failures which were dumped on American shores made a real aristocracy impossible. The older gentry of the South and New England both succumbed to materialism and industry — the one in the civil war, the other around the turn of the twentieth century. America, in Spengler's judgment, has never been able to create a coherent social community or a viable government, partly owing to the spirit of laissez-faire individualism, partly to the racial melting pot that failed to melt. There is much talk in America, to be sure, of a distinct American type, the so-called one-hundred-percent American. In reality, however, this is an ideal rather than a fact. Those who talk about a strong Yankee race, Spengler said, confuse records and dollars with the real spiritual depth of a people.[52] A healthy race of people cannot flourish in a purely materialistic environment, in which all higher ideals are universally subject and where the only cultural aim is "mony mickles mak a muckle." If America pursues this goal, nothing can stay its eventual fall. On the other hand, Spengler knew that America possessed immense material riches which, properly harnessed, could make her the master of the world. This presupposed rigorous national leadership, self-discipline, and — above all — social cohesion. A country divided into gigantic egos, all attempting to enrich themselves at each other's expense, can never assume world leadership. America, Spengler argued, does indeed require a one-hundred-percent Americanism if it wants to avoid its impending fate — the collapse of capitalism.[53] To begin with, the ruling elite in America, as in the rest of Western Europe, had made too many power concessions to the lower classes or to the hordes of only recently enfranchized Americans. Spengler believed that the original West European elite in America had not perpetuated its kind and had failed to create a viable conservative tradition.

In the absence of firm political leadership by the old order, the country has degenerated into corruption and near anarchy under the *nouveaux riches*, now consisting largely of former peasants from east-central Europe. If we add to this the mounting racial struggle, the collapse of viable centralized government cannot be too far ahead. Time will tell, Spengler thought, whether America will grow strong or collapse under adversity. America is the last expression of the Faustian will to power. Can it rise to the task or will it collapse in a whimper?

Spengler did not know which nation would determine the future of the world. He was certain of one thing: the future master would be vigorous, confident in purpose, and impatient to restrain his aggressive impulses. The future most assuredly will not belong to liberal or pacifistic nations. In his last public utterance — a reply to an American poll entitled "Is World Peace Possible?" — Spengler returned to his tragic view of life. He said that the answer about world peace could only be answered by someone who was familiar with world history. Now, world history has shown that war is a fact and peace an illusion. From time immemorial, intellectuals have always preached peace, but to no avail. The problem today is that pacifism has become widespread among the white man, which is a sure sign of senility.[55] As Spengler warned:

> When whole peoples become pacifistic, it is a symptom of senility. Strong and unspent races are not pacifistic. To adopt such a position is to abandon the future, for the pacifist ideal is a static, terminal condition that is contrary to the basic facts of existence.[56]

Spengler went on to warn that there will always be wars; and if the white man should ever tire of war, the earth would fall victim to the colored races.

Whether this will be the destiny of the West two hundred

years hence is a possibility. In the meantime, however, the West has still to accomplish its final deed — to finish the death-symbolism of the thing-become. As Judith in Bluebeard's castle, the restless inquiring spirit of the Faustian West has yet to open the final door which conceals its ultimate and perhaps terrifying fate. We may squirm and rebel against these gloomy Spenglerian forebodings, but we can no longer afford to ignore them.

CONCLUSION

Spengler's real achievement has always been obscured by his overbearing personality and by his gloomy predictions. As to his personality, we have had occasion to observe both its positive and its negative side — its refreshing candor and its harsh dogmatism. Spengler was always at war with himself: he admired toughness, but he was soft to the core of his being; he championed a community of true believers; but he himself led a life of isolation and loneliness; he predicted the impending collapse of the West with a kind of intellectual glee, but privately shuddered at the consequences of his gloomy discoveries. The tug-of-war between his conflicting impulses naturally affected his public image. To this very day, Spengler is largely perceived as a harsh and dogmatic prophet whose language is shrill *in extremis* and whose imagery, as Northrop Frye has so aptly put it, is "Halloween imagery, full of woo-woo noises and shivery Wagnerian winnies about the 'dark' goings-on of nature and destiny."[1]

This image of Spengler as a harsh and shrill prophet of doom is quite accurate as far as it goes. The real question, however, is not whether Spengler's thought is gloomy or Halloween-like, but whether it is true! Nothing is easier, of course, than to discredit a man's perception of the world by attributing it to some inherent defect in his psychological make-up. The specter of Spengler cannot be exorcized this way, though there is undoubtedly a grain of truth to the accusation that Spengler frequently endowed events with his own pessimistic temperament.

Spengler's pessimistic views were often right, but they lost their sting by the way in which Spengler stated them. Thus, when he endowed his historical pessimism with his own fatalism, he ran the risk of being perceived as the worst sort of "doom and gloom" prophet. Temperamentally, as we have seen, Spengler saw life as inherently tragic, inexplicably mysterious, and unbearably painful. When he projected this feeling on history as a whole, Spengler undoubtedly twisted the shape of reality, which is never wholly one-dimensional.

In any case, it is precisely this apparently uncompromising pessimism about life and history which has always proved to be such a stumbling block towards a real understanding of Spengler's thought. Every fiber in us naturally rebels against the idea that our future is rigidly determined. We like to think that the future, if not rosy, is at least open-ended. Spengler denied this on the grounds that the past, which he claimed to be able to retrodict, was an index to the future. Once we grant him his basic premises, it necessarily follows that the future for Faustian man is indeed bleak. However, Spengler's vision is not wholly negative because it includes the idea of renewal and vitality. This is an important point that has been universally ignored by commentators of Spengler's thought.

An existing entity such as the Faustian culture is destined to wither away, but it does *not* follow from this statement that something new and vital cannot take its place on its *own* soil. Spengler merely argued that the Faustian culture, whose creative energy has now been spent after one thousand years, must give way to a more youthful, a more creative culture. He did not pretend to know whether this process would take place on the soil of the West or elsewhere.

Undoubtedly, there is a profound sense of tragedy about the prospect of our western culture as Spengler described it. We like to prolong or perpetuate ideas or institutions to which we have become accustomed. But why prolong something that has become irremediably decadent and senescent? On Spengler's own showing, the soil of the West is metaphysically barren and, therefore, incapable of producing a single great idea, a single compelling faith that could inspire a sense of purpose or mission. In view of this situation, is the impending collapse of western ideals and institutions really such a profound tragedy? Should we not rather look forward to the collapse of the whole decaying system with a profound sense of satisfaction? In other words, why should we perpetuate something that has become rotten and, therefore, incapable of regeneration? Spengler's ambivalent answer, which reveals how closely he was really tied to the survival of Faustian culture, was that we should hold fast to the declining ideals and institutions of the West, even though we know what the outcome will be! But without compromising a single premise of his system, Spengler could just as well have responded optimistically by welcoming the impending collapse and the growth of something more creative and more vital. In other words, pessimism is not intrinsic to the Spenglerian system at all. Just because Spengler endowed his conclusions with a temperamental pessimism peculiar to his own character, it does not follow that someone else, accepting both his premises and his conclusions, must reach the same pessimistic verdict. If we really accept the biological metaphor, what is so tragic about a culture fading away and, therefore, making it possible for something young to take its place? What could be more natural and less tragic? In sum, it is a great mistake to assume that to be a Spenglerian implies ipso facto to be either a pessimist or a fatalist.

Once we have overcome the stumbling block of Spengler's irascible personality and his tragic view of life as extraneous elements, we are in a far better position to appreciate his real accomplishments. What are his real contributions?

With the immodesty of the genius, Spengler several times referred to his achievements as a Copernican discovery. We may smile at Spengler's assertion that he was the Copernicus of the historical profession; but if we honestly canvass the field of history over the last two centuries, Spengler actually does stand out as a trailblazer who opened up entirely new vistas of historical research. Anyone who has seriously studied his thought is unlikely to read or write history in the old conventional manner. As man's history increases in length and in complexity of detail, historians are going to be forced to abandon their specialist bias and to write history along the lines indicated by Spengler. This does not mean that future historians will have to become Spenglerians but simply that they will have to write broad cultural histories.

Unfortunately, such histories do not exist at the present time. In surveying the present state of historical research, especially in the Anglo-American community, we still encounter nothing but specialized monographs on ever more restricted topics. The situation is worse today than it was in Spengler's day. Not only do historians continue to shred history in the conventional manner, but they continue to read and write and teach history as "Ancient," "Medieval," and "Modern." It is as though Spengler and Toynbee had not written a single line. In spite of all their caveats and suggestions, history continues to be written in the old tapeworm fashion and largely on political lines. In America, for example, there is not a single history department in which students are trained as cultural historians — that is, as generalists who can perceive the interrelationships between art, music, religion, science, politics, literature, and philosophy not only in their own culture, but in the cultures of other peoples. History today, more than ever, is written almost entirely from the narrow perspective of the specialist who defines the larger discipline by the smaller. This fragmentation of historical knowledge has reached truly ludicrous proportions as the academic establishment surrenders to the prevailing neophilia (love of novelty) by manufacturing Quantitative history, Black history, Chicano history, Women's history, Urban history, Ethno-history, Family history, etc. Plans are currently afoot to establish departments of "herstory" out of deference to the women's liberation movement. No wonder that broad cultural histories are a thing of the past. In fact, there is only one great cultural history that has been written by an American, and that man — Will Durant — is not a member of the historical profession.

Precisely what can the historical profession learn from Spengler? I believe that intensive study of Spengler will perforce break down the inertia of specialization and academic fragmentation. A synoptic view of the past, no matter from which perspective it may be guided, always has a liberating effect on the historical perception: it teaches us to see whole what was formerly a mere conglomeration of detail. Spengler may not have proved the logical validity of his holistic approach to history, but he did prove its practical validity. Experience has shown time and again that a meaningful knowledge of the past depends on the historian's ability to apprehend history as a whole rather than as a series of isolated parts. Knowledge of the past varies in proportion to a knowledge of its forms; and the apprehension of the larger historical forms (cultures) yields more meaningful insights than the perception of the smaller units. More simply put, synoptic vision broadens the understanding, whereas specialization restricts it.

Historians could also benefit from Spengler's organicist approach to history, if only as a corrective to the orthodox methods currently used by professional historians. Hayden White, in a recent fascinating study on the nature of historical consciousness, has pointed out that the professional historians have arbitrarily circumscribed historical inquiry to basically two modes of explanation: formism and contextualism.[2] By formism he means that kind of inquiry which seeks to identify the unique characteristics of historical objects. Such an inquiry, he said, considers an explanation to be complete "when a given set of objects has been properly identified, its class, generic, and specific attributes assigned, and labels attesting to its particularity attached to it."[3] On the contextualist model, events are explained by being set within the "context" of their occurrence. The way in which events have occurred is to be determined by showing how such events are related to other events in a "circumambient historical space."[4] The problem with both methods is that historical events, since they are viewed as particular and even unique, cannot be integrated into precise conceptualizations or universal generalizations. At best, the two approaches can adumbrate certain "trends" or general characteristics of historical periods.

Mechanism and Organicism — the two other modes of historical explanation mentioned by White — seek to integrate historical events under the aspect of some universal law or synthetic process. Both Organicism and mechanism are "metahistorical" inquiries of the type referred to in this work as grand-design history. Metahistory is based, as we have seen, on the idea that there is a general, sweeping, thematic unity in history which transcends particular historical epochs and which makes the course of history predictable and therefore meaningful. It is this kind of history writing which is widely rejected by professional historians on the grounds that it smacks of scientism. But the academic criticisms of grand-design history are not motivated by scholarly "objectivity." When academic historians reject grand-design models they do so in terms of implicit formist or contextualist biases. In other words, the hostility towards grand-design history, as White observed, appears to "lie in considerations of a specifically epistemological sort. For, given the protoscientific nature of historical studies, there are no apodictic epistemological grounds for the preference of one mode of explanation over another."[5]

If it is true, as White argued, that there are no apodictic epistemological grounds for preferring one method over another, what other grounds are there for choosing? At the present time it would seem advisable to adopt a pragmatic attitude in regard to historical explanation. A pragmatic explanation is one that can account for the "hows" and "whys" of historical events to the satisfaction of the general educated reader. It is clear that a number of methods can meet this basic requirement of what constitutes an explanation, provided, of course, that they are logically coherent. However, there is an added dimension to every explanation, and that is its ability to convince or persuade us. And the force of that persuasion is often determined by a kind of inward consent that we give to a particular explanation, an inward consent that has little to do with logical proof. In other words, we consent to explanations not only because they persuade us rationally, but also because they satisfy a deep emotional need in us. I submit that it is on this level of inward persuasion that Spengler is often at his most compelling. As we have seen, the reason for this is that he adopts a simple fact of life as the cornerstone of his whole system. Let us briefly recall what he meant by the metaphor of life. History and life, he believed, unfold through opposites and cycles in a never-ending rhythm of birth, maturity, and old age. This is an historic as well as a cosmic destiny because it encompasses the life of the lowliest protozoans to the mightiest cultures created by the hand of man. It was in this idea of the life cycle, as we have seen, that Spengler thought he had discovered the riddle of history. Applying the cycle to culture, he then showed that every culture passes through the age-phases of the individual man — that is, each culture has its childhood, youth, manhood, and old age. Each culture is also endowed with certain potentialities which it tries to actualize in the course of its life history. When a culture has fulfilled the potentialities of its prime symbol, when the source of its vital energy has dried up, it shrivels and ultimately decays. There can be no renewals of a decaying culture, just as there can be no rejuvenation of a man who has become old and senile. The life cycle, however, moves on relentlessly, creating new vital life where there was once senescence and death.

Now, this metaphor of growth is beguiling because it speaks a profound and simple truth: history is an account of past life, and it must, therefore, be studied biologically. Moreover, since history is about past human life, it must be studied by transcendental biology (the biology of purpose). The objection that historical entities are not life entities does not detract from the validity of Spengler's biological approach. As Northrop Frye has recently said,

> it is no good saying that a culture is not an organism, and that, therefore, we can throw out his (Spengler's) whole argument. The question whether a culture "is" an organism or not belongs to what I call the fallacy of the unnecessary essence. It is an insoluble problem . . . The question is not whether a culture is an organism, but whether it behaves enough like one to be studied on an organic model.[6]

As we have seen, Spengler did succeed in studying cultures on an organic model, though his model contained serious limitations. Spengler's morphological explanations may not possess the degree of quantitative certitude of scientific explanations, but they can serve a very useful function in the study of cultural history. Intuitive flair, empathetic understanding, imaginative insight, analogy, or homology — all these explanatory aids are absolutely essential in the field of cultural history. Without them we could not understand a single play by Shakespeare, a single great picture by Rembrandt, or a single symphony by Beethoven. The scientific idéologue may sneer at these "heuristic" devices, but what is he going to put in their place? How is he going to explain the conflict between Othello and Iago; Bach's *Kunst der Fuge*; Bernini's Ecstasy of St. Theresa; or the motives of a complex historical personality? These cultural creations, as Spengler pointed out many times, are products of the imagination rather than the understanding and they must therefore be explained by the powers of the aesthetic faculty in man. To "explain" great works of art or literature scientifically — that is through the rational faculty of the understanding — is a futile enterprise because science apprehends the world through "facts," "laws," "true or false propositions," and "causal relationships." Science is a mode of inquiry that seeks to explain natural occurrences impartially and objectively. The human sciences (art, literature, history, music, religion), on the other hand, should adopt a different mode of inquiry because they picture a different world — a world of human joys, dilemmas, metaphysical questings, and tragedies.

The humanistic complex of meaning, as Albert William Levi has put it recently, revolves around such concepts as "appearance and reality, "illusion," "destiny," "fate," "tragedy," and "peace."[7] The chief aim of the humanities is not objective representation of reality, but imaginative reconstruction of men's moral, religious, and artistic questings. As Spengler and like-minded thinkers have repeated time and again, the language of the humanities is emotive, imaginative, and purposive, whereas the language of science is factual, objective, causal, and descriptive. The methods of the natural sciences cannot answer the questions posed by the humanities and vice versa. Let a scientist explain man's spiritual questings scientifically, Spengler observed, and he will spawn nothing but distortions and superficialities.

Spengler's contribution, then, lay in accentuating the differences between the natural and the human sciences and to raise the status of the latter to that of the former. His contribution to history was particularly noteworthy because it amounted to a declaration of independence and a corresponding call to the construction of a new science. I believe that Spengler's contribution to the study of history is a new point of departure, possibly analogous to that stage in the history of science represented by Copernicus. A century and a half separated Copernicus from Newton, a long period full of detours, false turns, and conservative reactions. Since the physical sciences have never progressed in a straight linear path, there is no reason to assume that the science of history will do so either. But let us make no mistakes, history *is* a science (*Wissenschaft*) which is trying, however slowly and conservatively, to develop its own method of discovery and its own rules of evidence. What the nature of that historical paradigm will be like and how it will resemble paradigms in the natural sciences, we do not know. One thing, however, is certain: Oswald Spengler will have had a large role in its creation.

CHAPTER I

INTRODUCTION: HISTORY AS A GRAND-DESIGN

NOTES

[1] On the various schools of historical thinking, see Patrick Gardiner (ed.), *Theories of History* (Glencoe, Illinois: 1959); Hans Meyerhoff (ed.), *The Philosphy of History in Our Times* (New York: 1959); Frank E. Manuel, *Shapes of Philosophical History* (Stanford: 1965); H. Stuart Hughes, *History as Art and as Science* (New York: 1965); and John Edward Sullivan, *Prophets of the West* (New York: 1970).

[2] This position is best represented by Karl Popper in his *The Poverty of Historicism* (New York: Harpers Torchbooks, 1964).

[3] The view that history has its own unique methods of explanation has been generally associated with the "Historical Idealists" such as B. Croce, Wilhelm Dilthey, and R. G. Collingwood. For an unbiased account of this school (which is hard to come by in the Anglo-American community), see John Edward Sullivan, *Prophets of the West,* Part Two.

[4] R. G. Collingwood, *The Idea of History* (New York: 1956), p. 213.

[5] *Ibid.*, p. 214.

[6] *Ibid.*, p. 215.

[7] Carl Hempel, "The Function of General Laws in History," in Patrick Gardiner (ed.), *Theories of History*, pp. 352-353.

[8] *Ibid.* p. 353.

[9] This issue is best summarized by John Edward Sullivan, *Prophets of the West*, Part Two.

[10] Leslie White, "The Concept of Culture," *American*

Anthropologist, LXI (April, 1959), pp. 241-242.

[11] Carl Hempel has argued this position at length in his "the Function of General Laws in History."

[12] H. R. Trevor-Roper, *Men and Events* (New York: Harper and Row, 1957), pp. 285-286.

[13] See, John Edward Sullivan, *Prophets of the West*, Part Two.

[14] Marx-Engels, *Selected Works*, Vol II (Moscow: Foreign Languages Publishing House, 1962), p. 442.

[15] Karl Marx, *The Poverty of Philosophy* (New York: International Publishers, 1963), p. 109.

[16] Marx, *Capital* (New York, Modern Library, n.d.), Preface, p. 15.

[17] H. A. L. Fisher, *A History of Europe* (London: Edward Arnold & Co., 1936), Preface.

[18] Philip Bagby, *Culture and History* (Berkeley: University of California Press, 1959), p. 54.

[19] Collingwood, *The Idea of History*, p. 49.

[20] Sullivan, *Prophets of the West*, p. 21.

[21] The best treatment of the metaphor of growth (the cycle) is by Robert Nisbet, *Social Change and History* (New York: Oxford University Press, 1969).

[22] Pitrim Sorokin quoted by Pieter Geyl, *Debates with Historians* (New York: Meridian Books, 1958), p. 153.

[23] Andrew Hacker, *The End of the American Era* (New York: Atheneum, 1971), p. 226.

[24] *Ibid.*, p. 229.

[25] Arnold Toynbee, *A Study of History*, abridged by D. C. Somervell, Vol I (New York: Oxford University Press, 1961), p. 246.

[26] Egon Friedell, *A Cultural History of the Modern Age*, trans. Charles Francis Atkinson, Vol. I (New York: Alfred A. Knopf, 1931), p. 57.

[27] F. L. Polak, *The Image of the Future*, Vol. II (New York: Oceana Publications, 1961), p. 342.

[28] *Ibid.*, p. 343.

[29] I owe this insight to Jose Ortega y Gasset, *The Revolt of the Masses* (New York: Norton, 1957), p. 166.

CHAPTER II

THE MAN BEHIND THE THEORY

NOTES

[1] Anton M. Koktanek, *Oswald Spengler in seiner Zeit* (München: Beck, 1968), pp. 4-5. In reconstructing Spengler's life and character, I have greatly benefited from Koktanek's study, which is the only reliable biography of Oswald Spengler.

[2] *Ibid.*, p. 12.

[3] *Ibid.*, p. 14.

[4] *Ibid.*, p. 87.

[5] *Ibid.*

[6] *Ibid.*, p. 88.

[7] *Ibid.*, pp. 102-103.

[8] *Ibid.*,p. 15.

[9] *Ibid.*, p. 26.

[10] *Ibid.*

[11] *Ibid.*, p. 19.

[12] A. L. Kroeber, *Style and Civilization* (Berkeley: University of California Press, 1963), p. 84.

[13] Koktanek, *Oswald Spengler,* p. 25.

[14] *Ibid.*, p. 14.

[15] *Ibid.*, p. 127.

[16] *Ibid.*, p. 108.

[17] "The Victor" bristles with images of "twitching bodies;" "hissing grenades;" "bloody boots and wildly flailing limbs;" "roaring canons;" and "glittering bayonets." (Spengler, *Reden und Aufsätze*), pp. 48-53.

[18] Heinrich von Treitschke, *Politics*, trans. Blanche Dugdale and Torben de Bille, Vol. II (London: Constable, 1916), p. 599. Elsewhere (I, 68) Treitschke says that "the demand for eternal peace is purely reactionary," and that "all movement and all growth would disappear with war, and that only the exhausted, spiritless, degenerate periods of history have toyed with the idea."

[19] Maurice Barres, *Les Traits Éternels de la France* (Paris: Emile-Paul Frères, 1916), p. 21 and 43.

[20] Quoted by Barbara Tuchman, *The Proud Tower, A Portrait of the World before the War* (New York: Macmillan, 1966), p. 250.

[21] Jacques Barzun, *Darwin, Marx, Wagner, Critique of a Heritage* (New York: Anchor, 1958), p. 92.

[22] Spengler, *Der Mensch und die Technik, Beitrag zu einer Philosophie des Lebens* (München: Beck, 1931), p. 34.

[23] Quoted by Koktanek, *Oswald Spengler*, p. 423.

[24] "The history of the Germans," writes A. J. P. Taylor, "is a history of extremes. It contains everything except moderation, and in the course of a thousand years the Germans have experienced everything except normality ... 'German' has meant at one moment a being so sentimental, so trusting, so pious, as to be too good for this world; and at another a being so brutal, so unprincipled, so degraded, as to be not fit to live. Both descriptions are true: both types of German have existed not only at the same epoch, but in the same person." [(A. J. P. Taylor, *The Course of German History* (New York: Capricon Books, 1962), p. 13].

[25] Friedrich Meinecke, *The German Catastrophe*, trans. Sidney

Fay (Boston: Beacon Press, 1963), p. 10.

[26] Hans Kohn has written extensively and perceptively on the surrender of German liberalism to Bismarckian *Realpolitik*. See, especially, his *The Mind of Germany* (New York: Harpers Torchbooks, 1960).

[27] Quoted by Koktanek, *Oswald Spengler*, p. 1.

[28] August Albers, "Oswald Spengler," *Preussische Jahrbücher*, CLXXXXII, (1923), p. 132.

[29] In the *Decline of the West* (I, 46), Spengler observes that it was in 1911 that the major ideas of his work took shape. In his "Pessimismus?" he writes that his philosophy was greatly influenced by the Agadir (the Moroccan) crisis. In any case, the year 1911, which saw the Agadir crisis, seems to have been the germinal year for Spengler's ideas.

[30] On this issue, see Ernst Troeltsch, "Die Ideen von 1914," in Hans Baron (ed.), *Deutscher Geist und Westeuropa* (Tübingen: 1925); Rudolf Kjellen, *Die Ideen von 1914, Eine Weltgeschichtliche Perspektive* (Leipzig: 1915); Werner Sombart *Handler und Helden* (München: 1915); and Klaus Schwabe, *Die deutschen Professoren und die politischen Grundfragen des ersten Weltkrieges,* Diss. (Freiburg: 1958).

[31] Koktanek, *Oswald Spengler,* p. 212.

[32] H. Stuart Hughes, *Oswald Spengler, A Critical Estimate* (New York: Charles Scribner's Sons, 1962), p. 89.

[33] The best summary of the Spengler controversy is by Manfred Schroter, *Der Streit um Spengler: Kritik seiner Kritiker* (München: 1922).

[34] *Ibid.*

[35] *Ibid.*, pp. 44-45.

[36] Anton M. Koktanek (ed.), *Spengler Briefe: 1913-1936* (München: Beck, 1963), p. 180.

[37] Spengler, *Reden und Aufsätze* (München: Beck, 1937), p. 75.

[38] *Ibid.*, p. 64.

[39] See, Eduard Meyer, *Spenglers Untergang des Abendlandes* (Berlin: Crusius, 1925).

242

[40] H. Stuart Hughes, *Oswald Spengler*, p. 94.

[41] *Ibid.*, pp. 94-95.

[42] *Ibid.*, p. 95.

[43] R. G. Collingwood, "Oswald Spengler and the Theory of Historical Cycles," *Antiquity*, Vol. I, No. 3 (December, 1927), p. 313.

[44] Koktanek, *Oswald Spengler*, p. 299.

[45] *Ibid.*, p. 212.

[46] Spengler, *Briefe*, p. 159.

[47] Klemens von Klemperer, *Germany's New Conservatism* (Princeton, New Jersey: Princeton University Press, 1957), p. 175.

[48] Anton M. Koktanek (ed.), *Spengler-Studien, Festgabe für Manfred Schröter zum 85. Geburtstag* (München: Beck, 1965), especially the article by Bodo Herzog "Die Freundschaft zwischen Oswald Spengler und Paul Reusch," pp. 77-97.

[49] Koktanek, *Oswald Spengler*, p. 366.

[50] Spengler, *Frühzeit der Weltgeschichte, Fragmente aus dem Nachlass* (München: Beck, 1966), p. 34.

[51] The notes of Spengler's projected cultural study have been published recently in two books: *Urfragen* (1965) and *Frühzeit der Weltgeschichte* (1966).

[52] Koktanek, *Oswald Spengler*, p. 366.

[53] See, Leo Frobenius, *Peideuma: Umrisse einer Kultur-und Seelenlehre* (Munchen: Beck, 1921).

[54] Spengler, *Mensch und Technik*, p. 89.

[55] H. Stuart Hughes, *Oswald Spengler*, p. 99.

[56] August Albers, *Oswald Spengler*, p. 129.

[57] Koktanek, *Oswald Spengler*, p. 423.

[58] Koktanek (ed.), *Spengler-Studien*, p. 17.

[59] Koktanek, *Oswald Spengler*, p. 190.

[60] *Ibid.*, p. 2.

[61] *Ibid.*, p. 15.

[62] *Ibid.*, p. 422.

[63] Alan Bullock, *Hitler: A Study in Tyranny* (New York: Harper and Row, 1962), p. 218.

[64] Koktanek, *Oswald Spengler*, p. 427.

[65] *Ibid.*, p. 441.

[66] See, *Decline of the West*, Vol. II, Chap. V (People, Races, Tongues).

[67] Spengler, *Frühzeit der Weltgeschichte*, p. 61.

[68] Spengler, *Jahre der Entscheidung* (München: Beck, 1933), p. 3.

[69] Spengler, *Briefe*, p. 749.

[70] *Ibid.*, p. 710.

[71] *Ibid.*, p. 699.

[72] Albert Speer, *Inside the Third Reich*, trans. Richard and Clara Winston (New York: The Macmillan Company, 1970), p. 12.

[73] *Ibid.*, p. 16.

[74] Koktanek, *Oswald Spengler*, p. 457.

CHAPTER III

FLAME: THE METAPHYSICS OF THE LIFE CYCLE

NOTES

[1] Spengler, *Reden und Aufsätze* (München: Beck, 1937), pp. 28-29.

[2] Robert A. Nisbet, *Social Change and History, Aspects of the Western Theory of Development* (New York: Oxford University Press, 1970).

[3] *Ibid.*, p, 20.

[4] *The Dialogues of Plato*, trans. B. Jowett, II (New York: Random House, 1937), pp. 296-302. See also Vol. I., pp. 803-805.

244

[5] Quoted by Nisbet, *Social Change and History,* p. 15.

[6] Aristotle, *Politics,* Bk. III, Chap. 15.

[7] Lucius Annaeus Florus, *The Epitome of Roman History* (Cambridge, Massachussetts: Loeb Classical Library, 1957).

[8] Hesoid, *The Poems and Fragments,* A. W. Mair (ed.), (Oxford: Clarendon Press, 1908), pp. 5-8.

[9] Nisbet, *Social Change and History,* p. 48.

[10] Philip Wheelwright (ed.), *The Presocratics* (New York: The Odyssey Press, Inc., 1966), p. 71.

[11] W. K. C. Guthrie, *A History of Greek Philosophy,* I (Cambridge, England: Cambridge University Press, 1967), pp. 419-424.

[12] *Ibid.,* I, p. 426.

[13] *Ibid.,* I, p. 428.

[14] Philip Wheelwright, *Heraclitus* (Princeton, New Jersey: Princton University Press, 1959), p. 32.

[15] Wheelwright, *The Presocratics,* p. 71.

[16] W. C. K. Guthrie, *History of Greek Philosophy,* I, p. 452.

[17] Wheelwright, *The Presocratics,* p. 71.

[18] *Ibid.*

[19] See, Ferdinand Lassalle, *Die Philosophie Herakleitos des Dunklen von Ephesus,* 2 Vols. (Berlin, 1858). For a more comprehensive treatment of Dialectics in ancient thought: Livio Sichirollo, *Dialektik von Homer bis Aristoteles* (Hildesheim: Olms Verlag, 1966).

[20] Spengler, *Reden und Aufsätze,* p. 2

[21] *Ibid.,* p. 28.

[22] *Ibid.,* p. 11.

[23] Wheelwright, *The Presocratics,* p. 76.

[24] Spengler, *Reden und Aufsätze,* p. 32.

[25] For the idea of eternal recurrence: Mircea Eliade, *The Myth of the Eternal Return,* trans. Willard R. Trask (London: Routledge & Kegan Paul, 1955); Karl Löwith, *Meaning in History* (Chicago: University of Chicago Press,

1949); and the same author's *Nietzsches Philosophie der ewigen Wiederkehr des Gleichen* (Stuttgart: Kohlhammer, 1956).

[26] Eliade, *Myth of the Eternal Return*, p. 143.

[27] For the German cultural revival of the eighteenth century: W. H. Bruford, *Germany in the Eighteenth Century, the Social Background of the Literary Revival* (Cambridge: 1965); Friedrich Meinecke, *Die Entstehung des Historismus*, 2d ed. (München: 1959); and Wilhelm Dilthey, *Gesammelte Schriften*, Vol. III (Stuttgart: 1959).

[28] Voltaire, *The Age of Louis XIV*, trans. Martyn P. Pollock (London: Dent, 1961), p. 1.

[29] This historical bias particularly distorted the philosophes' conception of the Middle Ages, a period which they viewed as a time of horrible superstition and ignorance.

[30] R. G. Collingwood, *The Idea of History* (New York: Oxford University Press, 1956), p. 77.

[31] For the rise of the new historical consciousness (*Historismus*) in Germany: Friedrich Meinecke, *Die Entstehung des Historismus* (1959); and George G. Iggers, *The German Conception of History* (Middletown, Connecticut: Wesleyan University Press, 1968).

[32] Novalis quoted by Paul Kluckhohn, *Das Ideengut der Deutschen Romantik* (Tübingen: Max Niemeyer, 1966), p. 43.

[33] This development is discussed by R. G. Collingwood in his *Idea of History*. For the German view, consult Ernst Troeltsch, *Der Historismus und seine Probleme* (Tübingen: 1922).

[34] Oswald Spengler, *The Decline of the West*, trans. Charles Francis Atkinson, I (New York: Alfred A. Knopf, 1926), p. 49.

[35] There is a fine study of Goethe's thought by Karl Vietor, *Goethe, the Thinker* (Cambridge, Massachussetts: Harvard

University Press, 1950).

[36] The best discussion of Goethe's philosophy of history is by Friedrich Meinecke, *Die Entstehung des Historismus*, Chap. X.

[37] Johann Wolfgang von Goethe, *Faust II*, final stanza.

[38] Goethe, *Dichtung und Wahrheit*, Bk. 13.

[39] Goethe, *Die Metamorphose der Pflanzen* (1790).

[40] See, Hans Joachim Schoeps, *Vorläufer Spenglers, Studien zum Geschichtspessimismus im 19. Jahrhundert* (Leiden: E. J. Brill, 1955).

[41] The most reliable books in English on Friedrich Nietzsche are: Walter Kaufmann, *Nietzsche, Philosopher, Psychologist, Antichrist*, 3d ed., (New York: Vintage Books, 1968); and R. J. Hollingdale, *Nietzsche, The Man and his Philosophy* (Baton Rouge, Louisiana: Louisiana University Press, 1965).

[42] The quotation comes from the *Gay Science*, No. 62. For a slightly different translation: *The Gay Science*, trans. Walter Kaufmann (New York: Vintage Books, 1974), p. 67.

[43] Friedrich Nietzsche, *On the Use and Abuse of History*, No. 9.

[44] An excellent study of Nietzsche's eternal return is Joan Stambaugh, *Nietzsche's Thought of Eternal Return* (Baltimore: Johns Hopkins University Press, 1972).

[45] Nietzsche quoted by R. J. Hollingdale, *Nietzsche, The Man and his Philsophy*, pp. 177-178. The passage is from the *Gay Science*, No. 341.

[46] Walter Kaufmann (ed.), *The Portable Nietzsche Reader* (New York: The Viking Press, 1968), p. 332.

[47] Nietzsche quoted by Joan Stambaugh, *Nietzsche's Thought of Eternal Return*, p. 45.

[48] *Ibid.*

[49] Hollingdale discusses this problem in his *Nietzsche, The*

Man and his Philosophy, p. 312.

[50] Nietzsche, The Antichrist, No. 4.

[51] Nietzsche, The Will to Power, No. 339.

[52] See, Walter Kaufmann, Nietzsche, Philosopher, Psychologist, Antichrist, p. 154.

[53] Nietzsche, Untimely Meditations, I, p. 1.

[54] Spengler, Decline, II, p. 3.

[55] Ibid., II, p. 5.

[56] Ibid.

[57] Spengler, Urfragen, Fragmente aus dem Nachlass (München: Beck, 1965), p. 9.

[58] Spengler, Decline, II, p. 9.

[59] Ibid., II, p. 10.

[60] Ibid., II, p. 11.

[61] Ibid., II, p. 12.

[62] Ibid., II, p. 15.

[63] Ibid., II, p. 17.

[64] Ibid.

[65] Goethe quoted by Spengler in the Decline, I, p. 49.

[66] Collingwood discusses this process of re-thinking a past thought in his Idea of History, pp. 215 ff.

[67] Spengler, Decline, I, p. 165.

[68] Ibid., I, p. 168.

[69] Ibid.

[70] Spengler, Reden und Aufsätze, p. 66.

[71] Spengler, Decline, I, p. 120.

[72] Ibid., I, p. 122.

[73] Ibid., I, p. 129.

[74] Ibid., I, p. 118.

[75] Ibid., I, p. 117.

[76] Ibid., I, p. 95.

[77] This is especially apparent in Spengler's posthumous papers entitled Urfragen. For Freud's cultural pessimism: Civilization and Its Discontents (1930).

[78] Spengler, *Decline*, I, p. 54.

[79] *Ibid.*

[80] Spengler, *Urfragen*, p. 29.

[81] Spengler, *Decline*, p. 79.

[82] Spengler, *Urfragen*, p. 46.

[83] *Ibid.*, p. 39.

[84] *Ibid.*, p. 1.

[85] *Ibid.*, p. 221.

[86] Spengler, *Der Mensch und die Technik* (München: Beck, 1931), p. 26.

[87] Spengler, *Urfragen*, p. 188.

[88] As Spengler put it, "the predatory animal man is opposed to culture; he has caught himself in his own trap, the clever hunter." (*Frühzeit der Weltgeschichte*, p. 62). Elsewhere, he remarked that "culture encapsulates man in a brass armor." (*Ibid.*, p. 56).

[89] Spengler, *Frühzeit der Weltgeschichte, Fragmente aus dem Nachlass* (München: Beck, 1966), p. 34.

[90] Spengler, *Urfragen*, p. 343.

CHAPTER IV

AMOEBA AND MONAD

NOTES

[1] Spengler, *Decline,* I, pp. 18-19.

[2] *Ibid.*, I, p. 17.

[3] *Ibid.*, I, p. 22.

[4] *Ibid.*, I, p. 21; also, I, p. 44.

[5] *Ibid.*, I, pp. 97 ff.

[6] *Ibid.*, I, p. 104.

[7] *Ibid.*, I, p. 107.

[8] *Ibid.*, I, p. 106.

[9] *Ibid.*, I, p. 31.

[10] *Ibid.*

[11] *Ibid.*, I, p. 106.

[12] *Ibid.*, I, p. 353.

[13] *Ibid.*, I, p. 21.

[14] Spengler, *Frühzeit der Weltgeschichte*, p. 27.

[15] *Ibid.*, p. 12.

[16] Spengler, *Decline*, II, p. 170.

[17] Spengler's conception of culture as both spiritual and material is clearly brought out in the following statement: "I distinguish the *idea* of a Culture, which is the sum total of its inner possibilities, from its sensible phenomenon or appearance upon the canvas of history as a fulfilled actuality. It is the relation of the soul to the living body, to its expression in the light-world perceptible to our eyes." (*Decline,* I, p. 104).

[18] Spengler, *Mensch und Technik*, p. v.

[19] The major guardian of Spengler's posthumous writings has been his niece Dr. Hildegard Kornhardt (1910-1959).

[20] Spengler, *Decline*, II, p. 33.

[21] *Ibid.*, I, p. 33.

[22] Spengler, *Mensch und Technik*, pp. 27-28.

[23] *Ibid.*, p. 30.

[24] Spengler, *Frühzeit der Weltgeschichte*, p. 29; also p. 45.

[25] Spengler, *Mensch und Technik*, pp. 38-39.

[26] Spengler, *Frühzeit der Weltgeschichte*, p. 210.

[27] *Ibid.*, pp. 225-226.

[28] Spengler, *Reden und Aufsatze*, p. 152.

[29] Spengler, *Decline*, II, p. 36.

[30] *Ibid.*, I, p. 106.

[31] *Ibid.*, I, p. 21.

[32] *Ibid.*, II, p. 233.

[33] *Ibid.*, I, p. 183.

250

[34] *Ibid.*

[35] *Ibid.*

[36] *Ibid.*, I, p. 83.

[37] For a thoughtful criticism of Spengler's cultural monism, see R. G. Collingwood "Oswald Spengler and the Theory of Historical Cycles," *Antiquity*, I, No. 3 (December, 1927), pp. 311-325.

[38] Spengler, *Decline*, I, p. 202.

[39] *Ibid.*, I, p. 175.

[40] *Ibid.*, I, p. 231.

[41] *Ibid.*, Preface to the revised edition.

[42] *Ibid.* I, p. 189.

[43] Spengler, *Frühzeit der Weltgeschichte*, p. 270.

[44] Spengler, *Decline*, I, p. 184.

[45] *Ibid.*, II, p. 287.

[46] Spengler, *Frühzeit der Weltgeschichte,* p. 464.

[47] Spengler, *Decline*, I, pp. 172-174.

[48] *Ibid.*, I, p. 184.

[49] *Ibid.*, I, p. 183.

[50] *Ibid.*, II, p. 237.

[51] *Ibid.*,I, p. 200.

[52] *Ibid.*, I, p. 174.

[53] *Ibid.*, II, p. 287.

[54] *Ibid.*, I, p. 190.

[55] *Ibid.*, I, p. 189.

[56] *Ibid.*, I. p. 145.

[57] Spengler developed this theme at much greater length in his *Prussianism and Socialism* (1920).

[58] Spengler, *Decline*, II, p. 96.

[59] *Ibid.*

[60] *Ibid.*, I, p. 358.

[61] *Ibid.*, I, p. 226.

[62] *Ibid.*, I, p. 239.

[63] *Ibid.*, I, p. 226.

[64] Spengler, *Preussentum und Sozialismus,* p. 48.

[65] Spengler, *Decline*, I, p. 353.

[66] *Ibid.*, II, p. 330.

[67] See, *Decline*, I, pp. 420-424.

[68] Spengler, *Jahre der Entscheidung*, pp. 28-29.

[69] Spengler, *Decline*, II, p. 99.

[70] *Ibid.*, II, p. 103.

[71] *Ibid.*, II, p. 310.

[72] *Ibid.*, I, p. 289.

[73] *Ibid.*, I, p. 294.

[74] *Ibid.*, I, p. 293.

[75] Spengler, *Reden und Aufsätze*, p. 63.

[76] Spengler, *Decline*, II, p. 435.

[77] *Ibid.*

[78] Spengler tried to illustrate the morphological nature of events in his cultural charts, appended to the first volume of the *Decline*.

CHAPTER V
MORPHOLOGY AND PHYSIOGNOMIC TACT

NOTES

[1] For a good selection of Leibniz's ideas in English translation, see Philip P. Wiener (ed.), *Leibniz Selections* (New York: Scribner, 1951). The best commentaries of Leibniz's philosophy are by Louis Couturat, *La Logigue de Leibniz* (Paris: 1901); R. W. Meyer, *Leibniz and the Seventeenth Century Revolution* (Cambridge, England, 1952); and Bertrand Russell, *A Critical Exposition of the Philosophy of Leibniz* (London: 1900).

[2] The concept of entelechy was first systematically developed by Aristotle, who used the term in order to describe a

condition in which a potentiality has become an actuality.

[3] This issue is discussed at length by Bertrand Russell in his *Critical Exposition of the Philosophy of Leibniz.*

[4] Although Spengler often exaggerated the uniqueness of a culture, his keen eye for the unique enabled him to make some profound observations about the differences in cultural styles of expression. For his discussion of the differences in mathematics in the various cultures, see the *Decline*, I, Chap. 2; for ethics, *Decline*, I, p. 315, pp. 345-347; and for law, *Decline* II, pp. 78 ff.

[5] Spengler's monodological view of culture has been most persistently attacked by anthropologists. For a typical objection, see A. L. Kroeber, *Style and Civilization* (Berkeley: 1963), pp. 83-107; and the same author's *Configurations of Culture Growth* (Berkeley: 1944).

[6] Spengler, *Decline*, II, pp. 189 ff.

[7] *Ibid.*, II, p. 189.

[8] *Ibid.*, II, pp. 191-192.

[9] *Ibid.*, II, p. 192.

[10] See, A. L. Kroeber, *Style and Civilization;* and Philip Bagby, *Culture and History* (Berkeley, 1958).

[11] Spengler, *Decline*, II, p. 59.

[12] Spengler, *Frühzeit der Weltgeschichte,* p. 10.

[13] A fine discussion of Goethe's scientific theories may be found in Karl Vietor, *Goethe, the Thinker* (Cambridge, Massachusetts: Harvard University Press, 1950). For a more detailed treatment, see Adolf Meyer-Abich, *Die Vollendung der Morphologie Goethes durch Alexander von Humboldt* (Gottingen: Vandenhoeck, 1970).

[14] See, Philip C. Ritterbush, "Organic Form: Aesthetics and objectivity in the Study of Form in the Life Sciences," in G. S. Rousseau (ed.), *Organic Form* (London: Routledge and Kegan Paul, 1972), pp. 37-38.

[15] *Ibid.*, pp. 41-42.

[16] On this issue of transcendental biology, the reader should

consult Ludwig von Bertalanffy, *Modern Theories of Development: An Introduction to Theoretical Biology* (New York: Harpers Torchbooks, 1962); and Edmund W. Sinott's readable *Cell and Psyche* (New York: Harpers Torchbooks, 1961).

[17] Philip C. Ritterbush, *Organic Form,* p. 42.

[18] Spengler, *Decline,* I. p. 4.

[19] *Ibid.,* I, p. 104.

[20] *Ibid.*

[21] The most recent developments in the study of homology are treated by Adolf Remane, *Die Grundlagen des natürlichen Systems der vergleichenden Anatomie und der Phylogenetik* (Leipzig: Geest und Portig, 1956).

[22] *Ibid.,* p. 60.

[23] Spengler, *Decline,* I, p. 111.

[24] *Ibid.*

[25] *Ibid.*

[26] *Ibid.*

[27] Remane, *Grundlagen des natürlichen Systems,* p. 30.

[28] Spengler, *Decline,* I, p. 112.

[29] *Ibid.*

[30] *Ibid.,* I, p. 113.

[31] *Ibid.* I, p. 95.

[32] *Ibid.* I, p. 3.

[33] *Ibid.* I, p. 94.

[34] *Ibid.,* I, p. 155.

[35] Carl Hempel, "The Function of General Laws in History," in Patrick Gardiner (ed.), *Theories of History* (Glencoe, Illinois: The Free Press, 1959), pp. 348-349.

[36] Sidney Hook, "A Pragmatic Critique of the Historico-Genetic Method," in *Essays in Honor of John Dewey on the Occasion of His Seventieth Birthday* (New York, 1929), p. 156.

[37] In his posthumously published fragments (*Frühzeit der Weltgeschichte,* p. 38), Spengler refers to the search for causes in history as "practicing physics in the wrong place."

254

[38] Spengler, *Decline*, I, p. 96.

[39] *Ibid.* I, pp. 5-8.

[40] As Alfred Baemler rightly observed, "the history of a nation or a state cannot be turned into a biography because the existence of these living entities cannot be severed from the *relations* to other nations or states. The biographer deals with a substantial unity, whereas the historian always treats relations." (Alfred Baemler, "Kulturmorphologie und Philosophie," in Anton M. Koktanek (ed.), *Spengler-Studien*, p. 101).

[41] Spengler, *Decline*, I, p. 104.

[42] *Ibid.*, I, p. 299.

[43] *Ibid.* II, pp. 16-17.

[44] *Ibid.* I, p. 7.

[45] Zevedei Barbu, *Problems of Historical Psychology* (New York: Grove Press, Inc., 1960), pp. 19-42.

[46] Tieck quoted in *Deutsche National Literatur*, Vol. CXLV, p. 300.

[47] Spengler, *Decline*, I, p. 224.

[48] *Ibid.* I, p. 202.

[49] *Ibid.*, I, pp. 221 ff.

[50] *Ibid.*, I, p. 260.

[51] *Ibid.*, I, pp. 260 ff.

[52] *Ibid.*, I, pp. 275-276.

[53] *Ibid.*, I, pp. 273-281.

[54] *Ibid.*, I, p. 197.

[55] *Ibid.*, I, pp. 348-351.

[56] *Ibid.* I, p. 101.

[57] Spengler, *Frühzeit der Weltgeschichte*, pp. 19-20.

[58] *Ibid.*, p. 31.

CHAPTER VI

THE VOICE OF CASSANDRA

NOTES

[1] Koktanek, *Oswald Spengler*, pp. 314-315.

[2] Koktanek (ed.), *Oswald Spengler: Briefe*, p. 104.

[3] The flood of criticism directed against Spengler's *Decline of the West* is ably summarized by Manfred Schröter in his *Metaphysik des Untergangs*.

[4] The millennial impulse in modern history owes its inspiration primarily to science. The following books shed light on this optimistic strain in the western soul: Carl Becker, *The Heavenly City of the Eighteenth Century Philosophers* (1932); J. B. Bury, *The Idea of Progress* (1932); Frank Manuel, *The Prophets of Paris* (1962); Charles van Doren, *The Idea of Progress* (1967); and John Passmore, *The Perfectibility of Man* (1970).

[5] Spengler, *Reden und Aufsätze*, pp. 73-74.

[6] *Ibid.*, p. 79.

[7] Spengler admired those who believe deeply, but he also insisted that an inseparable gulf divided religion and politics. Religion deals with eternity, politics with the facts: "A statesman can be deeply religious, a pious man can die for his country — but they must, both, know on which side they are really standing." (*Decline*, II, p. 216).

[8] Spengler, *Decline*, II, p. 364.

[9] *Ibid.*, II, p. 367.

[10] *Ibid.*, II, p. 414.

[11] Spengler, *Politische Schriften*, pp. 14-15.

[12] Spengler, *Decline*, II, p. 393.

[13] *Ibid.* II, p. 430.

256

[14] *Ibid.* II, p. 447.

[15] Kemens von Klemperer, *Germany's New Conservatism*, p. 197.

[16] For the History of the Weimar Republic, see William Halperin, *Germany Tried Democracy* (1946); and Erich Eyck, *History of the Weimar Republic*, 2 Vols. (1962-1963).

[17] Koktanek, *Oswald Spengler*, pp. 276-277.

[18] *Ibid.*

[19] See, von Klemperer, *Germany's New Conservatism*, pp. 172 ff.

[20] *Ibid.*, p. 175.

[21] *Ibid.*, p. 50.

[22] *Ibid.*, pp. 51-52.

[23] These men styled themselves "Socialists of the Chair" *Kathedersozialisten*).

[24] Two excellent studies of Walther Rathenau are by Count H. Kessler, *Walther Rathenau* (1928); and by James Joll, *Intellectuals in Politics* (1960).

[25] Relatively little of substance has been written on Weimar culture. The best study is by Peter Gay, *Weimar Culture: The Outsider as Insider* (1968). A good study on popular culture in Berlin in the 1920's is Otto Friedrich, *Before the Deluge* (1972).

[26] Quoted by Gay, *Weimar Culture*, p. 75.

[27] *Ibid.*, p. 74.

[28] Spengler, *Jahre der Entscheidung*, p. 66.

[29] Spengler, *Politische Schriften*, p. 189.

[30] Spengler, *Decline*, II, p. 456.

[31] *Ibid.*, p. 200.

[32] In this sense, Peter Gay is not exaggerating when he refers to Spengler and other conservatives as "gravediggers" of the Republic (*Weimar Culture*, p. 48).

[33] Spengler, *Preussentum und Sozialismus*, p. 76.

[34] *Ibid.*, p. 46.

[35] *Ibid.*, p. 32 ff.

[36] *Ibid.*, p. 34.

[37] *Ibid.*, p. 76

[38] *Ibid.*, p. 48.

[39] Spengler, *Jahre der Entscheidung*, pp. 54-55.

[40] Spengler, *Preussentum und Sozialismus*, p. 48.

[41] Spengler, *Jahre der Entscheidung*, p. 89.

[42] Spengler, *Preussentum und Sozialismus*, pp. 98-99.

[43] Spengler, *Frühzeit der Weltgeschichte*, p. 61.

[44] Spengler, *Politische Schriften*, p. 145.

[45] Spengler, *Jahre der Entscheidung*, pp. 4-8.

[46] Spengler, *Mensch und Technik*, p. 89.

[47] Spengler, *Jahre der Entscheidung*, p. xii.

[48] *Ibid.*, pp. 58 ff.

[49] *Ibid.*, p. 151.

[50] *Ibid.*, p. 12.

[51] Spengler, *Decline*, II.

[52] Spengler, *Jahre der Entscheidung*, p. 48.

[53] *Ibid.*, pp. 51-52.

[54] *Ibid.*, p. 49.

[55] Spengler, *Reden und Aufsätze*, pp. 292-293.

[56] *Ibid.*, p. 292.

CHAPTER VII

CONCLUSION

NOTES

[1] Northrop Frye, "The Decline of the West by Oswald Spengler," *Daedalus* (Winter, 1974), p. 9.

258

[2] Hayden White, *Metahistory: The Historical Imagination in Nineteenth-Century Europe* (Baltimore: Johns Hopkins University Press, 1973), p. 13.

[3] *Ibid.*, p. 14.

[4] *Ibid.*, pp. 17-18.

[5] *Ibid.*, p. 20; also 429 ff.

[6] Northrop Frye, "The Decline of the West," pp. 5-6.

[7] Albert William Levi, *Literature, Philosophy and the Imagination* (Bloomington, Indiana: Indiana University Press, 1962), pp. 7-8.

BIBLIOGRAPHY

I

WORKS BY SPENGLER

Der Untergang des Abendlandes, Umrisse einer Morphologie der Weltgeschichte; Vol. I: *Gestalt und Wirklichkeit.* Wien: Braumüller, 1918; all subsequent editions, München: C. H. Beck, 1923 ff; Vol. II: *Welthistorische Perspektiven.* München: Beck, 1922.

Preussentum und Sozialismus. München: Beck, 1919.

Der Mensch und die Technik, Beitrag zu einer Philosophie des Lebens. München, Beck, 1931.

Politische Schriften. München: Beck, 1932.

Jahre der Entscheidung, Deutschland und die Weltgeschichtliche Entwicklung. München: Beck, 1933.

Reden und Aufsätze. Edited by Hildegard Kornhardt. München: Beck, 1937.

Gedanken. Edited by Hildegard Kornhardt. München: Beck, 1941.

Briefe 1913-1936. Edited by Anton M. Koktanek. München: Beck, 1963.

Urfragen, Fragmente aus dem Nachlass. Edited by Anton M. Koktanek. München: Beck, 1965.

Frühzeit der Weltgeschichte, Fragmente aus dem Nachlass. München: Beck, 1966.

260

II

WORKS BY SPENGLER IN ENGLISH TRANSLATION

The Decline of the West. 2 Vols. trans. Charles Francis Atkinson. New York: Alfred A. Knopf, 1926.
The Decline of the West. Abridged edition by Helmut Werner. New York: Alfred A. Knopf, 1961.
Man and Technics, A Contribution to a Philosophy of Life. Translated by Charles Francis Atkinson. New York: Alfred A. Knopf, 1932.
The Hour of Decision. Translated by Charles Francis Atkinson. New York: Alfred A. Knopf, 1934.
Selected Essays. Translated with an introduction by Donald O. White. Chicago: Henry Regnery Company, 1967.
Aphorisms. Chicago: Henry Regnery Company, 1967.
Letters of Oswald Spengler, 1913-1936. Edited by Arthur Helps. New York: Alfred A. Knopf, 1966.

III

COMMENTARIES ON SPENGLER

Albers, August. "Oswald Spengler." *Preussische Jahrbücher,* CLXXXII, 1923, pp. 129-137.
Collingwood, R. G. "Oswald Spengler and the Theory of Historical Cycles." *Antiquity*, I, No. 3, December, 1927, pp. 311-325.
Dakin, Edwin F. *Today and Destiny: Vital Excerpts from the Decline of the West of Oswald Spengler.* New York: Alfred A. Knopf, 1940.

Fauconnet, Andre. *Un Philosophe Allemand Contemporain, Oswald Spengler.* Paris: Librairie Felix Alcan, 1925.

Frye, Northrop. "The Decline of the West by Oswald Spengler." *Daedalus,* Winter, 1974, pp. 1-13.

Gauhe, Eberhard. *Spengler und die Romantik.* Berlin: Junker und Dunnhaupt, 1937.

Hughes, H. Stuart. *Oswald Spengler, A Critical Estimate.* New York: Charles Scribner's Sons, 1962.

Koktanek, Anton M. *Oswald Spengler in seiner Zeit.* München: C. H. Beck, 1968.

Logos, Internationale Zeitschrift fur Philosophie der Kultur. Vol IX, 1920-1921, pp. 133-295.

Mazlish, Bruce. "Spengler," in *The Riddle of History, the Great Speculators from Vico to Freud.* New York: Harper & Row, 1966.

Meyer, Eduard. *Spenglers Untergang des Abendlandes.* Berlin: Curtius, 1925.

Schröter, Manfred. *Der Streit um Spengler, Kritik seiner Kritiker.* München, 1922.

——. *Metaphysik des Untergangs, Eine Kultur-kritische Studie über Oswald Spengler.* München: R. Oldenbourg, 1949.

Spengler-Studien, Festgabe für Manfred Schröter zum 85. Geburtstag. München: C. H. Beck, 1965.

Stier, H. E. "Oswald Spengler, Erinnerungen und Betrachtungen," in *Die Welt als Geschichte.* Stuttgart, 1937.

Stutz, Ernst. *Oswald Spengler als Politischer Denker.* Bern: Franke Verlag, 1958.

Vogt, Joseph. *Wege zum historischem Universum, Von Ranke bis Toynbee.* Stuttgart: Kohlhammer, 1961.

IV

USEFUL COLLATERAL READING

Adams, Brooks. *The Law of Civilization and Decay*. 2nd ed. New York, 1951.

Adams, Henry. *The Degradation of the Democratic Dogma*. New York, 1919.

Bagby, Philip. *Culture and History*. Berkeley: University of California Press, 1963.

Becker, Carl. *The Heavenly City of the Eighteenth Century Philosophers*. New Haven, Connecticut: Yale University Press, 1932.

Bury, J. B. *The Idea of Progress*. New York, 1932.

Collingwood, R. G. *The Idea of History*. New York: Oxford University Press, 1956.

Doren, Charles van. *The Idea of Progress*. New York: Praeger, 1967.

Dray, William H. *Philosphy of History*. Englewood Cliffs, New Jersey: Prentice-Hall, Inc., 1964.

Fleischer, Manfred P. (ed.). *The Decline of the West?* New York: Holt, Rinehart and Winston, Inc., 1970.

Freud, Sigmund. *Civilization and Its Discontents*. Edited by James Strachey. New York: W. W. Norton, 1962.

Gardiner, Patrick (ed.). *Theories of History*. Glencoe, Illinois: The Free Press, 1959.

Hacker, Andrew. *The End of the American Era*. New York: Grove Press, Inc., 1959.

Iggers, Georg G. *The German Conception of History*. Middletown, Connecticut: Wesleyan University Press, 1968.

Kroeber, A. L. *An Anthropologist looks at History*. Berkeley: University of California Press, 1966.

——. *Configurations of Culture Growth*. Berkeley: 1944.

——. *Style and Civilization.* Berkeley: University of California Press, 1966.

—— and Kluckhohn, C. *Culture, A Critical Review of Concepts and Definitions.* New York: Vintage Books, n. d.

Löwith, Karl. *Meaning in History.* Chicago: University of Chicago Press, 1949.

Manuel, Frank E. *Shapes of Philosophical History.* Stanford: Stanford University Press, 1965.

Meyerhoff, Hans (ed.). *The Philosophy of History in our Time.* Garden City, New York: Anchor Books, 1959.

Nisbet, Robert A. *Social Change and History, Aspects of the Theory of Development.* New York: Oxford University Press, 1969.

Ortega y Gasset, José. *The Revolt of the Masses.* New York: W. W. Norton, 1932.

Pareto, Vilfredo. *The Rise and Fall of the Elites.* Totowa, New Jersey, 1968.

Polak, F. L. *The Image of the Future.* 2 Vols. New York: Oceana Publications, 1961.

Schoeps, Hans Joachim. *Vorläufer Spenglers, Studien zum Geschichtspessimismus im 19. Jahrhundert.* Leiden: B. J. Brill, 1955.

Sorokin, Pitrim A. *The Crisis of our Age.* New York: E. P. Dutton & Co., Inc., 1941.

——. *Social and Cultural Dynamics.* New York: 1937-1941.

Sullivan, John Edward. *Prophets of the West.* New York: Holt, Reinhart and Winston, Inc., 1970.

Teggart, Frederick J. *Theory and Processes of History.* Berkeley: University of California Press, 1941.

Toynbee, Arnold J. *Civilization on Trial.* New York: 1948.

——. *Experiences.* Oxford, 1969.

——. *A Study of History.* 2 Vols. Abridged by D. C. Sumervell. Oxford, 1957.

Walsh, W. H. *Philosophy of History.* New York: Harpers Torchbooks, 1960.

INDEX

TABLE I. "CONTEMPORARY" SPIRITUAL EPOCHS

	INDIAN (from 1500)	CLASSICAL (from 1100)	ARABIAN (from 0.)	WESTERN (from 900)
SPRING. (Rural-intuitive. Great creations of the newly-awakened dream-heavy Soul. Super-personal unity and fulness)	**I. BIRTH OF A MYTH OF THE GRAND STYLE, EXPRESSING A NEW GOD-FEELING. WORLD-FEAR. WORLD-LONGING**			
	1500-1200 Vedic religion	1100-800 Hellenic-Italian religion of the people. "Demeter"	0-300 Primitive Christianity (Mandaeans, Marcion, Gnosis, Syncretism (Mithras, Baal) Gospels. Apocalypses	900-1200 German Catholicism Edda (Baldr) Bernard of Clairvaux, Joachim of Floris, Francis of Assisi Popular Epos (Siegfried)
	Aryan hero-tales	Homer. Heracles and Theseus legends	Christian, Mazdaist and pagan legends	Western legends of the Saints
	II. EARLIEST MYSTICAL-METAPHYSICAL SHAPING OF THE NEW WORLD-OUTLOOK ZENITH OF SCHOLASTICISM			
	Preserved in oldest parts of the Vedas	Oldest (oral) Orphic, Etruscan discipline	Origen (d. 254). Plotinus (d. 269), Mani (d. 276), Iamblichus (d. 330)	Thomas Aquinas (d. 1274), Duns Scotus (d. 1308), Dante (d. 1321) and Eckhardt (d. 1329)
		After-effect; Hesiod, Cosmogonies	Avesta, Talmud. Patristic literature	Mysticism. Scholasticism
SUMMER. (Ripening consciousness. Earliest urban and critical stirrings)	**III. REFORMATION: INTERNAL POPULAR OPPOSITION TO THE GREAT SPRINGTIME FORMS**			
	Brahmanas. Oldest parts of Upanishads (10th and 9th Centuries)	Orphic movement. Dionysiac religion. "Numa" religion (7th Century)	Augustine (d. 430) Nestorians (about 430) Monophysites (about 450) Mazdak (about 500)	Nicolaus Cusanus (d. 1464) John Hus (d. 1308) Savonarola, Karlstadt, Luther, Calvin (d. 1564)
	IV. BEGINNING OF A PURELY PHILOSOPHICAL FORM OF THE WORLD-FEELING. OPPOSITION OF IDEALISTIC AND REALISTIC SYSTEMS			
	Preserved in Upanishads	The great Pre-Socratics (6th and 5th Centuries)	Byzantine, Jewish, Syrian, Coptic and Persian literature of 6th and 7th Centuries	Galileo, Bacon, Descartes, Bruno, Boehme, Leibniz. 16th and 17th Centuries

V. FORMATION OF A NEW MATHEMATIC CONCEPTION OF NUMBER AS COPY AND CONTENT OF WORLD-FORM

(lost)	Number as magnitude (proportion) Geometry. Arithmetic Pythagoreans (from 540)	The indefinite number (Algebra) (development not yet investigated)	Number as Function (analysis) Descartes, Pascal, Fermat (ca. 1630) Newton and Leibniz (ca. 1670)

VI. PURITANISM. RATIONALISTIC-MYSTIC IMPOVERISHMENT OF RELIGION

(lost)	Pythagorean society (from 540)	Mohammed (622) Paulicians and Iconoclasts (from 650)	English Puritans (from 1620) French Jansenists (from 1640) Port Royal

AUTUMN.

VII. "ENLIGHTENMENT." BELIEF IN ALMIGHTINESS OF REASON. CULT OF "NATURE." "RATIONAL" RELIGION

(Intelligence of the City. Zenith of strict intellectual creativeness)

Sutras; Sankhya; Buddha; later Upanishads	Sophists of the 5th Century Socrates (d. 399) Democritus (d. ca. 360)	Mutazilites Sufism Nazzam, Alkindi (about 830)	English Rationalists (Locke) French Encyclopaedists (Voltaire) Rousseau

VIII. ZENITH OF MATHEMATICAL THOUGHT. ELUCIDATION OF THE FORM-WORLD OF NUMBERS

(lost) (Zero as number)	Archytas (d. 365) Plato (d. 346) (Conic Sections)	(not investigated) (Theory of number. Spherical Trigonometry)	Euler (d. 1783), Lagrange (d. 1813), Laplace (d. 1827) (The Infinitesimal problem)

IX. THE GREAT CONCLUSIVE SYSTEMS

Idealism Yoga, Vedanta *Epistemology* Vaicashika *Logic* Nyaya	Plato (d. 346) Aristotle (d. 322)	Alfarabi (d. 950) Avicenna (d. ca. 1000)	Goethe { Schelling, Hegel } Kant { Fichte }

WINTER.

(Dawn of **Megalopolitan** Civilization. Extinction of spiritual creative force. Life itself becomes problematical. Ethical-practical tendencies of an irreligious and unmetaphysical cosmopolitanism.)

X. MATERIALISTIC WORLD-OUTLOOK. CULT OF SCIENCE, UTILITY AND PROSPERITY

Sankhya, Tscharvaka (Lokoyata)	Cynics, Cyrenaics. Last Sophists (Pyrrhon)	Communistic, atheistic, Epicurean sects of Abbassid times. "Brethren of Sincerity."	Bentham, Comte, Darwin. Spencer, Stirner, Marx. Feuerbach

XI. ETHICAL-SOCIAL IDEALS OF LIFE. EPOCH OF "UNMATHEMATICAL PHILOSOPHY." SKEPSIS

Tendencies in Buddha's time	Hellenism. Epicurus (d. 270). Zeno (d. 265)	Movements in Islam	Schopenhauer, Nietzsche. Socialism, Anarchism. Hebbel, Wagner, Ibsen

XII. INNER COMPLETION OF THE MATHEMATICAL FORM-WORLD. THE CONCLUDING THOUGHT

(lost)	Euclid, Apollonius (about 300). Archimedes (about 250)	Alchwarizmi (800). Ibn Kurra (850). Alkarchi, Albiruni (10th Century)	Gauss (d. 1855). Cauchy (d. 1857). Riemann (d. 1866)

XIII. DEGRADATION OF ABSTRACT THINKING INTO PROFESSIONAL LECTURE-ROOM PHILOSOPHY. COMPENDIUM LITERATURE

The "Six Classical Systems"	Academy, Peripatos, Stoics, Epicureans	Schools of Baghdad and Basra	Kantians. "Logicians" and "Psychologists"

XIV. SPREAD OF A FINAL WORLD-SENTIMENT

Indian Buddhism	Hellenistic-Roman Stoicism from 200	Practical fatalism in Islam after 1000	Ethical Socialism from 1900

From Oswald Spengler's *Decline of the West*, New York: Alfred A. Knopf, 1926.

TABLE II. "CONTEMPORARY" CULTURE EPOCHS

	EGYPTIAN	CLASSICAL	ARABIAN	WESTERN
PRE-CULTURAL PERIOD.	CHAOS OF PRIMITIVE EXPRESSION FORMS.		MYSTICAL SYMBOLISM AND NAÏVE IMITATION	
EXCITATION	Thinite Period (3400-3000)	Mycenean Age (1600-1700) Late-Egyptian (Minoan) Late-Babylonian (Asia Minor)	Persian-Seleucid Period (500-0) Late-Classical (Hellenistic) Late-Indian (Indo-Iranian)	Merovingian-Carolingian Era (500-900)
CULTURE.	LIFE-HISTORY OF A STYLE FORMATIVE OF THE ENTIRE INNER-BEING. FORM-LANGUAGE OF DEEPEST SYMBOLIC NECESSITY			
I. EARLY PERIOD (Ornament and architecture as elementary expression of the young world-feeling.) (The "Primitives")	OLD KINGDOM (2900-2400)	DORIC (1100-500)	EARLY-ARABIAN FORM-WORLD. (Sassanid, Byzantine, Armenian, Syrian, Sabræan, "Late-Classical" and "Early Christian") (0-500)	GOTHIC (900-1500)
1. Birth and Rise. Forms sprung from the Land, unconsciously shaped	Dynasties IV-V. (2930-2625)	11th to 9th Centuries	1st to 3rd Centuries	11th to 13th Centuries
	Geometrical Temple style Pyramid temples Ranked plant-columns Rows of flat-relief Tomb statues	Timber building Doric column Architrave Geometric (Dipylon) style Burial urns	Cult interiors Basilica, Cupola (Pantheon as Mosque) Column-and-arch Stem-tracery filling blanks Sarcophagus	Romanesque and Early-Gothic vaulted cathedrals Flying buttress Glass-painting, Cathedral sculpture
2. Completion of the early form-language.			*Exhaustion of possibilities.*	*Contradiction.*
	VI Dynasty (2625-2574) Extinction of pyramid-style and epic-idyllic relief style Floraison of archaic portrait-plastic	8th and 7th Centuries End of archaic Doric-Etruscan style Proto-Corinthian-Early-Attic (mythological) vase painting	4-5th Centuries End of Syrian, Persian, and Coptic pictorial art Rise of mosaic-picturing and of arabesque	14-15th Centuries Late Gothic and Renaissance Floraison and waning of fresco and statue. From Giotto (Gothic) to Michelangelo (Baroque). Siena, Nürnberg. The Gothic picture from Van Eyck to Holbein. Counterpoint and oil-painting

II. LATE PERIOD (Formation of a group of arts urban and conscious, in the hands of individuals) ("Great Masters")	MIDDLE KINGDOM (2150–1800)	IONIC (650–350)	LATE-ARABIAN FORM-WORLD (Persian-Nestorian, Byzantine-Armenian, Islamic-Moorish) (500–800)	BAROQUE (1500–1800)
		3. Formation of a mature artistry		
	XIth Dynasty. Delicate and telling art (Almost no traces left)	Completion of the temple-body (Peripteros, stone) The Ionic column; Reign of fresco-painting till Polygnotus (460)	Completion of the mosque-interior (Central dome of Hagia Sophia) Zenith of mosaic painting	The pictorial style in architecture from Michelangelo to Bernini (d. 1680) Reign of oil-painting from Titian to Rembrandt (d. 1664)
		Rise of free plastic "in the round" ("Apollo of Tenea" to Hageladas)	Completion of the carpet-like arabesque style (Mschatta)	Rise of music from Orlando Lasso to H. Schütz (d. 1672)
		4. Perfection of an intellectualized form-language		
	XIIth Dynasty (2000–1788) Pylon-temple, Labyrinth	Maturity of Athens (480–350) The Acropolis	Ommayads (7th–8th Century)	Rococo Musical architecture ("Rococo")
	Character-statuary and historical reliefs	Reign of Classical plastic from Myron to Phidias	Complete victory of featureless arabesque over architecture also	Reign of classical music from Bach to Mozart
		End of strict fresco and ceramic painting (Zeuxis)		End of classical oil-painting (Watteau to Goya)
		5. Exhaustion of strict creativeness. Dissolution of grand form. End of the Style. "Classicism" and "Romanticism"		
	Confusion after about 1750	The age of Alexander	"Haroun-al-Raschid" (about 800)	Empire and Biedermeyer
	(No remains)	The Corinthian column Lysippus and Apelles	"Moorish Art"	Classicist taste in architecture Beethoven, Delacroix

CIVILIZATION. EXISTENCE WITHOUT INNER FORM. MEGALOPOLITAN ART AS A COMMON-PLACE: LUXURY, SPORT, NERVE-EXCITEMENT: RAPIDLY-CHANGING FASHIONS IN ART (REVIVALS, ARBITRARY DISCOVERIES, BORROWINGS)

1. "Modern Art." "Art problems." Attempts to portray or to excite the megalopolitan consciousness. Transformation of Music, architecture and painting into mere craft-arts.

Hyksos Period	Hellenism	Sultan dynasties of 9th-10th Century	19th and 20th Centuries
(Preserved only in Crete; Minoan art)	Pergamene Art (theatricality)	Prime of Spanish-Sicilian art	Liszt, Berlioz, Wagner
	Hellenistic painting modes (veristic, bizarre, subjective)		Impressionism from Constable to Leibl and Manet
	Architectural display in the cities of the Diadochi	Samarra	American architecture

2. End of form-development. Meaningless, empty, artificial, pretentious architecture and ornament. Imitation of archaic and exotic motives.

| XVIII Dynasty (1580-1350) Rock temple of Dehr-el-Bahri. Memnon-Colossi. Art of Cnossos and Amarna | Roman Period (100-0-100) Indiscriminate piling of all three orders. Fora, theatres (Colosseum). Triumphal arches | Seljuks (from 1050) "Oriental Art" of the Crusade period | From 1800 |

3. Finale. Formation of a fixed stock of forms. Imperial display by means of material and mass. Provincial craft-art.

| XIX Dynasty (1350-1205) Gigantic buildings of Luxor, Karnak and Abydos. Small-art (beast plastic, textiles, arms) | Trajan to Aurelian Gigantic fora, thermæ, colonnades, triumphal arches Roman provincial art (ceramic, statuary, arms) | Mongol Period (from 1250) Gigantic buildings (e.g. in India) Oriental craft-art (rugs, arms, implements) | |

From Oswald Spengler's *Decline of the West.* New York: Alfred A. Knopf, 1926.

TABLE III. "CONTEMPORARY" POLITICAL EPOCHS

	EGYPTIAN	CLASSICAL	CHINESE	WESTERN
PRE-CULTURAL PERIOD. PRIMITIVE FOLK. TRIBES AND THEIR CHIEFS. AS YET NO "POLITICS" AND NO "STATE"	Thinite Period (Menes) 3400-3000	Mycenean Age ("Agamemnon") 1600-1100	Shang Period (1700-1300)	Frankish Period (Charlemagne) (500-900)

CULTURE. NATIONAL GROUPS OF DEFINITE STYLE AND PARTICULAR WORLD-FEELING. "NATIONS." WORKING OF AN IMMANENT STATE-IDEA

I. EARLY PERIOD. *Organic articulation of political existence. The two prime classes (noble and priest).*
Feudal economics; purely agrarian values

	EGYPTIAN	CLASSICAL	CHINESE	WESTERN
1. Feudalism. Spirit of countryside and countryman. The "City" only a market or stronghold. Chivalric-religious ideals. Struggles of vassals amongst themselves and against overlord	OLD KINGDOM (2900-2400) Feudal conditions of IV Dynasty Increasing power of feudatories and priesthoods The Pharaoh as incarnation of Ra	DORIC PERIOD (1100-650) The Homeric kingship Rise of the nobility (Ithaca. Etruria, Sparta)	EARLY CHOU PERIOD (1300-800) The central ruler (Wang) pressed hard by the feudal nobility	GOTHIC PERIOD (900-1500) Roman-German Imperial period Crusading nobility Empire and Papacy
2. Crisis and dissolution of patriarchal forms. From feudalism to aristocratic State	VI Dynasty. Break-up of the Kingdom into heritable principalities. VII and VIII Dynasties, interregnum	Aristocratic synoecism Dissolution of kinship into annual offices Oligarchy	934-904. I-Wang and the vassals 84. Interregnum	Territorial princes Renaissance towns. Lancaster and York 1254. Interregnum

II. Late Period. *Actualizing of the matured State-idea. Town versus countryside. Rise of Third Estate (Bourgeoisie).*
Victory of money over landed property

	MIDDLE KINGDOM (2000–1800)	IONIC PERIOD (650–300)	LATE CHOU PERIOD (800–500)	BAROQUE PERIOD (1500–1800)
3. Fashioning of a world of States of strict form. Frondes	XIIth Dynasty. Overthrow of the baronage by the rulers of Thebes. Centralized bureaucracy-state	6th Century. First Tyrannis. (Cleisthenes, Periander, Polycrates, the Tarquins.) The City-State.	Period of the "Protectors" (Ming-Chu 685–591) and the congresses of princes (~460)	Dynastic family-power, and Fronde (Richelieu, Wallenstein, Cromwell) about 1650.
4. Climax of the State-form ("Absolutism") Unity of town and country ("State" and "Society." The "three estates")	XIIth Dynasty (2000–1788) Strictest centralization of power. Court and finance nobility	The pure Polis (absolutism of the Demos). Agora politics. Rise of the tribunate. Themistocles, Pericles	Chun-Chiu period ("Spring" and "Autumn"), 590–480. Seven powers. Perfection of social forms (Li)	Ancien Régime. Rococo. Court nobility of Versailles. Cabinet politics. Habsburg and Bourbon. Louis XIV. Frederick the Great
5. Break-up of the State-form (Revolution and Napoleonism). Victory of the city over the countryside (of the "people" over the privileged, of the intelligentsia over tradition, of money over policy)	1788–1680. Revolution and military government. Decay of the realm. Small potentates, in some cases sprung from the people	4th Century. Social revolution and Second Tyrannis (Dionysius I, Jason of Pherac, Appius Claudius the Censor) *Alexander*	480. Beginning of the Chan-Kwo period. 441. Fall of the Chou dynasty. Revolutions and annihilation-wars	End of XVIIIth Century. Revolution in America and France (Washington, Fox, Mirabeau, Robespierre). *Napoleon*

CIVILIZATION. THE BODY OF THE PEOPLE, NOW ESSENTIALLY URBAN IN CONSTITUTION, DISSOLVES INTO FORMLESS MASS. MEGALOPOLIS AND PROVINCES. THE FOURTH ESTATE ("MASSES"), INORGANIC, COSMOPOLITAN

1. Domination of Money ("Democracy") Economic powers permeating the political forms and authorities	1680 (1788)–1580. Hyksos period. Deepest decline. Dictatures of alien generals (Chian) After 1600 definitive victory of the rulers of Thebes	300–100. Political Hellenism. From Alexander to Hannibal and Scipio royal all-power; from Cleomenes III and C. Flaminius (220) to C. Marius, radical demagogues	480–230. Period of the "Contending States." 288. The Imperial title. The imperialist statesmen of Tsin. From 289 incorporation of the last states in the Empire	1800–2000. XIXth Century. From Napoleon to the World-War. "System of the Great Powers," standing armies, constitutions. XXth-Century transition from constitutional to informal sway of individuals. Annihilation wars. Imperialism

2. Formation of Caesarism. Victory of force-politics over money. Increasing primitiveness of political forms. Inward decline of the nations into a formless population, and constitution thereof as an Imperium of gradually-increasing crudity of despotism	1580–1350. XVIIIth Dynasty Thuthmosis III	100-0-100. Sulla to Domitian Cæsar, Tiberius	250-0-26. House of Wang-Cheng and Western Han Dynasty 211. Augustus-title (Shi) of Emperor Hwang-Ti 140–80. Wu-ti	2000–1200
3. Maturing of the final form. Private and family policies of individual leaders. The world as spoil. Egypticism, Mandarinism, Byzantinism. History less stiffening and enfeeblement even of the imperial machinery, against young peoples eager for spoil, or alien conquerors. Primitive human conditions slowly thrust up into the highly-civilized mode of living	1350–1205. XIXth Dynasty Sethos I Rameses II	100–300. Trajan to Aurelian Trajan, Septimius Severus	25-220 A.D. Eastern Han Dynasty 58–71. Ming-ti	after 1200

From Oswald Spengler's *Decline of the West*. New York: Alfred A. Knopf, 1926.